404293

MATERIAL MATTERS

D1477020

EDITED BY
KATIE LLOYD THOMAS

MATERIAL MATTERS
ARCHITECTURE
AND MATERIAL PRACTICE

Routledge
Taylor & Francis Group

LONDON AND NEW YORK

First published 2007 by Routledge

2 Park Square, Milton Park, Abingdon, Oxon, OX14 4RN

Simultaneously published in the USA and Canada by Routledge
270 Madison Avenue, New York, NY10016

Routledge is an imprint of the Taylor & Francis Group, an informa business

Design concept by Claudia Schenk
Typeset in Gothic by
Keystroke, 28 High Street, Tettenhall, Wolverhampton
Printed and bound in Great Britain by
The Alden Press, Oxford

British Library Cataloguing in Publication Data
A catalogue record for this book is available from the British Library

Library of Congress Cataloging-in-Publication Data
Material matters : architecture and material practice / edited by Katie Lloyd Thomas.
     p. cm.
   Includes index.
   ISBN-10: 0-415-36325-X (hardback : alk. paper)
   ISBN-10: 0-415-36326-8 (pbk. : alk. paper)
   ISBN-10: 0-203-01362-X (ebook)
   ISBN-13: 978-0-415-36325-9 (hbk.)
   [etc.]
   1. Building materials. 2. Architecture. I. Thomas, Katie Lloyd.
   II. Title.
   NA2540.M385 2006
   720'.28—dc22   2006010010

ISBN10 0-415-36325-X (hbk)
ISBN10 0-415-36326-8 (pbk)

ISBN13 978-0-415-36325-9 (hbk)
ISBN13 978-0-415-36326-6 (pbk)
ISBN13 978-0-203-01362-5(ebk)

CONTENTS

CONTRIBUTORS

MARTIN BECHTHOLD

Martin Bechthold is an architect and Associate Professor of Architecture at Harvard University Graduate School of Design, where he teaches Building Structures and Technology. For his work on wood-foam sandwich roof shells he was awarded the Snyder Prize for Innovation in Fabrication, the Peter Rice Prize and the Tsuboi Award. He co-authored *Digital Design and Manufacturing* (2004).

ANDREW BENJAMIN

Andrew Benjamin is Professor of Critical Theory in Design and Architecture at the University of Technology, Sydney. He teaches regularly at the Architectural Association in London. His recent publications include *Architectural Philosophy* (2001), *Disclosing Spaces: On Painting* (2004) and *Style and Time* (2006).

RAOUL BUNSCHOTEN

Raoul Bunschoten is founding director both of the practice CHORA architecture and urbanism, and of its not-for-profit sister, CHORA research. Planning methodologies developed by CHORA research are now being commissioned and CHORA is working on a small multiple arts pavilion for Homerton, Hackney and a Future Centre for the National Board for Water and Infrastructure in the Netherlands.

ALAN CHANDLER

Alan Chandler is Senior Lecturer running Technical Studies within the Architecture programme at the University of East London, and Co-Director of architectural practice 'Arts Lettres Techniques' with a particular interest in sustainability and conservation. He has collaborated with artists, including Danny Lane, Richard Wentworth, Elisa Sighicelli and Richard Woods.

NICHOLAS COETZER

Nicholas Coetzer's Ph.D., 'The Production of the City as a White Space: Representing and Restructuring Identity and Architecture, Cape Town, 1892–1936', was awarded from the Bartlett, University College London, in 2004. He is presently a senior lecturer at the University of Cape Town's architecture department and the Bachelor of Architectural Studies Programme Convenor.

RACHEL CRUISE

Rachel Cruise is a dissertation tutor at the Bartlett School of Architecture and is currently studying for a Ph.D. in the civil and environmental engineering department at Imperial College, London. Her area of research is the effect of production routes on the material properties of stainless-steel sections and their resulting structural behaviour.

ANDREW FREEAR

Andrew Freear is Associate Professor at Auburn University and Co-Director of the Rural Studio in Newbern, Alabama. He has practised in London and Chicago, taught design at the University of Illinois, and lectured internationally on the Rural Studio. He was recently made honorary citizen of Marion for his work on the Perry Lakes Park Project.

CONTRIBUTORS

JON GOODBUN
Jon Goodbun is a senior lecturer and design tutor at SABE, University of Westminster, and a founder member of the Polytechnic Research Group. Prior to co-founding WaG Architecture, he worked on a range of architectural, digital media, urban and exhibition design projects. He is currently jointly editing a book on architecture and surrealism.

SUSANNAH HAGAN
Susannah Hagan is Reader in Architecture at the University of East London, where she set up and still runs the MA 'Architecture: Sustainability+Design'. Her 2001 publication *Taking Shape* examines the effect of environmental design on the future of architecture and vice versa. Her next book, *Digitalia*, will look at the 'invasion' of architecture by computers, and its environmental potential.

KATIE LLOYD THOMAS
Katie Lloyd Thomas was a senior lecturer at the University of East London, where in 2004 she organised the symposium 'Material Matters: Materiality in Contemporary Architectural Practice and Theory' – out of which this book developed. She is currently completing a Ph.D. about material and the architectural specification at Middlesex University. She is a founder of 'taking place', a group of architects, artists and writers working with questions of feminism and space, and collaborates regularly with artist Brigid McLeer. Katie has published articles on materiality, feminism and architectural representation, and lectured in France, Iceland, Slovakia, Australia, Germany and the UK.

NIALL MCLAUGHLIN
Founder, in 1991, of Niall McLaughlin Architects. The practice places strong emphasis on the inventive use of materials, qualities of light and the relationship between buildings and their surroundings. Awards and international recognition for its buildings, exhibitions and publications include UK Young Architect of the Year (1998) and honorary fellow of the Royal Institute of Architects in Ireland (2001).

CLARE MELHUISH
Clare Melhuish is engaged in cross-disciplinary research in architecture and anthropology, and is a doctoral candidate at Buckinghamshire and Chilterns University College. She was guest-editor of Architecture and Anthropology (1996), author of *Modern House 2* (2000), and most recently co-author of *Housey Housey: a Pattern Book of Ideal Homes* (2005).

PABLO MIRANDA CARRANZA
Pablo Miranda Carranza is an architect and researcher at the KTH School of Architecture and the Built Environment, Stockholm, Sweden. He is currently involved in the project 'Autopoiesis and Design: Authorship and Generative Strategies' (developed together with Rolf Hughes), and in the architecture collective Krets. His main concern is the effects of computation in architecture.

DOINA PETRESCU
An architect and writer based at Sheffield University and the Architectural Association, Doina Petrescu has worked with activist associations and feminist research groups in Europe and Africa. She co-founded Atelier d'Architecture

Autogérée, developing alternative 'strategies' and 'tactics' in architecture and urban planning; has edited *Altering Practices: Feminist Politics and Poetics of Space* (2006); and co-edited *Architecture and Participation* (2005).

SCOTT POOLE

Director Designate of Virginia Tech. School of Architecture + Design, Poole has lectured in the USA and Scandinavia – where he ran design workshops at the Royal Danish Academy of Art, Copenhagen, and Stockholm's Royal Institute of Technology. He is author of *The New Finnish Architecture* and moderated the 2003 Alvar Aalto Symposium, 'Permanence and Change in Architecture'.

PEG RAWES

Peg Rawes is Departmental Tutor and Coordinator of Diploma History and Theory at the Bartlett School of Architecture, University College London. Her writing and teaching on architecture, art and philosophy explores theories of embodiment and spatio-temporality. She co-edited *Spatial Imagination* (2006) and has published chapters in *Reflexive Architecture* (2002) and *Architecture: the Subject is Matter* (2001).

ELIZABETH SHOTTON

Elizabeth Shotton coordinates the Architectural Technology and Thesis programmes at University College Dublin. This teaching is supported by a research-based practice involving building projects and other forms of investigation such as curatorial work and writing. Exhibitions include Peter Cardew: Ordinary Buildings and RE POSE. Her current research explores the role of memory and perception in design.

HELEN STRATFORD

Through exhibitions, papers and performances, architect Helen Stratford addresses intersections of power relations and spatial practices. Fellow at Akademie Schloss Solitude, Stuttgart (2004/5), she curated 'Compendium' at the RIBA (2006) and is Creative Practitioner for Creative Partnerships. Her essays have appeared in *Recoveries and Reclamations* (2002), the *Journal of Architectural Education* (2001) and RFR *Journal of Feminist Research* (2002).

STEPHEN WALKER

Stephen Walker trained as an architect and has worked at Sheffield University School of Architecture since 2001. His research focuses on the relationships between the disciplines of art and architecture, and has been published widely. He is currently completing a monograph on the artist Gordon Matta-Clark, and an edited collection on architecture and the contemporary body entitled BODY: SPACE.

RICHARD WILSON

One of Britain's most renowned sculptors, Wilson is celebrated for his interventions in architectural space, drawing inspiration from engineering and construction. Representing Britain in the Sydney, São Paulo and Venice Biennales, Wilson has twice been nominated for the Turner Prize. His seminal '20:50', permanently installed in the Saatchi Collection, was hailed 'one of the masterpieces of the modern age'.

ILLUSTRATION CREDITS

The authors and publishers would like to thank the following individuals and institutions for giving permission to reproduce illustrations. We have made every effort to contact copyright holders, but if any errors have been made we would be happy to correct them at a later printing.

5th Studio 18.2
Per-Erik Adamsson 13.5
© ADGAP, Paris and DACS, London 2005 8.2
American Air Museum, Duxford 18.1
© ARS, NY and DACS, London 2005 4.1, 4.2, 4.3, 4.4
Martin Bechthold 12.2, 12.3, 12.4, 12.5, 12.6, 12.7, 12.8, 12.13
Hélène Binet 9.2
Ian Bramwell 11.10
Cape Town Archives Repository 16.5
Alan Chandler 10.2
CHORA 7.1, 7.2, 7.3, 7.4, 7.5, 7.6, 7.7, 7.8, 7.9, 7.10, 7.11, 7.12, 7.13, 7.14, 7.15
Nicholas Coetzer 16.3 (right)
Peter Davies 9.8
Guy Dickinson 3.2
Claudia Dutson 10.1
© FLC/ADGAP, Paris and DACS, London 2005 8.3, 8.4, 8.5, 8.6
Susannah Hagan 21.1, 21.2, 21.3, 21.4, 21.5, 21.6
Jason Halaby 12.10, 12.11, 12.12
Timothy Hursley 20.1, 20.2, 20.3, 20.4, 20.9, 20.10, 20.11, 20.12, 20.14, 20.19, 20.20, 20.22
Justin Lee 12.9
Dirk Lellau 10.5, 11.1,11.2, 11.3, 11.4, 11.5, 11.6, 11.7, 11.8, 11.12, 11.13, 11.15, 11.17, 11.18, 11.19, 11.21, 11.26
Jan Liebe 11.20
Niall McLaughlin Architects 3.3, 3.4, 3.5, 3.6, 3.7, 3.8, 3.9, 3.10, 3.11, 3.12
MAK-Austrian Museum of Applied Arts/Contemporary Art, Vienna 3.9
Karoline Mayer 11.8, 11.9, 11.14, 11.16, 11.22, 11.23, 11.24, 11.25, 11.27
Clare Melhuish 17.1, 17.2, 17.3, 17.4, 17.5, 17.6
Pablo Miranda 13.1, 13.2, 13.3, 13.4
Tze Ting Mok 10.3, 10.4
Jason Oliviera 12.14
Oxford University Press 16.1, 16.2 (left)
Doina Petrescu 19.1, 19.2, 19.3, 19.4, 19.5, 19.6, 19.7, 19.8, 19.9, 19.10, 19.11, 19.12, 19.13
Pinakothek, Munich 3.1
Scott Poole 9.1, 9.3, 9.4
Rural Studio 20.5, 20.6, 20.7, 20.8, 20.13, 20.15, 20.16, 20.17, 20.18, 20.21
William Sevebeck 9.5, 9.6
Elizabeth Shotton 8.1, 8.7, 8.8
Smout Allen 5.1
Monika-Sprueth/Philomene Magers © DACS, London 2006 3.13
Helen Stratford 18.3,18.4,18.5, 18.6, 18.7, 18.8
Heidi Svenningsen 11.11
Kei Takeuchi 12.1
Maria J. Villacreces 9.7
WaG Architecture 6.1
Steve White 15.8
Richard Wilson 15.1, 15.2, 15.3, 15.4, 15.5, 15.6, 15.7, 15.9, 15.10, 15.11,15.12, 15.13

ACKNOWLEDGEMENTS

This book has developed out of an international conference I organized, 'Material Matters: Materiality in Contemporary Architectural Practice and Theory', which was held in the adapted unoccupied studios of the fine art school and in the architecture school of Architecture and the Visual Arts at the University of East London between 29 March and 3 April 2004. For encouraging me to take a leap into the unknown in inaugurating and managing such an event, I thank Andrew Higgott and Nick Weaver, and for their practical support I am very grateful to Signy Svalastoga and Cliff Nicholls. The assistance of David Ring was invaluable; and other colleagues – particularly Vicki Anne Heyday, Alan Chandler, Raphael Lee, Czes Bany, Mark Hayduk, Michele Roelofsma, Christian Derix, Heidi Svenningsen and Jonathan Dawes – contributed time and skill. In the spirit of UEL, many students offered their help freely and enthusiastically – building canopies to transform studios into lecture spaces; looking after technical equipment, reception and catering – but two former students Ani Berg and in particular David Knight, were absolutely indispensable and I cannot thank them enough.

Caroline Mallinder and Katherine Morton from Routledge have been patient and helpful guides with the editing of this book. We were very lucky to have Claudia Schenk working on the design. Stephen Walker, Peg Rawes, Brigid McLeer, Andrew Higgott, Helen Stratford and David Knight have given valuable advice. This endeavour would never have happened without four very different teachers of mine, whom I take the opportunity to make a special mention of – Peter Carl, Michele Roelofsma, Jane Rendell and Adrian Rifkin.

Just after I had begun working on this book my son Max was born, three months early. I want to extend my great appreciation to the staff in SCBU at Homerton Hospital for their wonderful work with all of us, and to special-care baby units and their patients and carers around the country. I am also very grateful to the contributors for their understanding and willing when finally I picked the book up again. Many friends and family helped us during this time – most especially my parents, Anne and David Lloyd Thomas, and my sister, Sally Lloyd Thomas; but also Jean Copping, Gisela Malnig and Karin Watzke. To Christian Malnig, whose calm and hope sustained us, just love.

KATIE LLOYD THOMAS >INTRODUCTION: ARCHITECTURE AND MATERIAL PRACTICE

The practice of architecture and the discourses surrounding it are, as so many ways of understanding and constructing the world, structured around a distinction between form and matter where the formal (and conceptual) is valued over the material. On the one hand, historically, discourses and theories of architecture have tended to concern themselves with formal questions and to establish the architect as form giver. On the other, the very method we use to develop architectural proposals – orthographic drawing – describes only form, and relegates material to the empty spaces between the lines. The privileging of form is deeply embedded into our working practices, and material is rarely examined beyond its aesthetic or technological capacities to act as a servant to form. The essays and projects collected here each insist on making the material matter, and in doing so something exciting and potentially important happens. From this simple shift in attention towards the material a very wide range of issues emerge: issues otherwise invisible or excluded from architectural discourse; issues that shape and determine the buildings we make, the processes we use and the ways in which we understand them.

Like any building, the book you have in your hands right now is a material object. But as you read it you will be unlikely to think of it this way. The materiality of the book has probably gone unnoticed: at most you might be aware of its weight, or the smell and texture of its pages – and even these immediate sensory qualities are secondary while you are concentrating on the contributors' ideas through their words and images. To shift your attention to the book as a material object would be to see that it is not only the ideas of the authors which shape it. Like any building, this book is in fact the result of a vast network of practices. There are conventions of its structure and of the English language in written form; the designs of typefaces and the software in which the print is set; the manufacture of papers, glues and inks from which it is constructed. Behind each of these materials is a complex history of development, extraction, technique, transportation and exchange. Economies of production, regulation of standards and labour shape this object, as do the lives and contexts of the many persons who have handled it along the way.

To move beyond the ideas behind this book and the physical experience of its 'objecthood' involves the recognition of the social and material practices in which its generation is embedded and the forces at work in the realization of objects (and their continuing lives) which range from the conceptual to the practical and technical, to the institutional. In shifting attention from the formal to the material, it is precisely these forces and practices which become visible in the contributions which make up *Material Matters*. To reverse the usual hierarchy and valorize matter over form does of course leave the opposition intact, and some of the essays try to dismantle this opposition altogether and suggest alternative ways of conceiving the material world, which may in turn help to explain why attention to materials sets so many questions in motion.

Before moving to a discussion of the individual contributions I want first to elaborate on the form/matter distinction and the particular problems that architectural discourse might inherit from it. I will go on to suggest that the surge of interest in materiality in architecture at the present time results from the convergence of a number of rather different areas of endeavour – particularly from technological developments, environmental concerns and current philosophical debates. Taken together, these developments might be seen to be shifting discourse about material towards questions of practice and challenging the dominance of formal concerns. My own concern in putting this collection of writings and images together is to ask how this current interest in materiality might open architectural discourse up to social and political questions of material practice, rather than simply providing us with some new form-making techniques which are inflected by their material realization.

ARCHITECTURE AND HYLOMORPHISM
The privileging of form over material is central both to the theoretical discipline and to the profession of architecture. It is also a preference that many architects display in their own design work. Material's secondary status not only lends it a certain invisibility that leaves it under-discussed but also creates a number of problems for the discipline and its critical accounts. Materials tend to be discussed in guides to construction rather than in theoretical works, where formal concerns are dominant, or in historical works, where, as Andrew Benjamin discusses, an idealist approach tends to prevail. As Pablo Miranda notes in his contribution, the 'craft' of the architect is not building but drawing. The descriptive geometry we traditionally use did not so much enable communication between designer and builder, as is often commented upon, but produced that separation, and affiliated the design of buildings with the high-minded and ideal disciplines of mathematics and the pure sciences. In contemporary professional practice the split appears again in the tender package, where drawings describe form but language is used for the materials of building in notes on working drawings and in the specification.[1] Furthermore in architectural education, as Alan Chandler discusses, the formal aspects of design are usually developed first in student projects with material considerations only brought in at a later stage and left to 'technical' studies.

The form/matter split which structures architecture also has a long philosophical tradition. It is one of many foundational binary oppositions in which one member of the pair is privileged and the other is secondary. In Plato's theory of forms the material realization of a pure form is always imperfect and degraded. The perfect form can only exist in the ideal realm where it is untainted by matter. In a typical account of 'hylomorphism' such as Aristotle's, matter, or 'hyle', is given shape by form, or 'morphe'. Matter in itself is inert and undifferentiated; it is the servant of form and gives it presence. It does not determine form.

In a hylomorphic account the form giver might appear as an architect, as in John Protevi's description of the typical conceptualization of material production as 'the transcendent imposition of the architect's vision of form on chaotic matter'.[2] Despite the properties of matter which might inform or resist the work of the form giver, as Protevi goes on to describe, 'the architect is blind to such traits and despises "surrender" to matter; he only sees and commands'.[3] The hylomorphic schema 'that a simple unchanging commanding origin is responsible for change in others' may not, he suggests, simply be of philosophical significance but may also be a model which supports systems of work such as slave labour[4] or industrialization.

By characterizing matter as inert – as that which is given form – the image of the architect as a kind of mythic form giver is reinforced and the processes and labour of construction are covered over. The very resistances that matter has to being formed are ignored. Materials must be extracted or manufactured, they must be worked and, once *in situ*, they must be maintained. And of course materials are themselves active; it is a transaction, rather than a one-way operation, that occurs in the shaping of stuff.

The valuing of form over matter relegates material in architecture to the practical underside of the profession and lifts the status of the architect to form giver. Hylomorphism also leaves architecture with another difficulty: while the concept of form may be transferable to architecture, the hylomorphic concept of matter, I want to suggest, cannot in fact account for materials (in the plural) as they are understood in architectural practice.

In the *Metaphysics* Aristotle understands substance (that which is separable) as a compound of form and matter.[5] The term Aristotle uses for matter, 'hyle', also means wood (and is occasionally used for other materials) and is, as I understand it, a positive term which refers to an instance of the material such as might be used in building. Aristotle uses a second term, 'hypokomenon', which is usually translated as 'substrate' and refers to prime matter. This word literally means 'that which lies beneath' – it has the sense of something behind, something perhaps which can be deduced rather than touched. In Aristotle's account a kind of elision occurs between the hypokomenon and the hyle. In trying to explain the concept of prime matter he uses examples of specific materials: 'In speaking of matter I have in mind say, the bronze of a statue, while by the shape-form I mean the geometry of the object's appearance.'[6] Not all materials would do as well as bronze in this example – a statue made of charcoal would become dust if you tried to change its shape – but we are happy to accept it as just one example of a generic material. The specific properties of bronze – its ability to become liquid and be moulded, and its own formlessness – lend conviction to a concept of matter that would be common to all materials. Aristotle is not alone in using a plastic material to support an argument concerning matter. In his sceptical account of matter, Descartes, for example, chooses wax.[7]

Hylomorphism understands matter as singular; form is that which differentiates and matter is that which can be differentiated. But it imagines prime matter in reference to the properties of a particular material and passes over others which would not fit, and in doing so ignores or represses the plurality of materials. The hylomorphic concept of matter is not as easily conflated with materials as it would appear. Nevertheless architecture has this concept at its base and sets up a discourse in which form must be realized in matter, with the material being seen as merely interchangeable – just one instance of matter rather than another. In any binary opposition it is not only that the secondary term is degraded but that it is defined negatively, as 'not form'. Within such a definition there is no space for a positive appearance of the term, and therefore, for the possibility of differentiation.[8] Hylomorphism, which understands materials as a subset of matter, does not provide a way of positively distinguishing materials, and underscores the architectural tendency to use materials as mere finishes, exchangeable and superficial. In turn, it is no surprise that materials become supplementary in architecture and are used to decorate or to signify.

MATERIAL ATTENTION

This book, and the conference and workshops it has grown out of, emerges at a time when there is a renewed interest in questions of materiality in architecture. The essays and practices presented here respond to very different forces and concerns within (and without) the discipline and use a variety of strategies to do so. Some posit an alternative philosophical approach which does not split the world into form and matter but instead considers it in terms of force, setting up equivalence between persons, objects, words, solar systems and so on, which all act on each other. In such a view the real and the virtual, or the material and the idea, are part of a continuum of potentiality and actualization. Interestingly, at least for architecture, developments in practice support these conceptual frameworks, particularly in relation to digital-based mechanistic processes such as Computer Numerically Controlled (CNC) milling operations and Rapid Prototyping which make possible a direct link between conceptualization and production, undoing a gap which has been such an important part of the discipline's structuring.

A number of the essays consider materials in terms of effect, either on the process of design or on performance. In this view, form emerges out of a transaction with the material or the material demands or invites certain practices in terms of maintenance or behaviour. New products, particularly those using 'smart materials', add to the persuasiveness of these kinds of analyses. Façade components which are responsive to changes in the environment, for example, challenge a view of materials as inert or acted upon, and encourage us to consider the active aspects of all materials.[9]

Most of the essays however, would seem to generally accept the hylomorphic account of architecture and object making. Their approach is to redress the balance, and to replace neglect with what I have called 'material attention'. Inevitably, in adopting this strategy, the primacy of form is reiterated rather than avoided, but out of the attention to material a number of very different and interesting issues emerge, ranging from temporality to economics. Attentiveness to material does not, of course, only happen through intellectual research, but is part of the manual work of craft or fabrication. A problem for any book dealing with material attention, then, is how to give making a presence. Here there are a number of written accounts of making, from sewing and tailoring to slicing a disused sand dredger in two, and also a number of sections which allow the visual to dominate and punctuate the textual in an effort to evoke the attention of the hand and eye within the limits of the printed page.

The contributions here, then, are distinguished more by the variety of their approaches to materiality than by a commonality but in choosing to put them together, and in using the term 'material practice' in the title, I have tried to draw attention to what is a shared refusal to consider materials in purely visual (and static) terms and an insistence on examining materials as part of a network of forces and actions (although few of the contributors would use this terminology). Architecture must explore materials in this way if it is to use them responsibly, to open itself to the potentiality of new and 'old' materials and to reach an understanding of how materials may be productive of effects, both experiential and political, as it already has to some extent in relation to space. An emphasis on practice accepts that materials can only be understood (and even defined) within the terms of a specific discourse and in relation to when, where and how they are produced and used.

In his influential account of a woodworker making a table, Brian Massumi describes how the qualities of the piece of wood have a future potential to affect (to resist gravity when a glass is placed upon it) and be affected (to submit to 'the pressure of salt shakers and discourteous elbows') and arise out of its individual past ('the evolution of the tree's species . . . the cultural actions that brought that particular wood to the workshop for that particular purpose').[10] The material, at any particular point in time, is brought into its existence through a developing chain of events, both 'natural' and cultural, and has the potential for a myriad of future interactions and transformations. Massumi suggests that what is important in this encounter is not the distinction between form and matter for:

> There is substance on both sides: wood; woodworking body and tools. And there is form on both sides: both raw material and object produced have determinate forms, as do the body and tools. The encounter is between two substance/form complexes, one of which overpowers the other.[11]

Rather it is this power differential that determines that we understand the wood as merely 'content' and the craftsman as 'agent of expression'. Massumi points out that if we see the craftsman instead as produced by 'the apprenticeship system or technical school that trained him' he becomes content – content and expression are relative, and they themselves can be seen as organized into forms of qualities or of functions. Such a form is not separable from its substance but '*is* that substance seen from the point of view of the actions to which it submits and the changes of state through which it passes.'

Massumi provides us with an (Deleuzian materialist) alternative to the hylomorphic account of the architectural material, which suggests that material is itself active and does not distinguish between the physical forces (the plane smoothing it) and immaterial forces (the building standard that determined its fire treatment in a certain way) that produce it. Within this account the line that is a string of code in a computer or an idea is no less material than a piece of wood or a spoken sentence; each acts. While only a few essays in this book take such a position – and it may even be problematic to think of a material as a constellation of forces when we are trying to stage a discussion about architectural materials (since how are we to separate them, then, from tools, treatises, tables, institutions, geometries and so on?) – Massumi's account suggests how the simple undertaking of attending to the material can yield the extremely wide range of issues that emerge in the essays collected here.

Massumi's account also problematizes the reason that is often given for the contemporary interest in materials. It has become commonplace to understand the recent interest in materials in architecture as a response to the impact of the computer on our discipline, or, in a more sophisticated version of the same argument from Sheila Kennedy entitled, tellingly, 'Material Presence: The Return of the Real',[12] to consider it as a broader cultural phenomenon in an increasingly mediated world – a longing for the material we have lost. But although we may live in an image-saturated world, it is just as material as it ever was. And for architects and architecture students, the shift to designing on the computer has not really altered their relationship with the materials of building. Orthographic drawing, whether produced digitally or manually, has always operated in the virtual realm, and always concerned itself with the formal aspects of architecture rather than the material. And if we are to take Massumi's account on board, then these distinctions – between real and ideal, between digital and manual, between formal and material – all disintegrate.

It seems more likely that the contemporary interest in materials has arisen from an intersection of concerns from rather different areas of architectural practice and theory. Firstly, after many years of research into sustainable architecture, we have had to pay more attention to the materials with which we build and, significantly, to recognize them as products. 'Green' specification requires a detailed knowledge of the sources, fabrication and transportation processes, labour and economic conditions in the construction of a material. Like the buildings they make, materials are themselves cultural artefacts, constructed in social and political contexts and subject to the same kind of critical analysis.

Secondly, changes in material production mean that we can specify the behaviour of a material rather than simply select it from an already existing range. In the United Kingdom, this shift gained momentum in the 1960s when the advent of the performance specification allowed a contractor to use any material as long as it conformed to particular standards (in terms say of fire-rating or acoustic separation). Now, the use of nanotechnologies to engineer new materials offers the possibility of designing materials with tailor-made behaviours, and smart materials can incorporate what would once have been independent building services. Materials are increasingly considered in terms of their performance as well as their appearance.

This emphasis on the performance of materials is also to be found in current philosophical discourse. As Lars Spuybroek points out, these theoretical shifts passed architecture by while it was 'caught in the local politics of language'.[13] While the architectural discipline considered the building as a representational system, material remained invisible. As Jacques Derrida showed time and time again, the medium of language remains invisible – a mirror through which we look to see meaning perfectly reflected and undistorted (as if it is a given – natural not produced). The material is as invisible as the glass and silvering through which we look to see our reflection staring back at us. Now that architectural discourse has moved away from a linguistic model which limited the role of the material to the (singular) medium of representation, it is able to engage with materials as individuated through the differences in their behaviours. Theorists such as Massumi and Manuel De Landa are concerned with the active and generative nature of materials, and practitioners such as Nox use the emergent behaviours of materials in their design process.

One criticism, however, of these discourses and practices is that their concern with material seems always to return finally to form. The classic, now often-quoted, example of a starting from material rather than from form is Gaudí's hanging chain model, where the physical behaviour of the model generates the arches for the Sagrada Familia. Here the acknowledgement of the material's agency leads only to the development of a form, albeit one inflected materially. As such, the contemporary interest in the material remains within the 'interior' of architecture, ignoring the cultural and political issues that an engagement with the material might yield. Driving this collection is the intention that the essays presented here do more than ask what the formal possibilities of these shifts in thinking about material may be.

Building materials are constituted by a whole complex of practices, and contribute their specific properties to practices which in turn produce new objects and situations. They are social and cultural constructs, produced through the complexities of legislation and regulation, through techniques of production and fabrication, through language and use. In turn they create possibilities and limitations, ways of working and experiential conditions which are specific and individuated.

SHAPING THESE MATERIALS

In putting together a book which is concerned with the specificity of material practice I have chosen to avoid the imposition of a strong editorial structure and to attend instead to the specificity of the pieces which are collected here. Rather than divide the book into titled sections, four more visual essays punctuate the text, each put together by a practitioner whose approach to material is of particular interest. A fifth piece, at the centre of the book, illustrates the hands-on workshops which preceded the symposium at 'Material Matters: Materiality in Contemporary Architectural Practice and Theory' which generated this collection.[14] In shifting the emphasis from text to image in these sections I hoped that the book could in some way acknowledge that materiality always exceeds language and offer a second kind of experience for the 'reader'. This is of course a partial and flawed strategy that perhaps serves, more than anything else, to remind us of the necessary inadequacy of a book that purports to be about material practice.

Between these visual essays, the more conventional chapters have been grouped in clusters of shared concerns. The workshop section is at the heart of the book between two clusters about making: the first is mostly concerned with the experience and expression of making, the second focuses more on the techniques and tools involved. Before these comes a cluster of more philosophically grounded texts, which each posit alternatives to the form/matter division, and the last cluster in the book is concerned with the political and cultural construction of material practices.

The book is framed by two stand-alone essays: the first looks to the history of architectural discourse to uncover possible approaches to history and materiality, and the last considers material and 'the new' or 'renewed' as foundational concerns of modernism and environmentalism, and asks how future material technologies might disrupt this model. Andrew Benjamin looks at the work of three architectural historians – Emil Kaufmann, Colin Rowe and Kenneth Frampton – in order to consider how a history of architecture as 'material possibility' might be constituted that would be different to a history of architecture as 'plan' (or ideal form). Benjamin is interested in Kaufmann's work because although it discusses plans, it locates moments of historical rupture in which new formal systems emerge. Although Rowe makes the plan central to his analysis and Frampton focuses instead on 'tectonics', for Benjamin *both* writers set up a historical continuity that is idealist. A history of material possibility must also be a materialist history, and must, he says, pay attention to differences and potentials. The importance of this essay is that it argues that a methodological shift is necessary to an architectural discourse which concerns itself with material, which would produce different historical accounts of architecture, but also understand ideas, plans, tools and the stuff of building as material in as much as each is productive in terms of their potentiality. Although only a small number of the contributors are self-conscious about the methodology they adopt, attention to the material is often described as an opening to possibility, or leads to a concern with the precise conditions and specificity of a situation. Benjamin's ideas can be traced in various guises throughout *Material Matters*, in particular in their challenge to the distinction that is all too easily made between the virtual world of the digital and the drawing, and the 'material' world of bricks and cement.

The work of architect Niall McLaughlin's practice also throws many of these distinctions into question. For McLaughlin processes, construction, site, climate, time, electronics, services and inhabitants are all the materials of building. His figure of 'the thicket' is architectural space as a kind of expanded porous boundary. In the thicket branches, poles, pigs, persons, eating and chasing are indistinguishable and intertwined, as in our increasingly networked space.

The first cluster of essays explores alternative conceptual structures in which to think about material assisted in each case by a particular philosopher. Stephen Walker thinks through the work of the artist Gordon Matta-Clark in relation to Bergson's critique of the Cartesian and scientific understanding of matter as inert and predictable, and in particular to his idea that thinking concerned with fabrication cannot stop at the form of things and must consider matter as 'indifferent to its form'. The selection of artworks discussed here demonstrate matter's refusal to be subordinated to form or cultivation, and that it has its own life force and differs from itself. Peg Rawes takes Leibniz's concept of the plenum and shows how it might offer an understanding of experience that is embodied both materially and psychically. The plenum is at once continuous and differentiated; differentiation makes possible internal differences by degree. In the final section, 'Plenum III', a young woman is described at work on an architectural drawing in relation to the space she is in, her thoughts and sensations, and a phone conversation. For Rawes the plenum challenges the belief that geometry is abstract and suggests that qualitative differences produce geometries. Jon Goodbun is interested in relationships between mind, body, space and society, particularly in terms of the materialist philosophy of Marx and the empathy theory of Schmarsow. Even within these accounts, he suggests – and in notions of architectural space, in cybernetic concepts of networks and the contemporary desires of architects such as David Greene to create an 'immaterial' architecture – we can still locate 'spiritual forms'.

Raoul Bunschoten describes the interest of his practice CHORA in the 'dynamic' of material. This dynamic is present in the 'thinking hand' moulding a ball of clay and in the processes of human activities, exchanges and emotions at an urban scale, which Bunschoten also terms 'materiality'. The idea of dynamic materiality allows a continuity between projects at 1:1 scale and urban analysis, or at the scale of building as will be realized in the pavilion in Homerton in 2006.

Following from Bunschoten's interest in the dynamism of material, the central core of essays explore making, the most obvious form of material practice. The first cluster of these texts is particularly concerned with the experience and expression of making. Elizabeth Shotton revisits the intense and imprecise materiality of Le Corbusier's later work, but uses painting to think about approaches to materials which might either impose order on them or utilize the order they offer. She argues that Le Corbusier's own painting practice brought about a realization of the power of materiality which transferred to his later architectural work. This idea, that the experience of making might inform and develop a heightened understanding of material is also explored in Scott Poole's meditation on the importance of slowness in architectural education. For Poole the speed with which students can generate forms digitally does not allow for the acquiring of a more durable and particular knowledge which comes from careful attention to making. Alan Chandler is concerned that materials are too often an afterthought in architectural design, and he too asks how making and risk-taking can contribute to architectural pedagogy. He outlines three possible approaches to technical study: the technical strategy as developed by Peter Salter, the 'negotiated item', and the hands-on workshop – an event, he suggests, in which students can engage with the potentials of material and begin to understand that construction is a social process. Chandler's essay acts as an introduction to the visual collection of workshops which lies at the heart of the book. From the tea house erected in a week with traditional Japanese techniques to the physical computer built of sash pulleys and ropes, the workshops explore materiality through construction, modelling, drawing, ornament, taste, smell, sound and light.

The second cluster of making-related essays investigates 'crafts', as Pablo Miranda puts it, in terms of their techniques and practices. Martin Bechthold describes his research into building ferrocement shells in combination with parametric digital design tools and manufacturing techniques. He suggests that these techniques can do more than simply develop more complex forms and have the potential to reinvent defunct building techniques and transform our reliance on standardized components. Pablo Miranda suggests that the craft of the architect is drawing, and looks at how the tools of drawing delimit and prescribe design and reinforce traditional techniques. The computer further cements these structures, but they become hidden from the user and cannot evolve. In Dendroid, Miranda's project for a chemical drawing computer, the pattern of material deposits in the computer's electrochemical bath can grow different forms of projective transformations and allow for the possibility of change. Rachel Cruise turns to the sewing of bespoke clothing to explore two very different methodologies of material practice. The tailor's method is highly standardized and is set up precisely to overcome the 'abnormalities' of the cloth and the gentleman's body. The home-sewer's method is iterative and intuitive and produces and works out of the irregularities and differences of fabric and wearer. Her analysis hints at the architectural possibilities of the home-sewer's method, and suggests that it is not so much a formal idea which determines the artefact as the constellation of practices which go into its making.

Richard Wilson's sculpture re-uses materials and alters them at an architectural scale. It might be seen to have some formal similarities with Gordon Matta-Clark's building dissections, but he reveals rather different preoccupations and ways of working. While Wilson acknowledges that in his earlier work materials were put to work in the service of an idea, his newer work is more concerned with developing from its material context and processes.

In his piece which looks at how building materials in late-colonial Cape Town were politicized through legitimization, exclusion and their relation to the colonized 'other', Nicholas Coetzer issues a pertinent warning. He explains that 'material-based phenomenology . . . is political in its *erasing* of any overt political traces . . . this text is also a cautionary note against a material-based phenomenology that valorises building materials – particularly "natural" ones in rural conditions – as these can "bewilder the senses" and subdue our critical faculties.' Material is not prior to the constructive act, it is as much a social construction itself and this is all too easily forgotten in much architectural discourse. For the authors of this final cluster of essays, material attention opens up questions of legislation, regulation, maintenance and use. Clare Melhuish takes architectural history's placing of the Brunswick Centre as a piece of brutalist concrete expression to task. Its realization in concrete was not the intention of its architect but a result of economy and expedience, and in her careful use of residents' experiences she resists easy stereotypes and develops a complex and social understanding of the Brunswick's materiality. Helen Stratford compares two very different pieces of architecture: the paper room, an installation by 5th Studio in an existing paper mill, and the American Air Museum at Duxford by Foster and Partners. The first uses found waste products – cardboard panels, paper sheets and bales – to construct a visitors' centre, while the second must constantly remove dust, dirt and debris from its hi-tech glass and steel spaces and displays. Stratford looks particularly at how the paper room had to conform to building regulations and at how it challenges notions of a proper public space. The Air Museum is seen as an architecture which is constantly reproduced through its heavily regulated maintenance activities. Material and buildings are always implicated, in and of the world. In discussing her work with a group of African women who are beginning the process of making their own homes, Doina Petrescu asks how their principle of 'putting together and sharing' might be realized in an architectural project. The specificities of place, culture, gender and local forms of negotiation make an 'architecture' that is more fluid than solid, and more matter than form, and demonstrate the radical alterity of building in another context.

Many of the book's themes appear in Andrew Freear's reflective discussion of his work with Rural Studio: self-building as pedagogy, the particularities of local legislative and social context, material experimentation and re-use. Because they work with limited means, Rural Studio's buildings invent from what they have and try to make insertions which are responsible and appropriate.

In the closing essay Susannah Hagan identifies modernism's longing for the new as a version of the myth of resurrection which has been pursued at great environmental cost. We need, she argues, to return to a cyclic model where matter is only ever reformed and make (or adapt) architecture accordingly – but without necessarily returning to old forms of building. In a responsible future, architects may have to relinquish their role as form givers, and 'grow' materials rather than give them shape. Social imperatives and new technologies may well, finally, be the undoing of the grip that hylomorphism has held on architectural and material practices for so long.

1 >For more on the specification as representation, see my 'Specifications: Writing Materials in Architecture and Philosophy' in *ARQ* 8/3–4, 2006, pp. 227–83.
2 >John Protevi, *Political Physics: Deleuze, Derrida and the Body Politic*, London: The Athlone Press, 2001, p. 7.
3 >*Ibid.*, p. 8.
4 >*Ibid.* Protevi makes this point in relation to the work of Gilbert Simondon.
5 >This discussion is based mostly on Aristotle's account in Book Zeta of the *Metaphysics.* See Aristotle, *Metaphysics*, trans. Hugh Lawson-Tancred, London: Penguin, 1988.
6 >*Ibid.*, p. 174.
7 >René Descartes, *Discourse on the Method* and the *Meditations*, trans. F.E. Sutcliffe, London: Penguin, 1968, pp. 108–12.
8 >Gaston Bachelard is a rare example of a philosopher concerned with this problem. Not only is he aware of philosophy's tendency to privilege form over matter, he also raises the question of individuation: 'I was immediately struck by the neglect of the material cause in aesthetic philosophy. In particular it seemed to me that the individualizing power of matter had been underestimated. Why does everyone always associate the notion of the individual with form?' Gaston Bachelard, *Water and Dreams: An Essay on the Imagination of Matter*, trans. Edith Farrell, Dallas: Dallas Institute Publications, 1983, p. 2.
9 >For recent developments see, for example, Michelle Addington and Daniel Schodek, *Smart Materials and Technologies for the Architecture and Design Professions*, Oxford: Architectural Press, 2005.
10 >Brian Massumi, *A User's Guide to Capitalism and Schizophrenia*, Cambridge, Massachusetts: The MIT Press, 1992, p. 10.
11 >*Ibid.*, p. 12.
12 >Sheila Kennedy, *KVA: Material Misuse*, London: AA Publications, 2001, p. 4.
13 >Lars Spuybroek, *NOX Machining Architecture*, London: Thames & Hudson, 2004, p. 4.
14 >The varying formats of academic texts and practice-based essays here reflect the different forms of presentation at the conference. Practitioners tended to speak ad lib to images, or, in the case of the workshop presentations and tours, by showing the work. They were asked how they would like to transform their contributions into a book format.

PLANS TO MATTER: TOWARDS A HISTORY OF MATERIAL POSSIBILITY

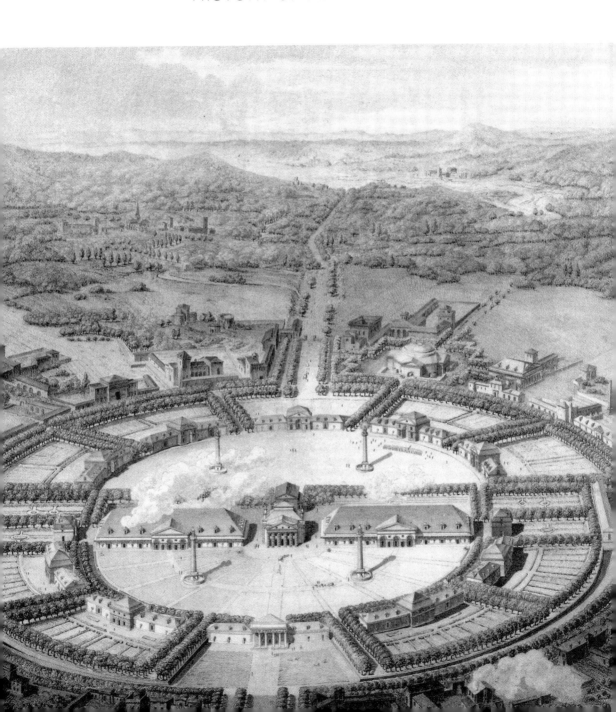

CHAPTER 2

ANDREW BENJAMIN >PLANS TO MATTER: TOWARDS A HISTORY
OF MATERIAL POSSIBILITY

A concern with the history of any practice has to recognize that the status of the
object, and thus its presence within differing fields of activity, is always
negotiable.[1] And yet, objects are never determined absolutely; rather, they are
always in a state of construction. Forms of determinacy, therefore, have a type of
inevitability. To be specific, this means that arguments to do with breaks and
ruptures as marking the history of any discursive practice cannot be taken as ends
in themselves. Breaks and ruptures – forms of discontinuity – are not just internal
to the history of any practice; more significantly, they are internal to the way the
object of that history is constituted. These opening considerations, ones that
clearly demand greater precision, nonetheless allow for differences within the way
the history of architecture is thought of. The result of this reformulation is that
history cedes its place not just to histories but also to their intentions or uses.

Within this frame of reference a distinction can be drawn between a history
of architecture that becomes the history of the plan and a history of architecture as
the history of material possibilities. It should be added that the former will still
maintain a concern with materials and the latter will also be bound up with the
presence of plans. (While recognizing that the term 'plan' has a certain elasticity
within discussions of architectural practice and history, in this context the term is
taken as identifying architecture's drawn presence where that presence is defined
by the project of instantiation defined in terms of representation and scale.) The
conjecture will be that, to the extent that emphasis moves from the centrality of
the plan to that of material possibility, there is a concomitant rethinking of how
both materials and plans are to be understood. Moreover, they will have a different
status depending upon the nature of the practice involved. The use value of these
differing conceptions of history will also change. The implicit project at work here
concerns the relationship between history and design. Once a form of relationality
is central, then history cannot be taken as an end in itself – nor is there just history.
History *for* design may have a status that begins to allow for its separation from
any immediate conflation with a history *of* design.

Central to the overall argument is the understanding of materials as sites of
potentiality. Material possibilities can be understood in a number of different ways.
Three of the most immediate are the following. In the first instance, the potentiality
of a given material; in the second, using the properties of one material to open up
architectural possibilities within other materials; finally, allowing drawings or
diagrams to suggest spatial relations given through material possibilities as
opposed to form creation. The affinity between each of these positions is located in
the definition of the architectural in terms of the relationship between materiality
and potentiality. What is also reconfigured is what counts as the image of
architecture. The aim of this text is to move towards the position in which
materiality could begin to play an important role in the creation of architectural
histories that, to use the formulation advanced above, are written *for* design.

Pursuing these possibilities will occur via three approaches to the question
of history. For the sake of brevity they will be identified with three proper names:
Emil Kaufmann, Colin Rowe and Kenneth Frampton. Their strengths and
limitations will open up another path of engagement, namely one defined by
material possibility. Questions immediately arise. How is the potential of a material
to be identified? What, in such a context, would 'material possibility' involve? Is
possibility potentiality? It is not as though these are new questions: while they

have a certain ubiquity, more specifically they play a fundamental role in the German style debate inaugurated by Heinrich Hübsch's pamphlet of 1828, *In welchem Style sollen wir bauen?*[2]

After taking up the central concern of this text – preparing the way for the argument that a fundamental shift occurs if material possibility is taken as providing aspects of architecture's history with a form of coherence rather than explicating that history in terms of the centrality of the plan – the problem of the relationship between materiality and potentiality will still have to be addressed. The problem is as much philosophical as it is central to architectural theory. This is especially the case firstly when the latter is delimited by the complex and divergent demands of design and secondly when the material is not reducible to mere matter – such a move equates materialism with empiricism – but allows for a connection between the material and the digital.[3] (While this latter point – the connection between the material and the digital – is not the direct concern of this text, it is important to note that once representation is moved to one side as the framework within which architectural diagrams are to be understood, then it becomes possible to see a relationship between the immateriality of the digital image [e.g. a spline-based geometry] and a different form of connection to material realization. A connection that, precisely because of its directness, eschews questions of representation while distancing at the same time the determinations of scale.)

DISCONTINUITY BETWEEN PLANS: KAUFMANN

In opening a space in which material possibility will be a concern for an approach to architectural history that is formulated in terms of design, a beginning can be made with the way Emil Kaufmann, in his *Von Ledoux bis Le Corbusier*, interprets what he takes as the fundamental shift from the Baroque to the Neo-Classical.[4] Kaufmann's significance does not lie in the limits that would be established by concentrating on the implicit operation of historicism within his text but in his commitment to an interpretation of the history of architecture in terms of interruption and discontinuity. However, it is not as though either discontinuity or interruption exist *in simpliciter*. The question that has to be posed, therefore, concerns how the locus of the disjunction is itself to be understood.[5]

For Kaufmann the fundamental moment that marks the end of what he refers to as the Baroque 'concatenation' (Verband) is the production of Ledoux's plans for The Salt Works (La Saline) at Chaux. What occurs with this movement is, in Kaufmann's words, the 'break up of the Baroque concatenation' (die Zertrümmerung des Barocken Verbandes).[6] He then goes on to argue that,

> in a remarkable parallelism with general historical evolution,
> the pavilion system, the free association of autonomous existence is
> substituted for the concatenation henceforth becoming the dominant
> system.[7]

In regards to the master plan for the city of Chaux, in Kaufmann's formulation of the argument the plan has even more autonomy in regards to nature than is found in 'medieval cities', while the planner (Der Baumeister) 'no longer attempts to raise up the countryside as was done by artists in the Baroque.'[8]

Vue perspective de la Ville de Chaux

An examination of the 'Vue perspective de la Ville de Chaux' (figure 2.1) indicates the extent to which autonomy prevails. The intrinsic interrelatedness within the Baroque, from this perspective, has indeed been broken. The levels of autonomy are not simply external to each block, the blocks are autonomous in relation to each other. In addition, the wall separating the city from the countryside has to be interpreted as another marker of autonomy. It should be noted that the plate presenting this structuring of autonomy is called a 'Vue perspective'. The image of architecture – and as such what will count as 'the architectural' – is that which can be presented within a perspectival view. Autonomy, therefore, does not exist as an end in itself; it cannot be separated from a certain conception of the architectural. What is on view is the pavilion system. The methodological impetus guiding the analysis is advanced by Kaufmann in his later work *Architecture in the Age of Reason*, in which he argues that 'forms recur; systems don't'.[9] (Parenthetically, such a supposition would be the point of departure for any real engagement with Deleuze's claim in *Le Pli* that the Baroque should be understood not as a historical period but as an 'operative function'.[10])

What underpins the analysis that Kaufmann is undertaking is the centrality of a certain conception of the drawn line: a conception in which 'the line' (the graphic marks defining the plan) is of necessity representational. As such, not only is it delimited by the structure of representation – a structure in which representation becomes the image and thus the presence of architecture – it also cannot have a diagrammatic, and hence generative, quality.[11] On one level there is simply no doubt that if the plans for any of the walls of La Saline are compared with Borromini's drawings of plans for San Carlo alla Quattro Fontane (assuming such a drawing to be quintessentially Baroque), then it is clear that the autonomy

– and what could be described as a conception of relatedness that depends upon separation, and which structures the approach taken by Ledoux – sunders any possibility of an original conception of interrelatedness. (This point will be pursued presently in relation to the respective images.) Initial interrelatedness – a form of connection in which separation is always an after-effect rather than a point of origination – is another way of identifying what Kaufmann means by the Baroque 'concatenation'.

While, on one level at least, the reality of the distinction cannot be doubted there are two elements that warrant consideration. The first is the conception of line – and, by extension, the plan – that is implicit in the argument. The second is that once the process is repositioned in terms of the abstract conceptions of relation and separation on the one hand, and the temporal dimensions inherent in the initial versus the punctual on the other (the latter being the moment of separation that allows as much for autonomy as it does connection) then a possible transformation both of the line and of what is being staged becomes possible. And yet, while possible it need not be actualized. The question of actualization (a possibility held in place by abstraction) – bringing not just a link to material but an inscription of material possibility into the process – is integral to the move from the centrality of the plan. Conversely, part of the argument will also be that, despite appearances to the contrary, the convention both of the plan as well as the relation of separation and connection – including temporal determinations – will allow for the incorporation of a certain conception of materiality which can be thought in terms of these conventions. In other words, if there is to be a redefinition of the architectural object then the move from the plan is not a move to materiality *tout court*. Materiality cannot be simply invoked as though there were only one way of accounting for its presence; as though precisely because it is matter it would then only have determinant quality. Rather than simply positing the presence of matter, what is important is developing a materialist account of matter. As will emerge from the discussion of Frampton's evocation of tectonics – as if that evocation alone brought matter into play – it is all too easy to provide an idealist account of materials.

As was suggested, two images can be juxtaposed in order that what is implicit in Kaufmann's argument can be brought out. (It should be noted that these images do not form part of the textual detail of Kaufmann's argument; rather, they provide a way of privileging both the notion of interruption and the interarticulation of interruption and the drawn plan.) The first of these is *Albertina 175*, Borromini's drawing of the plan of San Carlo (figure 2.2). The second is Plate 11 of Ledoux's *L'Architecture*, which consists of the plans and elevations of the Hospice at Chaux (figure 2.3). Of central concern here is the interpretation of them as drawn plans. In other words, to the extent that architecture is equated with the plan such that plans not only represent architecture, they are also the objects of its history. Borromini's drawing brings the thick line that incorporates column and wall and locates the entrance (door/porch) as given by the relationship between the operation of the ellipse that generates the internal volume in relation to the line carrying the wall and column. All aspects of the drawing are interconnected. The particular relationship of architectural elements – wall, column, and internal volume – cannot be separated from each other. This is what Kaufmann refers to as the Baroque 'concatenation'. The drawing, therefore, has to be understood as the

2.2 >Borromini:
Half-plan for the
church of S. Carlo
alle Quattro Fontane,
Rome. From
reproduction in
Anthony Blunt,
Borromini, p. 62.

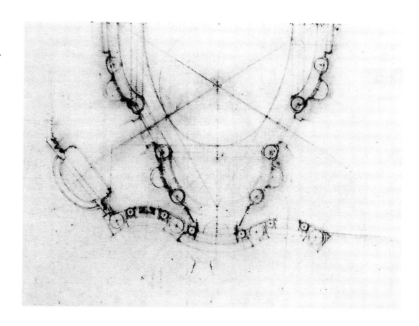

2.3 >Ledoux:
Hospice. Top Image:
Perspective View;
Bottom Image:
Elevation View.
From Claude
Nicolas Ledoux,
L' architecture,
Plate 11.

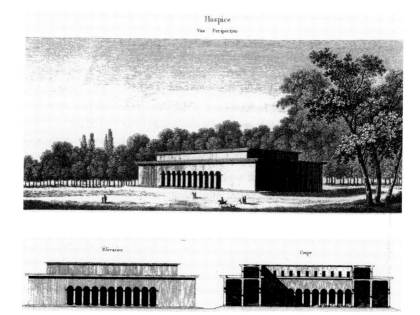

presentation of those concatenated elements. The relationship between the elements within Borromini's drawing – an interconnection that lends itself to the description of an already present interrelatedness – represents an actual possibility that, on the level of the plan, is discontinuous with the state of affairs present in Ledoux's drawing of the plans and elevation for L'hospice.[12]

What is presented by Ledoux is different. Our question, however, must concern the nature of that difference. Merely positing difference lacks any explanatory force; it is nothing more than a form of philosophical essentialism. Plate 11 includes floor plans and elevations. In addition, there is a contextual illustration. In every instance what is a work is a representation of autonomy. However, it is far from sufficient to understand autonomy as mere internal regulation. All architectural drawings, on that account, would tend towards the autonomous. The illustrations on the Plate define the architectural in terms of a system of additions and divisions. Lines demarcate space. Each block has, as a result of drawing, a separate existence. Each block can be further divided – a division that is regulated by the initial dimensions – such that subsequent divisions remain autonomous in relation to others. What coheres is a unity of separable, and thus isolatable, entities. The plans lack, therefore, the possibility of interwoven interconnection. Connection involves separation. In addition, it is not difficult to envisage – either on the level of the elevation or the plan – further addition. The system allows for such a possibility, while the Baroque concatenation precludes it by definition. Kaufmann sums up the position in the following terms:

> In place of the conception of architectural form as living organic nature, there enters the feeling for strict geometry.[13]

Finally, therefore, whatever force Kaufmann's argument has it is located in the incommensurability on the level of plan – where the plan is understood as a static representation rather than a dynamic play of forces – between these two images of architecture, i.e. between the Baroque and the Neo-Classical defined in terms of the pavilion system.

CONTINUITY BETWEEN PLANS: ROWE
Contrary to the spirit of Kaufmann – a spirit that seeks discontinuity – are the arguments of Colin Rowe. Rowe's position – first developed in his paper 'The Mathematics of the Ideal Villa' and continued throughout the differing attempts to forge relationships between Palladio on the one hand and Mies and Le Corbusier on the other – is preoccupied not simply with problem of continuity but with the more insistent one of how, were there to be discontinuities, they would be identified.[14] Rowe and Kaufmann can be seen, at least initially, as staging two radically different possibilities. Again, the question is the nature of this difference.

Rowe's early paper, in which his initial arguments are first formulated, involves the continual charting of differences and similarities between Palladio and Le Corbusier. The argument is not a general one. In the end it concerns the relationship between Villa Foscari and Villa Stein. Wary of too quick a generality, Rowe is always concerned to argue through specifics. Prior to any encounter with Rowe's actual positioning of these two buildings, the question that has to be addressed (and which must prefigure any encounter with analyses of this nature) concerns what it is that is being compared and thus what drives the analysis. In other words, what allows for such a comparison? What provides it with its ground?

The answer to these questions is given as much by the epigram from Wren's *Parentalia* as it is from the quotation from Le Corbusier that provides the opening moves of Rowe's argument. The central point in the passage cited from Wren concerns the status of the line within architectural drawing. The line is not just defined in representational terms; the representational and the aesthetic are combined. Wren, in Rowe's citation, writes, '(T)here are only two beautiful positions of straight lines, perpendicular and horizontal'.[15] Rowe uses the citation, in a description of the Villa Savoye, central to which is the formulation: 'Le plan est pur'.[16] This will come to predominate his argument. It is, of course, not just the purity of the plan that is central; it is the conception of line – 'perpendicular and horizontal' – that informs such a thinking about plans that will also play a structuring role. In other words, central to the identification of similarity and dissimilarity is the centrality of this conception of the line – a geometry with an inbuilt aesthetic dimension – and the possibility, one perhaps always mediated by the inevitability of its realization, of the plan's inherent purity.

Rowe's tracking back and forth between the two villas begins with the supposition that what is central in both instances is the 'block'. Variation is set by that centrality. Rowe argues, for example, that in both there is a 'dominant scheme' which then 'becomes complicated by interplay with a subsidiary system.'[17] The identification of difference within a 'subsidiary' component – indeed even the identification of such a component as 'subsidiary' – allows for the retained centrality of the block. Rowe, however, is not going to argue that the villas should be approached as though they were simply identical, or even the same in any straightforward sense. The relation between them is significantly mediated by an all-important 'almost'. There is no point arguing that there is a simple continuity. The worlds opened up by Palladio and Le Corbusier differ radically. The pretensions of Modernism versus Classicism involve obvious differences. And yet, even in recognizing such distinctions, the possibility of there being points of connection opens up the possibility for Rowe of having to rethink what is at stake in the departure from Palladio. Equally it necessitates rethinking as much the move to Modernism as it does Modernism's own self-theorization.[18] (This latter concern – Modernism's self-conception – is extensively treated by Rowe in later texts.[19])

The point of departure should not be the question of similarity but the ground of difference. On what basis can two buildings differing in time of construction by hundreds of years be compared? Asking this question opens up architecture's fascination with its own founding myths. Whether it is Laugier's 'primitive hut' or Semper's 'four elements', architecture continues to create myths of origin that then allow all of its variants to be versions of the same. On one level a similar narrative occurs here. What is important is how these differences come to be expressed. The roof in both instances furnishes, for Rowe, important 'differences'. Rowe argues that:

> Another chief point of difference lies in the interpretation of the roof. At the Malcontenta this forms a pyramidal superstructure, which amplifies the

volume of the house; while at Garches it is constituted by a flat surface, serving as the floor of an enclosure, cut from and thereby diminishing the house's volume. Thus, in one building the behaviour of the roof might be described as additive and in the other as subtractive; but, this important distinction apart, both roofs are then furnished with a variety of incidents, regular or random, pediment or pavilion, which alone enter into important – though very different – relations with vertical surfaces below.[20]

What is being staged here is the location of difference in terms of a relation to the centrality of the block. Addition and subtraction allow for distinctions to be noted and thus differences established. Even programmatic concerns, which are effects of structural variation, are occasioned because the retained centrality of the block allows for them to occur and for structure to sustain the programme.

Rowe, by incorporating a redrawing of the work of Palladio and thus allowing drawing to provide the basis of comparison, equally re-presents Le Corbusier's work in order to demonstrate firstly that organization and reorganization take the purity of the plan as the point of departure. However – and this is the second point – the identification of a commitment to 'elementary mathematical regulation' necessitates its location for Palladio in the floor plan, whereas in the case of Le Corbusier it is 'transposed' to the elevation. Questions of continuity and discontinuity are located in the way this transposition is presented and then commented upon. In other words, it is not only the case that the ground of the analysis lies in the way the redrawing is presented, it is equally important to recognize that what the drawings are taken to represent – the guarantee they possess as the image of architecture – is their relation to a mathematical ideal.

Two interrelated conclusions can be drawn here. The first is that the plan, while functioning as the representation of architecture, is itself governed by a form of ideality. In relation to the ideal, differences become epiphenomena. The second consequence is that precisely because of the interconnection – a connection present in and as the drawn line – between representation and a governing ideal, there cannot be any direct relation between geometry and materiality. The drawn line, as a consequence, will represent – of necessity – something other than a material possibility precisely because the lines are taken to represent spaces which are themselves understood in terms of ideals. What is opened up, therefore, as a question is how the relationship between the drawn line and the material presence could be brought about. Once the relation can be posed as a question rather than there being a sense of entailment, this reinforces the plan's purity and inscribes it further in the realm of ideals rather than material possibilities.

A final point needs to be added: while it can always be argued that Kaufmann's historicism may limit his project, much can still be gained by comparing his approach to Rowe's.[21] Kaufmann retains the centrality of the plan, and is therefore committed to a history of architecture as the history of plan even though that history allows for a form of discontinuity. Rowe, equally, is committed to a history of architecture in which the plan defines its object. Rowe's conception of continuity is, however, not structured by a form of historicism – rather it is structured by idealism. The important conclusion to be drawn – and part of that importance includes its implications in relation to a concern with materials – is that there is an ineliminable divergence within formulations of architectural history that are determined by the plan. While the plan has a history, it will also be the case that any one form it takes – a history as a discursive event – may diverge importantly from another. Not only does the recognition of this state of affairs have real implications for any understanding of historiography, it also indicates that the plan cannot, by definition, have an essential quality. The presence of conflict precludes from the start that very possibility. In sum, the history of the plan precludes its idealization.

IDEALIST TECTONICS: FRAMPTON

If the plan, as that which orientates or defines the object of architectural history, is put to one side precisely because a link between the representational line and materiality cannot be established, then it would seem to be the case that it looks, though only initially, that standing opposed to this insistence on the plan is a concern with tectonics. The reason for a necessary equivocation here is that there are fundamentally different conceptions of the tectonic. One of the most influential of these is the position argued for by Kenneth Frampton, which emerges from his engagement with Bötticher and Semper (and it needs to be emphasized that the engagement is Frampton's, the potential of both Bötticher and Semper is not exhausted by this one encounter).[22] Frampton's classic formulation of this position is found in his paper, 'Rappel à l'Ordre: The Case for the Tectonic',[23] and his explicit point of departure involves arguing against a conception of architecture that can be identified with 'spatial invention as an end in itself'.[24] The production of form cannot be taken as that which both delimits and defines the design process. Architecture cannot be reduced to form creation. For Kaufmann what marked Ledoux out was his 'will to form'.[25]

While only implicit in the formulation of Frampton's argument, the move against 'spatial invention' in which invention and creation come to be linked, is not just a position intended to open up the tectonic, it is equally, and as significantly, a claim that the site of criticality is not the plan. The important point is, therefore, that even if dominance involves the retention of the plan – retained within a history written from the position of either discontinuity or continuity – an engagement with dominance, and therefore the project of the critical has to dissociate itself from the varying possibilities that define a plan- or form-based history of architecture. (Equally, it has to differentiate itself from a conception of design that takes the plan as either the locus of continuity or of an enacted disruption brought about by a reworking of the plan.) To the extent, therefore, that 'deconstruction' in architecture takes the plan, and thus form creation, as its point of orientation (and it is not difficult to see Eisenman's engagement with Terragni in precisely this light) it becomes possible to argue that while 'deconstruction' may be a version of architectural autonomy it is so precisely because it is a critical practice – even if self-defined as such – that is structured around the centrality of the plan. The dominant plan becomes the object of a 'deconstruction'.[26]

Rather than 'deconstruction' or other variants of innovation as form creation, for Frampton there needs to be a radical alternative. The alternative position involves, at least in its formulation, the elimination of the plan as that which defines the object of the architectural. What has to occur is a return to 'the structural unit as the irreducible essence of architectural form'.[27] At the beginning, therefore, the actual formulation of the architectural, whilst not mythic in a direct sense, evokes nonetheless original and transcendental motifs. They function as that which falls outside history in order to provide history's transcendental condition of possibility. What other meaning could be attributed to the presence of an 'irreducible essence'? It must be transhistorical in order that it grounds the historical. Furthermore, Frampton's recasting of history pivots around the 'joint'. The centrality of the latter is found in its being the point of connection between the telluric and the immaterial. The joint, in Frampton's argument, brings together movement towards the earth and the opposing flight into space. Semper is invoked in the formulation of the argument:

> Semper's emphasis on the joint implies that a fundamental syntactical transition may be expressed, as one passes from the stereotomic base to the tectonic frame, and that such transitions constitute the very essence of architecture. They are the dominant constituents whereby one culture of building differentiates itself from the next.[28]

Prior to any consideration of the role of Semper in the argument, Frampton's formulation warrants attention.

In the passage cited above the 'joint' becomes the site in which the 'very essence of architecture' can be detected. This formulation reiterates the one noted above, in which the 'structural element' becomes the 'irreducible essence of architectural form'. The presentation of structural elements, and thus tectonics, in terms of essences is not the work of chance. Part of the result of this use of a productive essentialism is that it allows Frampton to connect Viollet-le-Duc, Wright and Kahn on the basis of structural similarities. Continuity, though it is a fundamentally different sense of continuity than the one already identified as at work in Rowe, is established through what can be described as the idealization of matter. Indeed a concern with materials actually becomes a concern within a complex sense of structure – and thus not a concern with materials at all. What defines this sense of structure, as opposed to one in which there is reduction of tectonics to structures and façades, is the operation of material possibilities and tectonics. What is meant by an idealization of matter is straightforward: instead of viewing matter – now understood as a general term for structure and the tectonic – in terms of matter's material qualities, it becomes the site in which the essential is at work. (And hence, matter would no longer matter.) Precisely because of this conception of matter, what then comes into play is the necessity for a relation of constancy – one almost bound by a conception of propriety, though linked too quickly to the visual – between the frame and building's appearance.

The necessity within Frampton's argumentation for an idealist, as opposed to materialist, conception of matter is clear from the use made of Semper. Not only is the already noted possibility that for Semper the joint has an essential quality, there is also the additional point that links between a number of architects (again Viollet-le-Duc, Wright and Kahn) can be discerned from the 'cultural priority that Semper gave to textile production and the knot as the primordial tectonic unit'.[29] While it is always possible to argue that there is a historicist dimension in Semper – and, moreover, that Semper has a mythic account of the origins of architecture; an account transformed almost as though it were unproblematic by Frampton – a more difficult argument to sustain is that Semper idealized the 'knot'. For Semper, it can be argued, the position is importantly different.[30] Part of the evidence for the real possibility of a different approach – and thus, 'another Semper' – can be found in his treatment of the wall.[31]

The detail of his position is formulated in *The Four Elements of Architecture* in the following terms:

> Hanging carpets remained the true walls, the visible boundaries of space. The often solid walls behind them were necessary for reasons that had nothing to do with the creation of space; they were needed for security, for supporting a load, for their permanence and so on. Wherever the need for these secondary functions did not arise, the carpets remained the original means for separating space. Even where building solid walls became necessary, the latter were only the invisible structure hidden behind the true and legitimate representatives of the wall, the colourful woven carpets.[32]

The importance of this formulation is that it moves the wall away from being no more than a structural element to having a clearly defined function within (or as part of) an overall structure. While for Semper there needs to be an accord between the outward appearance of structural elements and the nature of that function, such a relationship resists any reformulation in terms of a theory of ornamentation. What has to be opened up is the potential in Semper's conception of the wall.

The wall cannot be separated from the effect of space creation. Potentially what counts as a wall need not have anything necessarily to do with the literal presence of the wall as a structural element, but will be there in terms of what can be described as the 'wall-effect'. This position is argued for in considerable detail in §62 of *Der Stil*. In that context, walls are described as 'spatial concepts' (räumlichen Begriffe).[33] There is an important addition, namely that concerns for load bearing were 'foreign to the original idea of spatial enclosure (des Raumsabschlosses)'.[34] While this formulation holds to a distinction between wall and structure, it allows for the development of materials in which wall – again as an effect – and structure come to be interarticulated.

Semper's interest in materials – a key example is 'wickerwork' – is located in the way materials operated to realize such effects. There is no need to attribute an essentialism to Semper, since his chief concern was exploring the complex relationship between materials and their inherent possibilities. These possibilities lie as much in the creation of effects as they do in the potentiality within a material in terms of the realization of that effect. Materials become registers of what they allow. What they allow will, in the end, be specific to the materials in question. What can never be precluded are attempts to 'win' Semper round to the projects of idealism. However, there is enough in his work to deflect, if not resist, precisely that possibility.

Materials in the writings of Semper can be interpreted as resisting their idealization precisely because they are bound up with architectural effects. These effects necessitate that a distinction be drawn between, on the one hand, materials – understood as sites of potentiality and implicit geometries – and, on the other, the reduction of architecture's material presence to the strictly empirical and thus to brute matter. Flowing from Semper, there is the possibility of a connection between materiality and both the conceptual and the ideational. However, both of these elements are not external to the work of matter. On the contrary, as indicated by reference to the wall, they are realized within that work. The work of matter – matter understood as 'workful' – becomes another formulation of material possibility. In sum, therefore, Semper opens up, *pace* Frampton, the possibility for a materialist account of matter precisely because matter reconceived in terms of work becomes a locus of potentiality. Potentiality is a quality intrinsic to materials once they no longer have to bear the weight of being part of architecture's irreducible essence.

Tectonics, as a term, designates a range of divergent possibilities. In Frampton's work it cannot be readily separated from an idealization of matter. Were that not to be the project (and thus if what was actually at stake involved developing a materialist account of tectonics) then central to such an undertaking would be the theoretical necessity – a necessity imposed by design practice and therefore forming an intrinsic part of architectural theory – of developing a materialist account of materials. As such, idealism would have ceded its place to materials, and hence have avoided the hold of empiricism. This would have occurred to the extent that materials can themselves become sites of experimentation and research, and the latter takes place to the extent that diagrams, models and materials are approached in terms of their potentialities rather than as representations – potentialities to become the loci of meaning and the staging of ideals.

Perhaps there needs to be a word of warning here, by way of a conclusion. One way of taking the distancing of meaning, representation and the ideational would result in the reduction of architecture to a series of pragmatic operations – as though, thereby, a concern with experimentation and the critical were abandoned in the process. At its most polemical, it would be as if, in the move to the interrelationship of the digital and the material, what then became impossible was criticality in the age of digital reproducibility. (A concomitant casualty of this so-called impossibility would be the irrelevance of architectural theory theory having been effaced in the name of the pragmatic.) Two points need to be made in response.

In the first instance criticality is internal to architecture. Neither architecture nor the critical is to be understood in terms of teleological development. As such, innovation and experimentation remain possibilities. However, that possibility has to be situated in relation to the conception of the architectural object. Once a move is made from the centrality of the plan to the relationship between the material and the digital – a relationship in which, on the level of both theorization and practice, what has to dominate is a materialist account of the work of matter – then what counts as the experimental (and thus how the critical is to be understood) will become questions with as great an exigency as before. Nonetheless, with a shift in the conception of the object, in the move from the centrality of the plan to the materialist account of the relationship between the digital and the material, the architectural object acquires a different ontological status. This occurs precisely because the latter involves a repositioning of the immaterial and the material. As such, therefore, questions pertaining to the critical and the experimental demand new forms of response. Responding to those demands – response as the creation of a locus of research – is the distancing of the pragmatic.

The second point is related. Precisely because this repositioning demands conceptual innovation (therefore there has never been a greater need for architectural theory), both the repositioning and the possibility of research can always be resisted. However, that resistance needs to be analysed, it cannot be naturalized. Any analysis will give rise to further clarification of the repositioning of the architectural object, and of how techniques in relation to that object are themselves to be understood. While innovation and experimentation can always be dismissed as novelty (and, equally, novelty can always be presented as though it were experimental and innovative), once the historicist gesture of assimilation no longer dominates then a materialist account of the work of matter comes into play – especially when that work involves, of necessity, the productive presence of the immaterial (e.g. software). A materialist account, and not an empiricist or pragmatist one, will by the nature of the activity itself occur within the space created by allowing for the affirmation of the shift in the ontology of the architectural object to identify the parameters of research. The move to materialism will work to redefine both the nature and the project of architectural theory.

1   > I wish to thank Katie Lloyd Thomas, John Macarthur and Tony Vidler for comments on an earlier version. The direction of the interpretation is mine alone.
2   > The German text was published in Karlsruhe in 1828. Hübsch's text and other texts central to the Style Debates are available in English in *In What Style Should We Build? The German Debate of Architectural Style* (introduction and translation Wolfgang Herman), Santa Monica, California: The Getty Centre, 1992. I have examined this text and the context in which the question of style and its relation to material possibility is posed in greater detail in my *Style and Time. Essays on the Politics of Appearance*, Evanston: Northwestern University Press, 2005.
3   > This is the point at which the centrality of the work of Lars Spuybroek can be located. See his *Machining Architecture*, London: Thames & Hudson, 2004.
4   > Emil Kaufmann, *Von Ledoux bis Le Corbusier*, Vienna: Rolf Pesser, 1933 (all translations are my own). On the modernity of Kaufmann, see Detlef Mertins, 'System and Freedom. Sigfried Giedion, Emil Kaufmann and the Constitution of Architectural Modernity' in R. E. Somol (ed.) *Autonomy and Ideology. Positioning an Avant-Garde in America*, New York: The Monacelli Press, 1997, pp. 212–32. In addition Hubert Damisch has provided an excellent introduction to Kaufmann's work in relation to the general question of autonomy in his preface to the French translation of *Von Ledoux bis Le Corbusier*, see 'Ledoux avec Kant' in Emil Kaufmann, *De Ledoux à Le Corbusier*, Paris: Editions de la Vilette, 2002, pp. 7–13.
5   > The central text here is Michel Foucault, *Le Mots et les choses*, Paris: Gallimard, 1978. While Foucault's approach differs fundamentally from Kaufmann's, the productive point of comparison is the insistence on discontinuity. For Foucault the regimes that organize discrete configurations – 'episteme' – are themselves sites that can generate differences explicable in terms of the 'episteme' itself. Kaufmann's sense of discontinuity is itself articulated within a teleological conception of historical time. Discontinuity, therefore, as an operative principle within different conceptions of historiography will have its own complex history.
6   > Kaufmann, *op. cit.*, pp. 16–17.
7   > *Ibid.*, p. 17.
8   > *Ibid.*, p. 18. (This paper is available in an English translation in the edition of *Perspecta* noted below.) The most significant overview of 18th-century architecture, which situates Ledoux in relation to the question of modern architecture, is Anthony Vidler, *The Writing of the Walls. Architectural Theory in the Late Enlightenment*, London: Butterworth Architecture, 1987. In addition, Vidler has provided the most exacting and judicious overview of Kaufmann's project. Drawing on a range of sources, Vidler is able to position the centrality of Kaufmann's work for any discussion of architectural autonomy (see Anthony Vidler, 'The Ledoux Effect: Emil Kaufmann and the Claims of Kantian Autonomy' in *Perspecta* 33, 2002, pp. 16–30). In the context of the argument developed here, autonomy has not been the central concern – greater significance has been

attributed to the question of discontinuity and continuity. The argument developed in this paper is not antithetical to arguments concerning autonomy, or at least there is no intent that this be the case. Rather, what is at stake is the nature of the object – and thus its discursive construct – that is taken to be autonomous. Moreover, when Kaufmann begins to reformulate the propositions of his 1933 work in English the centrality of the autonomy argument shifts. What emerges is the importance of the historiographical argument that underpins it. In, for example, the paper given to the American Society of Architectural Historians in August 1942 (subsequently published as 'Claude-Nicolas Ledoux, Inaugurator of a New Architectural System' in *The Journal of the American Society of Architectural Historians*, Vol. 3, July 1943, pp. 12–20), Kaufmann is at pains to argue that with Ledoux there is the expression of 'an entirely new system' (p. 20) and that with the house designed for Bellevue Park 'the principle of unity, evoked by Alberti in his sixth book, and so dear to Baroque hearts was abandoned' (p. 17). Kaufmann's interest lies in the history of form and thus with the history of what he calls an 'architectural system' (p. 13). This is the aspect of Kaufmann's project that is being privileged. There is no doubt, however, that formal innovation is itself bound up with the Enlightenment project of autonomy.

9   > Emil Kaufmann, *Architecture in the Age of Reason. Baroque and Post-Baroque in England, France, Italy*, New York: Dover Publications, 1955, p. 132.

10   > Gilles Deleuze, *Le Pli*, Paris: Les editions de minuit, 1987. Even allowing for the significance of Deleuze's work on the 'fold' (le pli) for the presentation of architecture, the important question for a concern with writing history *for* design is accounting for what occurs when a form of thought and form creation at work in the 17th century acquires an insistent contemporary presence. John Rajchman has traced, with real philosophical acuity, the complex set of relations between Deleuze's writings and architecture. See his *Constructions*, Cambridge, Massachusetts: The MIT Press, 1998.

11   > What is opened up here does not concern the diagram per se. Rather, what is involved is the relationship between the drawn line and material presence. Clearly this treatment of the diagram draws on Delueze's discussion of the same in his work on Foucault and on Bacon. See Gilles Deleuze, *Foucault*, Paris: Les editions de minuit, 1986 and *Francis Bacon. Logique de la sensation,* Turin: Éditions de la difference, 1981.

12   > There are, of course, other ways of understanding the relationship between the Baroque – here present in the figure of Borromini – and the Modernism of Le Corbusier. For example, Giedion argues the following in relation to the Villa Savoye:

> It is impossible to comprehend the Savoye House by a view from a single point: quite literally, it is a construction in space-time. The body of the house has been hollowed out in every direction: from above and below, within and without. A cross section at any point shows inner and outer space penetrating each other inextricabley. Borromini had been on the verge of achieving the interpenetration of inner and outer space in some of his late baroque churches.

In Sigfried Giedion, *Space, Time and Architecture*, Cambridge: Harvard University Press, 1967, p. 529. The contrast that would need to be established between Giedion and other historians would have to incorporate the differing conceptions of the architectural object figured within the analyses.

13   > Kaufmann, *Von Ledoux bis Le Corbusier*, p. 20.

14   > This paper is collected in Colin Rowe, *Mathematics of the Ideal Villa and Other Essays*, Cambridge, Massachusetts: The MIT Press, 1987, pp. 1–29.

15   > *Ibid.*, p. 2.

16   > *Ibid.*

17   > *Ibid.*, p. 9.

18   > It is in relation to this point that Robin Evans argues that, within the structure of Rowe's argument, Mies and Le Corbusier remain Neo-Palladian. See Robin Evans, 'Translation of Drawing into Building' in his *Translation of Drawing into Building and Other Essays*, London: Architectural Association, 1997, p. 87.

19   > See, in this regard, Rowe's papers 'Neo-"Classicism" and Modern Architecture. I + II' in *The Mathematics of the Ideal Villa and Other Essays,* pp. 119–59.

20   > *Ibid.*, p. 9.

21   > For an interpretation of Semper that concentrates on this aspect of his work, see Mari Hvattum, *Gottfried Semper and the Problem of Historicism*, Cambridge: Cambridge University Press, 2004.

ANDREW BENJAMIN

22   > For a judicious evaluation of the importance of Bötticher in any evaluation of the history of tectonics, see M. Schwarzer, 'Ontology and Representation in Karl Bötticher's Theory of Tectonic' in *Journal of the Society of Architectural Historians*, No. 52, September 1993, pp. 267–80.

23   > Kenneth Frampton, 'Rappel à l'Ordre: The Case for the Tectonic' in his *Labour, Work and Architecture. Collected Essays on Architecture and Design*, London: Phaidon, 2002, pp. 90–106.

24   > Frampton, *op. cit.*, p. 92.

25   > Kaufmann, 'Claude-Nicolas Ledoux, Inaugurator of a New Architectural System' in *The Journal of the American Society of Architectural Historians*, Vol. 3, No. 3, July 1943, p. 15.

26   > I have developed this approach to both the 'deconstruction' in architecture and Eisenman's work on Terragni in my 'Passing Through Deconstruction: Architecture and the Project of Autonomy' in German Celant (ed.) *Architecture & Arts 1900/2004*, Milan: Skira, 2004, pp. 433–7.

27   > Frampton, *op. cit.*, p. 92.

28   > *Ibid.*

29   > *Ibid.*, p. 100.

30   > References to Semper will be to the following editions: Gottfried Semper, *The Four Elements of Architecture and Other Writings* (translated by Harry Francis Mallgrave and Wolfgang Herrmann), Cambridge: Cambridge University Press, 1989. *Vier Elemente der Baukunst*, Braunschweig, 1851. *Der Stil*, Munich: F. Bruschmann, 1878–9. The following discussion of Semper draws on my unpublished work, 'The Surface Effect : Borromini, Semper, Loos'.

31   > Another, and different, attempt to argue for the actuality of Semper can be found in the work of Bernard Cache. See his 'Digital Semper' in Cynthia Davidson (ed.) *Anymore*, New York, 1998 and 'Gottfried Semper: Stereotomy, Biology and Geometry' in *Perspecta* 33, 2002, pp. 80–6.

32   > Semper, *The Four Elements of Architecture*, *op. cit.*, p. 104.

33   > *Ibid.*, p. 255 (German edition, p. 214).

34   > *Ibid.*

A ROYAL GITTERN AT THE BRITISH MUSEUM

3.1 >Albrecht Altdorfer,
St. George in the Forest,
1510.

A ROYAL GITTERN AT THE BRITISH MUSEUM, ENGLISH 1280–1330, ROOM 42

I will write about a building that I have dreamt of but never built. Its properties have been forming in my mind for many years. It relates to my experience of living and working in Britain.

During my first year in London I spent many Sundays exploring the British Museum. I became attached to one artefact in particular. I have tried, without success, to draw it. It is a gittern, which is a kind of early guitar. The surface of the sounding box is very closely inscribed with a delicate filigree of dense foliage. If you look closely, you can make out plump acorns among the leaves, then pigs eating them at the foot of a tree. A man with a pole shakes the branches to drop the nuts for the pigs. Someone is chasing a rabbit through the thicket. The man, the rabbit and an arrow – flying from his bow – are all held within a dense maze of branches. These things are so intertwined that it takes your eye some time to distinguish detail in the continuous, enfolded fabric of leaves. If you follow the incidents across the carved surface, you eventually arrive back at the man with the acorns and the pigs. It is a world that unfolds and repeats endlessly.

As if by design, or happy coincidence, the object in the case next to it is an astrolabe. The date of its manufacture is not much later than that of the gittern, but it seems to occupy another world. Here is a device that used the elevation of stars relative to the horizon to objectively plot a person's position on the surface of the earth. You know where you are. This was the beginning of the modern world. This perception of the horizon as an objective datum altered everything. It lifted us off the dense, intertwined face of the world and asked us to see ourselves as separate from it. In some ways, it was a loss of innocence as profound as The Fall.

In 1510, Albrecht Altdorfer was painting in Regensburg on the Danube. In trying to create a specific northern identity for German painting, challenged by the great power of the Italian city states, he made the forest his subject. *St. George in the Forest* is a painting in which the whole space of the page is engulfed in a mass of minutely observed foliage (figure 3.1). The two protagonists are dwarfed by the profusion of growth. One tiny 'window' opens in the foliage to show a mountain and sky; it is the only thing to give spatial depth to the surface of the painting. I am interested in Altdorfer's deliberate denial of perspectival devices in his attempt to create a specifically Northern European identity for the work. Here, he suggests, in the woodland, the world is a dense unfolding thicket where pattern and line are more telling than surface or placement in space.

I am not, as William Morris was, sentimental about a medieval idyll – a better age in the past. Nor am I particularly interested in the undoubted craftsmanship of the pieces I have described. I am really interested in the spatial properties of these works and what kind of world they might suggest. I will call them thickets, and suggest that the spatial property they display is that of immersion; the sense that the space we inhabit is a continuous, dense weave without edges.

I began to think about architecture of line, where boundaries are no longer described by enclosing surfaces but are intuited somewhere in an enveloping matrix of interconnected networks. It is almost blasé to say that our increasingly linked world is thicket-like.

It was possible to develop this thinking through some of my teaching work with Unit 17 at the Bartlett School of Architecture, where I and my colleagues

3.2

Philip Tabor and Yeoryia Manolopoulou teased out some of the possibilities related to thickets. An experimental teaching environment is suitable for developing ideas such as these. I don't mean to be facile when I say that it is easier to think about architecture of line when you are not obliged to keep the weather out.

One project we set for students was a visit to the Aran Islands in Galway Bay, to make working pieces that they would place in the landscape, two of which I will discuss here.

Guy Dickinson made a patch for his back, gridded with tiny needles. Each one was electronically connected to a matrix of sensors on the rocky inter-tidal

3.2 >Aran project by
Guy Dickinson.

shore. The intermittent fragile activity of the rock pools was transmitted into a tiny tattooing on his back. His own posture (remembering a powerful moment in Tarkovsky's film *Stalker*) was entirely recumbent on the freezing rocks. The piece was both vicious and tender (figure 3.2).

Siobhán Sexton made a photosensitive object that she installed in the roof of a cave on the Atlantic-facing shore. Low sunlight entered the cave and reflected off rock pools to scatter occasional fragments of wavering light onto the ceiling of the cave. The sensor in a crack on the roof patiently harvested this light. When enough energy had been gathered, it was automatically discharged by triggering the piece to play back one recorded word. This word was the name of a local family, whose last surviving member had recently emigrated. This tiny object was left in place and, very occasionally, the name is pronounced against the thunder of the sea.

These pieces suggest that it is possible for technology to act in the environment in new ways. It is not placed in opposition to the natural world; rather the relationship is one of interdependence. Machines can deal with histories and the identity of place. They can exist within natural systems and patterns of inhabitation.

Silke Vosskoetter made an artificial oasis in the Western Desert of Morocco. A loose matrix of poles supports an array of solar panels, and energy gathered during the day is used to chill the panels at night. The cool panels precipitate moisture from the air coming off the Atlantic, and this condensation is directed down into collection bags. This desert piece provides shade and water and an escape from the open sand. Something on the scale of a building, it used the interweaving of lines to make a space in this great empty landscape. It might be like hiding in a hedge. Some of the models reminded me of paintings by Cy Twombly: dense structured scribblings, suggesting space.

Later on, Silke worked with us in the practice and we designed a houseboat. Here, for the first time, we tried to resolve the problem of how to keep weather out of a building without surfaces. We thought of the external wall as an assembly of woven layers: some would form the structural shell, others the inner lining, insulation and waterproofing. Differing densities of weave could perform each function. Geometric arrays of clear plastic underfloor heating pipes ran through the walls and were connected to copper coils under the water. This solar-powered system was used to moderate the environment of the building by connecting it to the more stable temperature in deeper water (figure 3.3).

We started to think about the interior as something different from the usual architect's photo-fantasy. Instead of immaculate empty interiors with strategically placed symbolic items, we considered the architecture of intense clutter. Where everything might be tucked out of sight, we turned the storage inside out. In the tall old Edinburgh tenements, they used to hoist their laundry into hanging racks up in the ceiling. In the houseboat, we had a hanging attic where everything could be put away but remained visible. You would live within the thick plenitude of your own possessions. I remember a photograph by Jeff Wall of a man in an interior like a spider's nest. His suspended arrays of lights, scraps and possessions make their own space. This intimate, domestic thickness has considerable power, but is often seen as beyond the scope of architectural imagining. There is something bourgeois about this denial.

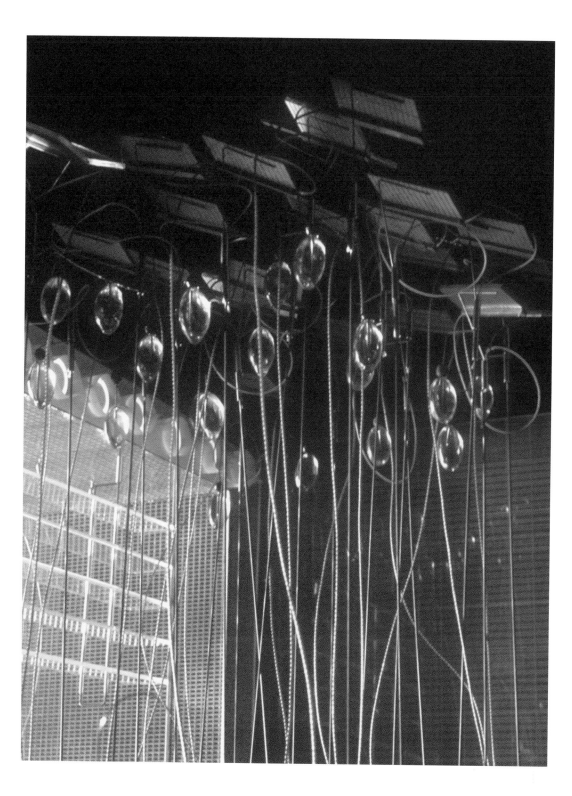

3.3 >Houseboat.

Anne Enright writes about childhood memories of pattern:

In my head is the cosy paranoia of an Irish sitting-room: Fifties curtains with an urn full of flowers woven into the net, Sixties leaves scattered all over the carpet, wallpaper from the Seventies embossed in damasked lines, and Sanderson flowers on the Eighties sofa, all of them in different shades of green perhaps, or peach, variations on a theme. All over the country people are looking at their sitting-rooms and seeing, not what they mean, but what other people think they mean, and painting the walls Magnolia Matt, painting over the pleasure and the trap, the fluid geometry that shifts and thickens from carpet to sofa to wall. The multiplication is pathological and easy, it spawns. The Irish sitting room is reproduction itself.[1]

Many ordinary environments that are considered beyond architecture have properties that we would associate with this thickened world. In our studio we collect examples and keep them on a pin board. They operate as partial versions of this building that we haven't built. Andreas Gursky's photograph of the Siemens factory shows a rain shower of tools hanging from the ceiling, suspended on airlines and cables (figure 3.13). The multi-coloured, coded, electrical and data lines fall with unstudied, casual elegance. There is so much of it that it makes a space, within which the workers gather at their tasks. For a moment you can see, in this industrial process, a glimmer of Altdorfer's wood. The image was so compelling that we tried to literally build it for the Digital Architecture Studio we designed at Oxford Brookes University. A regular cloud of acoustic baffles hangs below the concrete roof and a shower of data lines, power lines, drawing hangers and coat hangers drop through to the desks below (figure 3.5).

In two competitions we had the opportunity to literally weave our building between trees. Both are park pavilions. In each case, multiple woven layers and screens enclose the spaces. The trees appear to grow right through the interior, but this is an illusion. The building line wanders in and out to incorporate them. The roof is designed like a tree canopy with layers of gutters, solar shading, north-lights, lay-lights and festooned lighting. In some areas it is dense, while in others it thins out, and occasional lines wander out into the park. The trees and the elements of the buildings cast complex dappled shadows so that the projected lines double the architecture, weaving patterns on the ground. One pavilion – in Finsbury Park in London – is the first building of this kind that we were able to bring through the whole process of design and detailed development to a level of resolution that showed it could be viable (figure 3.4). The other – in Preston – did not win the competition. This is a great pity. It was designed like a linen-loom, one that gathers energy from its surroundings (figure 3.6). It responded particularly to the rain, because Preston is the wettest town in England. The whole roof was designed to noisily catch and delay the rainwater, sending it along chutes, across surfaces and gushing from gargoyles against windows. The rain becomes our way of animating the building and, like the shadows, it becomes a part of the architecture. In this way we began to design the building in time.

The screen has become a favourite device in our search. It is both surface and space. There is pattern, repetition and variation. Screens hold light within themselves, and this can manifest the passage of time across the day. Sometimes they seem like clocks.

3.4

3.5

3.4 >Model of Finsbury
Park pavilion, London.

3.5 >Digital Architecture
Studio, Oxford Brookes
University.

3.6

One screen, in a private house in London, is made from 300 computer-punched A4 sheets of silver-nickel suspended in a staggered array. South light is projected against the back of the screen. The arrangement of the sheets allows light to bounce around between and within each panel. Experiments decided the precise angle of the surfaces within the piece. As the sun's position changes throughout the day and the year, the screen reveals a range of luminous conditions: sometimes a glowing icon, sometimes a jagged silhouette (figure 3.7).

Rough Study for Revision of February 14 (B) is a drawing by Bridget Riley. She is patiently constructing the geometric orchestration of layers within a polychromatic array. The words I use to describe this piece are almost musical because the technique is close to music. I think that she has looked deeply into the work of Paul Klee. He was seeking connections between musical structures and the painted surface. It is the principle of polyphony applied to the use of colour.

We made a coloured screen on the face of a building. The project was for low-cost housing on an eerie site in Silvertown in East London. Derelict industrial buildings are being replaced with a weird combination of IBIS Hotels, conference centres and 'Noddy' houses. This old industrial complex had once created the cheap glory of Victorian manufactured goods – matches, coloured dyes, golden syrup, petroleum, primrose soap and fireworks; it is the home of the pearly kings and queens. Working with the artist Martin Richman, we tried to create iridescence. We used radiant light film in staggered layers behind cast glass. By developing minor variations within the geometric array between the layers, we could produce complex effects that varied throughout the day and the year. A stand of silver birch in front of the building casts fluttering indigo shadows and captures coloured particles of escaping light. On certain days, when the light is right, a coloured carpet appears briefly on the tarmac surface of the street (figure 3.8).

3.7

3.8

The effect of the running suitors in Banavari and Muhammad's painting, is electrifying – their fleeting trajectory against the sharp stillness of the earth. Figures are cast against the ground – flowers, creatures, hunters and the hunted (figure 3.9). It seems that depiction and representation were at the point where they had just recently been lifted off the woven surface of a carpet to become graphic images. Everything seems connected within an intertwined, deeply structured system. The image has neither a centre nor an edge.

Here is a fugitive dream world. One quality the thicket has is that of change. Within the spatial matrix, everything is in flux. This allows me to think of buildings as lacking a stable presence. It is a commonplace of most architectural representation that buildings have one perfect moment of being – sometime between completion and the day the photographs are taken. But the thicket has temporal properties. Connections extend back and forth. A building has no perfect moment of resolution. Its reality is equal in every phase of its conception, making, change and dissolution. The moment of the first sketch and the moment of ruin are equally pressing realities. One implication of this thinking is to challenge the idea of individual authorship. There is little scope for such a stable presence to exist in this fugitive lacework.

These two insights: that the building is never finished and that it is not the work of an individual mind, are liberating for me as an architect. It is possible to imagine my own identity as part of an interconnected network. A building project can draw into itself a thousand threads: uncertain histories, possible futures, collaborations, objections, surreal bureaucratic obstacles, microenvironments, revisions, occupation, extensions and unlikely changes of use. The identity that we

3.7 >Screen, private house, London.

3.8 >Housing in Silvertown, East London.

3.9 >Banavari and Muhammad, Untitled painting.

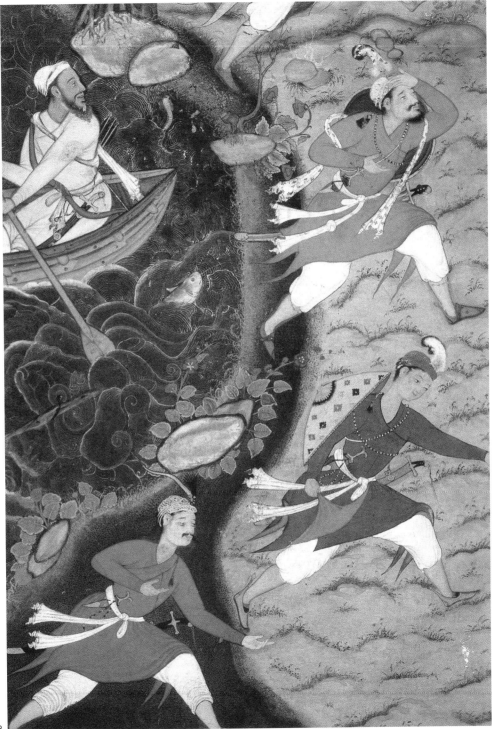

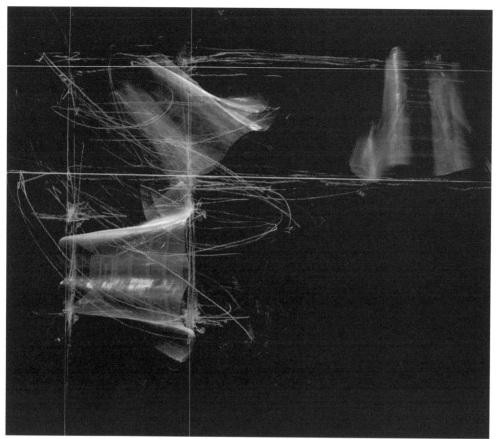

3.10

3.10 >Model of bandstand
for the De La Warr Pavilion,
Bexhill.

3.11 >Bandstand for the De
La Warr Pavilion, Bexhill,
under construction.

3.11

3.12 >Centre for the
Built Environment in Hull.

see at any point in design, construction, inhabitation, alteration and ruin is less
stable than it appears.

When we made a seafront bandstand for the De La Warr Pavilion in Bexhill,
we tried to work with this awareness. The design was carried out as a broad
collaboration between local schools. We observed and edited the process. From
time to time, we stole a version of the design to manifest it in a fixed image. We
concentrated on representing the building, not as an artefact but as a place where
invisible forces find an identity (figure 3.10). This naturally included wind, weight
and sound, but we also looked at how the occupation of the site would gradually
change, like the layout of deckchairs on a breezy day. Michael McHugh, who built
the project, took photographs of every stage of the fabrication. For me, it was more
beautiful during this period in the workshop than it was when complete (figure
3.11). The images taken during design and construction tell us something
important about the deeper identity of the piece, and when they were taken they
were the only reality.

3.13 >Andreas Gursky,
Karlsruhe, Siemens 1991.

3.13

A couple of years ago I was travelling to an interview for the commission to design a Centre for the Built Environment in Hull. I knew nothing about the place, so I asked the ticket inspector on Hull Trains to tell me what she knew about the town. For an hour she poured out stories. At least some were believable. I repeated the stories at the interview and got the job (I knew so much!). We continued the process by asking everyone the simple question, 'Why is Hull like it is?' What emerged was an imprint of the deep tissue of the place, not as fact but as myth and understanding. We used these stories to design the building. We contacted every significant manufacturer in the town to find out if their products could be incorporated into our building: caravans as rooms, shower trays as paving, beautiful Reckitts' Blue! It is clear that something of the form of the building has the fingerprint of our office, but the important things were made in Hull. In this process we saw our role as architect to be very different to the individual or master maker. We allowed ourselves to think of the architectural studio as a conduit that is intertwined, compromised, reliant, a patient conductor through which latent forces emerge (figure 3.12).

We have attempted to develop a specific architecture of line and immersion that could be said to have a thicket-like quality. I don't think that we have come close to achieving a compelling built synthesis of our ideas yet. We understand that the resolution of the ideal in a built project is not as important as the form of understanding that comes from thinking of buildings as time-bound, intertwined and fugitive. We will keep making fragments, feints and trial-pieces. In this sense, my dreamt-of building already exists in an emerging state.

1   > Anne Enright, 'Diary' in *London Review of Books*, 2 January 1997.

GORDON MATTA-CLARK: MATTER, MATERIALITY, ENTROPY, ALCHEMY

CHAPTER 4

STEPHEN WALKER >GORDON MATTA-CLARK: MATTER,
MATERIALITY, ENTROPY, ALCHEMY

Gordon Matta-Clark (1943–78) produced an extensive *œuvre* in a wide range
of media, although he is best known for his so-called 'building dissections'.
Although he worked as an artist, Matta-Clark had trained as an architect at Cornell
University in the 1960s, and discussions of his work have frequently alluded to this
background in order to contextualise it as being either against architecture, or
against object-based art, or indeed against the formal preoccupations of High
Modernism in general. But although Matta-Clark demonstrably attacked
Modernism's valorisation of form – his 'building dissections' exceed both the
architectural and artistic static object of Modernism – his work was no knee-jerk
destruction of form. His work went beyond a contestation of form brought about by
the revelation of stuff beneath the surface, where internal material could still be
understood to make up, and therefore remain subordinate to, the three dimensions
of form.

This essay will explore how his work treated this stuff beneath the surface
as *matter*, something different in kind to form, but also as something that could
differ from itself. Although Matta-Clark arguably 'looked upon all matter as if it
were carvable at will,'[1] his work nevertheless maintained matter in an intimate
(if complex) relationship to form, and in so doing it opened on to a wide variety of
issues that are usually overlooked or covered over. Indeed, it is this particular
characteristic of his *œuvre*, both contesting and maintaining assumptions made
by artists and architects, which lies behind the difficulty that art history has
experienced with Matta-Clark, and which can also go some way to explaining the
enduring interest his work exerts on architects in particular.

The various ways in which Matta-Clark's projects worked with matter
indicate the importance he attached to its particular relationship with location, and
to the kind of changes it underwent. These issues can be taken up with reference
to Matta-Clark's alchemical interest: his treatment of matter can be contrasted
with Minimalism's contemporaneous interest in entropy; and although he was
attracted to certain alchemical beliefs regarding the characteristics of matter,
his own approach called alchemy's broad project into question. In this situation,
matter is not overcome by form (although it is available to reason), and the
dynamic relationship between matter and materiality is demonstrated to involve
dimensions of nature, human culture, and individual memory.

MATERIAL MATTERS

It is difficult to begin without mentioning Plato. Not only do Neoplatonic
developments cast a certain shadow over Modernism's approach to form and the
fate of matter, there are aspects of Plato's treatment of matter which, though
frequently overlooked, can arguably anticipate Matta-Clark's own considerations.

For Plato, matter and form were incomplete co-principles of things.[2] In
various guises, whether as co-principle or (following Aristotle) essence, matter
remained a source of creative ambiguity until it was rationalised by the new
sciences of the seventeenth century, where, for René Descartes, '[t]he concept of
matter functioned . . . as a means of dividing the universe into two sorts of
substance, and consequently of dividing knowledge into two sorts of science.'[3]
Descartes referred to material substances (the things in the extended, physical
world) and to spiritual substances (in the non-extended, non-physical world), and,
while admitting that the two were linked, he clearly valorised the latter en route to

establishing his famous mind-body problem. With this move, Descartes laundered matter (as material substance) of any radical indeterminacy: it must give up all its secrets to physical science. Matter fell within the domain of modern physics, which sought a calculable and predictive understanding. The consequences of this move, of relevance in the present context, are that, ultimately, Isaac Newton replaced the concept of matter with that of 'mass' – and that natural science and philosophy parted company.

The philosopher Henri Bergson laments this move; for him it is a bad philosophy that leaves matter to science.[4] He argued against such Platonic or Cartesian approaches, suggesting that their ambitions to 'uncover' unchanging truth involved only the intellect,[5] which is predisposed to a spatialised understanding, and thus eliminates time. Just as the intellect spatialises, so the (bad) science that Bergson criticised was concerned with the repeatable, with an inert, measurable, discontinuous and predictable matter. In contrast, Bergson took time seriously, exploring the possibility that matter might differ from itself over time, and developing an understanding that exceeded the intellect: in order to get at what eludes scientific thought, he argued that 'we must do violence to the mind, go counter to the natural bent of the intellect. But that is just the function of philosophy.'[6] Although his main concern was to renovate philosophy, he suggests in the process that thought directed at action, at making, ought to consider things as provisional and capable of being carved up against the grain, arguing:

> An intelligence which aims at fabricating is an intelligence which never stops at the actual form of things nor regards it as final, but, on the contrary, looks upon all matter as if it were carvable at will . . . In short, it makes us regard its matter as indifferent to its form.[7]

Bergson's thought can help us approach the work of artists and architects, and to position and open up Matta-Clark's work in this respect. However significantly the meaning of 'form' has changed since the Classical era, it has retained its importance within art and architectural theory. Clearly, matter has suffered a different fate. Matta-Clark's œuvre consistently refuted concepts of matter that held it as either a simple problem, something to be overcome (through the use of quantifiable scientific method), or used up on the way to establishing a more important, unchanging truth. The various ways in which Matta-Clark's projects worked with matter reveal both the extent to which it can enjoy a continuing involvement in the operations of art and architecture, and the complexity of relationships it establishes as part of this process.

LOCATION OF MATTER: CULTIVATING NATURE

Matta-Clark's early work can easily be read as a reaction to his architectural education at the hotbed of Modernism which was Cornell School of Architecture in the 1960s: in contrast to the pure, discrete, whole-object buildings sanctioned by architectural High Modernism, his interest embraced matter and ongoing process.[8] The self-explanatory *Photo-Fry* (1969) marked a transition from Matta-Clark's earliest performances to more complex pieces where the production of an object involved a performative aspect of work (figure 4.1). Matta-Clark's *Photo-Fry*

4.1 >Gordon Matta-Clark
Photo-Fry (1969).

was part of a group exhibition, *Documentations*, at the John Gibson Gallery in New York, where the artist spent time cooking up Polaroid photographs of a Christmas tree. John Gibson recalled, 'It smelled terrible. After he finished his *Photo-Fry*, he just left it there. I stayed open all summer with all that in place and the awful smell.'9

Equally stinking and unpredictable were his series of *Agar* pieces, *Incendiary Wafers* and *Glass Ingots/Plants* (1969–71), in which Matta-Clark cooked up a variety of strange and unpredictable concoctions with no regard for the stable 'good form' expected of artworks (figure 4.2). These works addressed materials in such a way as to challenge matter's assumed relationships to space and to time by exploring how changes could be both brought to and brought about by matter: for the series of *Incendiary Wafers*, Matta-Clark experimented directly with 'batches of undefinable stuff . . . constantly brewing in large vessels or fermenting in large flat trays . . .'10 The undefinable stuff here included agar (a seaweed-based gelatine-like substance), glass, metals, minerals, food and non-foodstuffs, street debris and so on.

4.2 >Gordon Matta-Clark,
Agar (1969 71).

The ongoing project *Agar* involved mixing a variety of ingredients to an agar base and then leaving the mixtures to dry out (agar is a seaweed-based, gelatine-like substance). According to Jacob's catalogue, these ingredients included 'yeast, sugar, corn oil, dextrose, tryptone agar, sperm oil, NaCl, Pet concentrated milk, V-8, cranberry juice, Pet chocolate flavored Yoohoo, chicken broth, metal ingredients (gold leaf, local vines, galvanized pans, screw hooks, thumb tacks, Black Magic Plastic Steel) and known strains (*Mucor Racemosus, Rhizopus Apophysis, Aspergillus Niger, Penicillium Notatum, Streptomyces Griseur*)' and, later: various yeasts, juices, meat, vegetable extracts and minerals, non-food stuff and street debris. *Incendiary Wafers* developed from the Agar work, and involved similar batches of undefinable 'stuff', either constantly brewing in large vessels or fermenting in large flat trays. These acted as a host for micro-organisms in the air; as the stuff in the trays dried out, the growth rate of these organisms slowed down and the whole piece gradually solidified. One of the trays accidentally exploded. Following this occurrence, Matta-Clark took the remaining trays out of his studio and incinerated them.

His Agar pieces provided raw material for a subsequent piece, *Museum*
(Bykert Gallery, New York, June 1970), which was something of a reference
to the museal/mausoleal practice of gathering up and storing fragments of
the past. Here, his installation filled a wall with *Agar* pieces to mimic
the typical arrangement of a nineteenth-century picture gallery. In the
space in front of the wall he hung further stuff from a chaotic lattice of
vines; these mouldering pieces were supplemented with a microscope and
batches of contained organisms, provided to allow the visitor to make more
detailed inspections of the life of the agar-matter.

A more palatable development of these preoccupations came with Matta-
Clark's involvement in the collaborative 'restaurant' project, *Food* (Prince Street,
New York, 1971–3), where the object of art (and cooking) and the role of the artist
(and diner) enjoyed a similar ambiguity, all expanding their remit beyond 'proper'
definitions or clear end product. As well as being a going business concern, *Food*
was also an ongoing artistic project, providing work for artists both in the sense of
gainful employment and as an *œuvre*; as well as art, *Food* served up food: putting
on shows and food theatre, its operations drawing attention to the social mores
that usually governed the proper location for such things. (The shop premises for
Food was also the site of Matta-Clark's first 'building cut'.[11])

The approaches signalled by these early works were to become central
preoccupations of Matta-Clark's *œuvre*, developing initially to address the effect
of situation on matter, questioning in particular the modality of its classification
and the rules that policed such classification, and consequently opening onto the
social and political concerns that this exposed. Alongside the latent humour of
these experiments and the obvious, even explosive, hilarity of works they spawned
(one of the *Agar* pieces literally, unintentionally, blew up), there lay a more serious
concern. In notes from around 1970, he railed against the violence done to natural
materials by the 'American horde':

> The supremacy of the new modle [*sic.*] proposed by suburbia . . . dramatizes
> the exclusive domestication of nature . . . [I]t must sustain the battle against
> all spontaneous life forces so in one interpretation the docile, home life
> model becomes a repository for war trophies . . . Defoliation is allowed . . .
> because it is an alien chaotic form that is being destroyed.[12]

Matta-Clark took issue with the simplistic distinctions that underlay this
suburbanising approach, distinctions that exaggerate the desire to completely
control nature and that presume the relegation of matter to a scientific problem – a
presumption which Bergson so criticised. Considering this battle of the cultivated
against the naturally chaotic, Matta-Clark's work from this time set out to actively
involve both spheres of what he referred to as this 'dualistic conflict'. Projects such
as the *Agar* pieces or *Incendiary Wafers* demonstrated that matter stubbornly
remained beyond the controlling desires of 'cultivating' humanity: rather than
undergoing a predictable and controllable process and becoming subordinate to a
static, regular form, matter was shown here to be enjoying *spontaneous life forces*
of its own.

If these projects operated on matter's own terms, providing a demonstration
of its own uncontrollable life forces, projects such as *Garbage Wall* (1970; see figure
4.3) and *Jacks* (1971) demonstrated that, even within the domestication carried out

4.3 >Gordon Matta-Clark,
Garbage Wall (1970)
This project actively
demonstrated a life
cycle of the
'cultivating' process
beyond the specific
'cooking' work of 'time
and the elements', and
thus challenged the
claims these processes
made to timeless
supremacy. In contrast
to the *Agar* pieces, it
also clearly articulated
the 'selection' and
'preparation' operations,
by organising easily
recognisable urban
debris into deliberate
and useful arrangements.
Garbage Wall was an
ongoing investigation
undertaken in sketchbooks
and with physical
testing, the latter
often incorporated into
a performative work.
There have been several
Garbage Walls produced
subsequently.

by the suburbanising model, matter could be found that was *no longer* cultivated. Working with urban waste, these projects drew attention to this debris within the cultivated sphere. As Dan Graham observed, 'Matta-Clark came to the position that work must function directly in the actual urban environment. "Nature" was an escape; political and cultural contradictions were not to be denied.'[13]

The notion of escaping to nature picks up both Matta-Clark's criticisms of the 'new modle [*sic*.]' which attempted to domesticate a chaotic nature that it clearly situated beyond the boundary of the city, and the contemporary practice of many Land Artists, who similarly fled the gallery and the city to produce work in 'natural' environments. For Matta-Clark, nature didn't stop at the city boundary, and matter remained present in the formed materials of the cultivated realm. *Garbage Wall* and *Jacks* effectively recycled this stuff, giving it form and status, and thereby challenged both the assumed location of waste (as vaguely *somewhere else*) by celebrating its continuing location *within* this system, and challenging the belief that waste was useless and formless. One of the meals at *Food* followed a similar logic: Matta-Clark's *Bone Meal* consisted of a variety of bone-based dishes, the bones of which were quickly scrubbed, drilled, and returned to the diners as jewellery after they had finished various courses that Matta-Clark had prepared, so that they could take their leftovers home with them.[14]

Matta-Clark's interest in the multi-faceted properties of matter can already be recognised to be at play in these small works, which drew attention to the enduring insubordination of matter, demonstrating that it never fully submits to the process of making by taking up the 'correct' form and location, and upsetting expectations that it remain inert once 'cultivated'.

4.4 >Gordon Matta-Clark,
Conical Intersect (1975)
Photograph inside
completed work.
Conical Intersect was
produced for the Paris
Biennale in September
1975 within a twin town
house procured and
sanctioned by Georges
Boudaille, the General
Delegate of the Biennale;
the building was about
to be demolished to
make way for the new
Centre Pompidou. The
performative aspect
of the project was as
important to Matta-Clark
as the (short-lived)
final piece, wherein
the ongoing addition of
energy required to
produce the cuts is
clearly legible in the
rough edges that inscribe
the cone.

At this time he was already exploring the possibility of working this interest through at a bigger scale, in order to exercise the political and cultural dimensions that Dan Graham referred to more effectively. As Matta-Clark's work became more complex, the various facets of matter revealed separately by the *Agar* pieces (matter being formed in order to assume a position or meaning within the cultivated sphere) or by the *Garbage Wall* (demonstrating the presence of de-formed and 'meaningless' matter within the cultivated sphere) were combined, reflecting his broader interest in the role of matter both within the process of artistic production and within the formed object, in contrast to the various Modernist-idealist positions already mentioned.

In Matta-Clark's sketch books from this time, he likens the production of art to the process of cooking, 'where the flame, time and the elements are one's pallette.'[15] But 'cooking' was the last of three stages in this process; the preceding ones, 'selection' and 'preparation', were equally important to him in the constitution of 'a complete set of . . . operations.' His building dissections (see, for example, figure 4.4) effectively run this complete set of operations twice over: once from his own cutting and once from the repercussions of that cut, which exposed the secret, spontaneous and chaotic quality of the alien matter which must have been involved in the object's initial making and which continued to exist behind the apparently uniform, cultured façade of static form expected by established society. A balance is struck between the 'alien' and the familiar across the edge exposed around the cut; it is not a question as to which is out of place, but it is an operation that places a question for the observer that cannot easily be answered.

Matta-Clark held that the raw edges resulting from the process of cutting were much more informative than any manicured, cultivated version. Raw and cultivated were thus required to coexist in the work, though this was no easy co-existence; he emphasised the point: '. . . the edge is what I work through, try to preserve, spend this energy to complete, *and at the same time* what is read.'[16] Of particular importance here is the expenditure of energy to complete the work, as it raises questions that did not bear on the art produced under the aegis of Modernism, concerning when making occurs and when (and where) it stops. Although Matta-Clark refers to his own process of working the material, it was also a demand that was passed on to the observer, who was challenged by the contradictory modalities of matter, material and form revealed by these projects.

This demand for the ongoing addition of energy, both from the artist and the observer, distinguishes Matta-Clark's take on matter from the broad treatment it had received since the widespread adoption of Cartesian science in the late seventeenth century. Instead of the attenuation of matter, which this science achieved through its exclusively spatialised, quantifiable and located definition, Matta-Clark's work suggests that matter continues to carry temporal dimensions. He was entirely accepting of the fact that matter enjoyed an independent temporality, although he did not simply link this to decay, but to an active *life force*. Indeed, he stressed that he would avoid working in situations where he '[w]ould be competing with factual disintegration.'[17] It was through this dualistic aspect of his work, which established matter alongside culturally specific material form, that the aspect of decay was itself put alongside a broader movement of ongoing renovation and change.

ENTROPY AND ALCHEMY: CHANGING NATURE

Projects such as the building dissections, *Garbage Wall* and the *Agar* pieces worked in various ways to draw attention to the temporal insubordination of matter, demonstrating that it never fully submits to the process of making by taking up the 'correct' form and location, thus upsetting expectations that it remain inert once 'cultivated.' A contemporary review of Matta-Clark's *Museum* installation at the Bykert Gallery in New York (1970), which comprised an arrangement of several *Agar* pieces, picks up the relation between the natural and the cultivated within the work: Cindy Nemser wrote that 'Matta[-Clark] leaves only remnata of actions or gestures that have already taken place, and . . . the natural processes he has set in motion slow down to an almost imperceptible state of activity, we have only his stratified accumulation to tell us what has gone on in the past.'[18]

There was considerable interest in notions of slow-down and material decay, particularly among the Minimalist artists, who read it as an aspect of entropy, which they celebrated for providing an antidote to static, unchanging forms of Modernism. Interestingly, Robert Smithson suggested that the 'New Monuments' of Minimalist art cause us to forget the future rather than remember the past by enacting a 'destruction of classical time and space . . . based on an entirely new notion of the structure of matter.'[19] Matta-Clark's own *Museum* took up a more ambiguous position between past and future: it was clearly critical of traditional situations regarding both the production and reception of the art object. Although it has just been suggested that Matta-Clark's projects demand a reconsideration of the role of matter, his engagement with it demonstrated the need for ongoing involvement and an investment of energy to sustain his or any other 'work', in contrast to Minimalism's valorisation of the dissipation of energy characteristic of entropy.

The physical arrangement of *Museum* referred to beaux-arts picture galleries, and by implication to the particular expectations of spectatorship that would occur there. However, for a spectator regarding Matta-Clark's works their gaze would be met by a certain muteness, repeating aspects experienced by a visitor to his building dissections, where the polite, proper surface formalism of the building or the painting had been put in suspense. Beyond their obvious difference to figurative beaux-art oils, these 'exhibits' also differed from works such as the canvases of Abstract Expressionism championed by High Modernism in so far as they lacked a formal surface, offering instead an opening onto the raw mutating matter of the *Agar* pieces discussed earlier. (Matta-Clark provided a microscope and various phials of matter in different stages of mutation so that visitors could witness the 'imperceptible' changes Nemser alludes to.) This loss of surface is important, inasmuch as it distinguishes the operation of Matta-Clark's pieces from what Rosalind Krauss has read as the entropic dissolution of the figure-ground distinction undertaken by Abstraction Expressionism. Krauss's warning is that despite appearances, Modernism attempts to claim entropy as a move to a more purely formal art, where a spectator's experience would be purely visual and non-corporeal, and thus closer to a transcendental form (*eidos*) than previously available to figurative art.[20] Matta-Clark's *Museum* would have been looked at differently, and moved in a different direction: by offering a porous, changing, stinking surface, it would offer to remind an observer about the material make-up of the stuff of the world, rather than aiding their escape to an ideal realm. The awkward hanging of the *Agar* pieces, suspended on a tangle of vines in the gallery, would also have served to prevent the easy disinterested contemplation of these pieces, forcing the observer to negotiate the tangled routes through the piece.

So for Nemser to link *Museum's* remnata to slow-down is appropriate, but the link must be made with some care; while Matta-Clark's *Agar* slabs exposed an entropic slow-down, *Museum* was by no means an uncritical celebration of entropy laid bare. Alongside this reading, the various alchemical references within Nemser's review could just as persuasively suggest that alchemy's claims to speed up natural processes, and overcome natural time, might point in the opposite direction. Nemser's occasional references to Matta-Clark as an alchemist are understandable enough, nor was she alone; it was well known that he had studied alchemy in some detail during the late 1960s, and his seemingly endless, obsessive production of agar pieces and glass ingots seem to fit the alchemist's quest – a situation that is only reinforced by pictures of his studio from this time, which show it as more of a mad scientist's den than as an artist's place of work.

In this context, the particular material situation of Matta-Clark's projects warrants further attention, both to emphasise their distance from entropic Minimalism and Modernism and to clarify Matta-Clark's conception of 'nature', It has just been suggested that Matta-Clark's work was no celebration of entropy, but neither was his alchemical interest in matter focused on transmutation of base metals first and foremost. If there is any mileage in making an alchemical comparison, it must be prefaced with a warning that Matta-Clark's attempts at alchemy were serious and ridiculous at the same time.

Aside from the emblematic alchemical result that appears to treat matter as proto-gold, Matta-Clark's interest in alchemy was directed towards a more ambiguous balance of relationships between human beings, the cultural sphere and the natural world.[21] Here again, we can encounter a paradoxical situation where alchemists would hold that 'Nature can overcome Nature'. To read this as anything but a reductive contradiction required alchemists to understand the *solve et coagula* of matter, the possibility of an unending movement of matter from one state to another: although this was usually traced between an unconditioned state, *materia prima*, and formed objects, it can implicitly involve the cultural work done to establish matter in a certain form and position. On this account, to take natural or cultural forms as final and static would be erroneous, as Burckhardt notes: 'In the world of forms Nature's "mode of operation" consists of a continuous rhythm of "dissolutions" and "coagulations".'[22] If Matta-Clark's work enacts an alchemical position, it does so to the extent that energy is expended to sustain this rhythm.

But there is a more difficult issue that arises out of this situation, one that has led 'logically' to the *supremacy of the new model of suburbia*, and which Matta-Clark's entire *œuvre* opposed. Mircea Eliade has argued that, '[o]n the plane of cultural history, it is . . . possible to say that the alchemists, in their desire to supersede Time, anticipated what is in fact the essence of the ideology of the modern world.'[23]

The alchemical acknowledgement of *solve et coagula* of matter was qualified by a concomitant belief in the potential of nature not simply to change but, given favourable circumstances, to develop or mature, and it was this aspect of maturation that the alchemists sought to control. Vincent of Beauvais, writing in the fourteenth century, hints at this goal: 'These operations, which Nature achieves on minerals, alchemists set themselves to reproduce: *that is the very substance of their art.*'24 Alchemical operations attempted to replicate and, crucially, speed up the developments of nature from geological to experiential time in order to precipitate this natural potential to evolve towards perfection. In both its alchemical and modern guises, this ideology secularised nature, reducing it – and matter – to something that would be quantifiably accountable.

This alchemical desire to achieve perfection, and more importantly to attain control over the process, echoes certain aspects of Modernism's appropriation of entropy; although the role of matter is clearly different within these two processes, the fate it suffers is similar, ultimately being written out of human experience as Bergson lamented. In contrast, Matta-Clark's projects demonstrated the *solve et coagula* of matter, revealed and maintained its complexity, and offered this to the observer as a situation in which they could assume a role in holding together cultured material and natural, raw matter.

MATTER, FORM AND ENERGY

So, rather than adopting an alchemical temporality (subsuming natural time as matter falls under human control), and rather than adopting an entropic position (eliminating '[t]ime as decay or biological evolution'25 as matter slid towards total homogenisation), Matta-Clark's treatment of matter was resistant to these attempts at laundering its involvement in multi-faceted temporal dimensions. Bergson's work on matter similarly asserted that full human involvement in the world should be taken as a *resistance*: he argued that the creative evolution of human life marks an attempt to *retard* the natural course of material change, in contrast to alchemical speed-up or even entropic homogenisation.26 Matta-Clark's *œuvre* contested the transparent matter of modern physics by going against its repeatable predictability, instead reinvigorating matter that responds to a question, akin to the classical potency of matter in its 'creative' function.27

However, both Matta-Clark and Bergson differ substantially from classical positions by locating resistance in human agency rather than in things themselves. This resistance is played out in the relation between human beings and the world, where, on their account, human action can divide up matter or recombine it without following the 'objective articulations' (Plato) of nature's forms. This approach issues a challenge to theories of artistic and architectural design which treat matter as a 'transparent' medium, by establishing artistic form as an unobstructed conduit that an observer can traverse back to the mind of the artist (either artist-genius or artist as a relay to a divine creator). Bergson states this position in such a way as to suggest a re-consideration of the relationship between matter, form and human action:

> If the divisibility of matter is entirely relative to our action thereon, that is to say, to our faculty of modifying its aspect, if it belongs not to matter itself but to the space which we throw beneath this matter in order to bring it within our grasp, then the difficulty [of reconciling matter and memory in perception] disappears.28

This reformulation involves both reason and the imagination, and involves a negotiation between matter-as-stuff and cultivated matter, which produces in turn a contingent-form that is sufficiently stable to permit intelligibility while varying from itself sufficiently to exceed the domain of reason. For Matta-Clark form was an activity rather than a static principle of any particular thing.[29] In response to frequent criticisms of Matta-Clark's work as being simply destructive, this reading stresses that his projects didn't pit the cultivated world against the natural, but invested energy to maintain them in relief against each other. For Bergson, similarly, form was a contingent agreement between matter and intellect. Central to moments when reason is overshot is the expectation that energy is expended, either by the artist or by the observer, producing a different, 'obscure clarity' that draws on the imaginative alterations of contingent-form. This is a formal clarity that is not available to the intellect: a domain of form that escapes reason but allows it to function, effectively produced by balancing material and matter.[30] There is no 'proper' place from which to witness such obscure formal clarity, as works that operate in this way do so by playing out an active contradiction.

1   >Henri Bergson, *Creative Evolution*, trans. Arthur Mitchell, London: Macmillan and Co., 1911, pp. 164–5.
2   >Eslick stresses that 'Plato's matter . . . combines both the roles of existential actuation and differentiation, and achieves the former by means of the latter. The "creative" function of matter is its negation of essential reality.' Leonard J. Eslick 'The Material Substrate in Plato', in Ernan McMullin (ed.), *The Concept of Matter in Greek and Mediaeval Philosophy*, Indiana: University of Notre Dame Press, 1965, p. 53.
3   >Ernan McMullin (ed.) *The Concept of Matter in Modern Philosophy*, Indiana: University of Notre Dame Press, 1963 (revised edition 1978), p. 17.
4   >Bergson, *op. cit.*, pp. 205ff.
5   >See in particular Bergson's 'Second Introduction' to *The Creative Mind*, trans. Mabelle L. Andison, Philosophical Library, F. Hobner & Co., New York, 1946.
6   >Bergson, *op. cit.*, p. 31.
7   >*Ibid.*, pp. 164–5.
8   >Colin Rowe, 'architecture's Greenberg', started his studio at Cornell in 1963, the same year Matta-Clark enrolled. Matta-Clark's *œuvre* is comprehensively illustrated both by Maria Casanova (ed.), *Gordon Matta-Clark*, Valencia: IVAM Centre Julio González, 1992 and by Corinne Diserens (ed.), *Gordon Matta-Clark*, London and New York: Phaidon Press, 2003.
9   >John Gibson, interviewed by Joan Simon, in Mary Jane Jacob (ed.), *Gordon Matta-Clark: A Retrospective*, Chicago: Museum of Contemporary Art (ex. cat.), 1985, p. 23.
10   >*Ibid.*, *Incendiary Wafers* entry, pp. 26–7. Repeated (more or less) in Casanova, *op. cit.*, pp. 368–9.
11   >For a bigger helping of *Food*, including several 'apocryphal stories' about the goings-on there, see Klauss Bussmann and Markus Müller (eds.), *Food*, New York: White Columns Gallery (ex. cat.), 2000.
12   >Gordon Matta-Clark, 'Cannibalism, Suburbia and Defoliation,' in Matta-Clark's Sketchbook, Estate of Gordon Matta-Clark (cat. #828), *c.*1969–71, pp. 11–12 (unpublished).
13   >Dan Graham, 'Gordon Matta-Clark', in Casanova, *op. cit.*, p. 378.
14   >Caroline Yorke Goodden (co-founder of *Food*) interviewed by Joan Simon, in Jacob, *op. cit.*, p. 39.
15   >Gordon Matta-Clark, 'RECIPES' in Sketchbook, *op. cit.*, p. 7.
16   >Gordon Matta-Clark in Kirshner, 'Interview with Gordon Matta-Clark', in Casanova, *op. cit.*, p. 391 (my emphasis).
17   >Gordon Matta-Clark interviewed by Donald Wall, 'Gordon Matta-Clark's Building Dissections', *Arts Magazine*, May 1976, p. 77.
18   >Cindy Nemser, 'The Alchemist and the Phenomenologist', *Art in America* 59:2, March–April 1971, p. 102. (The phenomenologist of the title refers to another artist, Alan Sonfist.) Matta-Clark added his mother's surname to his own during 1971, in order to distinguish himself from his father.
19   >Robert Smithson, 'Entropy and the New Monuments' [*Artforum*, June 1966], in Jack Flam (ed.), *Robert Smithson: The Collected Writings*, Berkeley & London: University of California Press,

1996, p.11. By this entirely new notion he means entropy. The comments regarding destruction were addressed to Dan Flavin's work.

20   >See Rosalind E. Krauss, 'Entropy' in Yve-Alain Bois & Rosalind E. Krauss, *Formless: A User's Guide*, New York: The MIT Press/Zone Books, 1997, pp. 73–8.

21   >This approach comes through in several interviews. For example, he told Judith Russi-Kirshner that 'what I would love to do is to actually . . . extend the building above – I mean extend it below as much as above, like an alchemical motif where there is that definite dichotomy – or balance between the – above and below . . . Somehow I think that a building could be – in addition to a micro-archaeology – a kind of micro-evolution, or some kind of wholly internalised expression of a total genetic or evolutionary development.' Kirshner interview in Casanova, *op. cit.*, p. 391.

22   >Titus Burckhardt, *Alchemy: Science of the Cosmos, Science of the Soul* [1960], trans. William Stoddart, London: Stuart & Watkins, 1967, p. 123. This was in Matta-Clark's library, along with several other well-known texts on alchemy.

23   >Mircea Eliade, *The Forge and the Crucible: The Origins and Structures of Alchemy* [1956], trans. Stephen Corrin, Chicago: Chicago University Press, second edition 1978, p. 173.

24   >Vincent of Beauvais cited in Stephen Toulmin & June Goodfield, *The Architecture of Matter*, London: Hutchinson, 1962, p. 125. Toulmin and Goodfield trace the temporal underpinnings of alchemy in their chapter, 'The Redemption of Matter'.

25   >Robert Smithson argued that many Minimalist works celebrated entropy by eliminating time in this way: Smithson in Flam, *op. cit.*, p. 11.

26   >Bergson, *op. cit.*, pp. 259ff.

27   >'. . . post-Cartesian everyday usage of the term "matter" no longer responded to a question; it was no longer the case that matter was postulated to explain some general feature of the world . . .' McMullin, *The Concept of Matter in Modern Philosophy*, *op. cit.*, p. 19.

28   >Bergson, *Matter and Memory*, trans. Nancy Margaret Paul and W. Scott Palmer, New York: Zone Books, 1988, p. 219.

29   >'If needed we work to disprove the common belief that all starts with the plan. There are forms without plans – Dynamic orders and disorders.' Gordon Matta-Clark, Estate of Gordon Matta-Clark, #502 (two sheets detail paper, Anarchitecture period *c*.1972) (unpublished).

30   >This domain of form would approach Bataille's notion of *Informe* or Formless, an active principle that operates to prevent the domination of scientific or 'mathematical' systems of form (and, indeed, this is where entropy leads Krauss). For a fuller discussion of Bataille's *Informe* in the context of architectural production, see my 'Animate Form: Architecture's Troublesome claims to Formlessness', in Pat Cowley and Paul Hegarty (eds.) *Formlessness: Ways In and Out of Form*, Oxford: Peter Lang, 2004.

PLENUMS: RE-THINKING MATTER, GEOMETRY AND SUBJECTIVITY

PEG RAWES >PLENUMS: RETHINKING MATTER, GEOMETRY AND SUBJECTIVITY

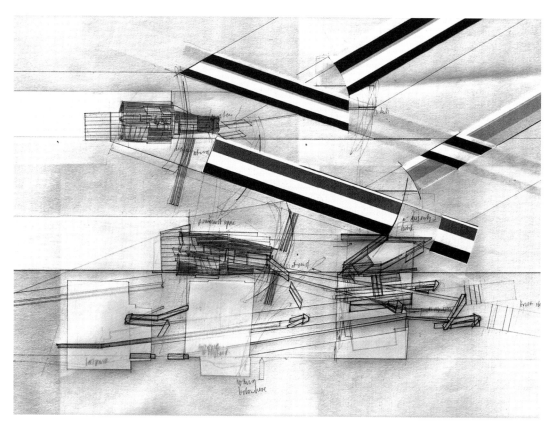

5.1

This chapter considers the scope for 'productive' relations that might be found between the disciplines of architecture and philosophy. By focusing on the construction of matter, space and the subject in Leibniz's philosophical figure, the 'plenum', it argues that architectural practice and events are made up of continuously changing occurences, spaces and relationships between people and the built environment. A plenum is therefore a spatial figure, which enables material and psychological qualities to assume equal importance in the production of architectural space. Concepts of space are transformed from abstract definitions of geometric quantity or measurement into particular figures, which have both material and psychic qualities.

    The chapter is organised into three sections, or plenums, each beginning with a descriptive figure of a plenum that highlights the extent to which spatio-temporal relations and architectural constituents continuously express different material and psychic qualities.

5.1 >Smout Allen,
The Retreating Village,
Happisburgh, Norfolk,
2005.

'Plenum I' draws attention to the importance of the psychic and material modes of embodiment that construct, *simultaneously*, our experiences of space and time. The section examines how the plenum embodies both the psychological experiences and the material, spatial or geometric relationships that we have with the built environment. Developing out of the time it takes a young family to travel from home to school it argues that the plenum is a *topological figure of embodiment*.

'Plenum II' explores the incremental differentiation of spatial and material relations that unfold in a public museum. It suggests that this building and its collections generate differences between objects, people and spaces by *degree*, not by kind. This *internal* concept of difference, it argues, is enabled by the plenum's scope for rethinking the relationship between material and immaterial properties, which are present in seventeenth-century discussions about 'substance' and anti-Cartesian debates about the mind and the body. Here, therefore, the plenum suggests a way out from the oppositionism that constructs many forms of binary relationships between architect/user, inside/outside, form/matter, and so on.

Finally, 'Plenum III' considers the technical qualities or differences which are generated in the production of the architectural drawing. In this context the plenum differentiates between the *technical and embodied* activities of material production and the embodied thoughts and feelings which constitute the architectural drawing. As a result, this section explores the extent to which the plenum is a *geometric figure* that is determined through processes of qualitative and internal change which are manifest in its material and psychic *activities*.

Plenums, the discussion concludes, therefore enable a reconfiguration of relationships between architecture and philosophy, and between architectural practice and the individual's engagement with the built environment, into a series of dynamic spatio-temporal events which are constituted by continuously differentiating material and psychic embodiments.

PLENUM I: DAILY LIFE

In a city in the north of England two girls are getting ready for school. It is a toing-and-froing process which has become more anticipated (and more of a palaver for whoever is doing the school run) because going to school now means going by bicycle. If school is to be reached by walking, the journey takes about fifteen minutes. In fact it doesn't take much less time with pedal-power. There is still some porridge to be eaten; it's gone cold and it's not going down the throat, but if it isn't eaten the end-of-the-day tiredness is too much for everyone to bear, given that this is only the start of the week. Hair has to be brushed: tugged, trapped, gripped. Packed lunches made. Baby loaded into the pram. Coats, shoes and scarves on. Running in and out of the house at least three times – why did we put those steps there? Brief tears and then, finally, it's time to put on the bike helmets, knee and elbow pads. There should be four apiece. There are only six altogether – one five-year-old elbow and one six-year-old knee are still visible. The two remaining pads are in the car. In the boot of the car. In the garage. Keys. Quick. Finally, there now, the last elbow and knee are strapped up under foam and Velcro and all are set to go. The youngest one with a push. We're off. At least until the end of the pavement, where we have to stop. Wait. Wait. OK, safe to cross. Quickly now. Past other families walking to school, past the junior school at the main road. At a pace. Down to the crossing where that Escort is, as-ever, parked over the pedestrian entrance. The youngest one's careering style has finally edged-off a bit now. Off the bike, pushed down to the sheds. Helmets and straps off. Lunch bags handed over and back up the playground to leave the pram to one side and to jostle in amongst the throng that is either over five foot tall or under three, depending upon who you are. Coats on hooks, felt-tip faces identifying whose hook is whose, a 'hello' to the class-teacher and a quick turn-about for a 'kiss' and back to the pram, where there are only seven knee and elbow pads. . .

Can a story about the 'school-run' draw you into a discussion about bridges; bridges between the material, psychic, emotional, fast, slow and physical relationship between a mother and children, in this scenario of daily life? Here, then, the plenum is a 'bridging' figure through which material and immaterial relations are brought together, simultaneously, to generate a continuously differentiating site.

If the plenum is seen as an architectural figure, insofar as it is both a geometric and a material embodiment, we can then suggest that it enables a way of discussing the architectural event in which both the formal and the sensory are simultaneously active. As a result, any 'unity' or 'amalgam' (i.e. a built form, subject or professional relationship) is not determined by discussions of form or matter which rely upon the exclusive oppositions that divide the idea of architecture from the ways in which it is played out, altered, misused or undone. These oppositions encompass, for example, the tendency of formalist accounts of architectural practice to rely upon the external application of ideas, or the tendency in materialist accounts of architectural experience (especially phenomenological ones) to suggest that contingency can *only* be found by promoting the role of the user or the subject.

This discussion attempts to draw out spatial relationships by exploring the ways in which the plenum operates in *at least two different modes* of material and psychological transformation at the same time. In particular, Leibniz's seventeenth-century figure provides the basis from which architectural practice, relations and products can be understood, not as expressions of the idealist division between matter and form, or subject and other, but through a series of material and spatio-temporal relations that are irreducible yet particular – embodiments, generated from an 'internal' form of geometry. As a result, the discussion focuses on the potential for *real embodied differences* to be expressed in architectural events, subjects, sites or practices.

The concept of the plenum appears in various forms in Leibniz's philosophical and scientific writings of the 1670s and 1680s, and again in the *Monadology* of 1714. It is a spatial figure that is defined as dynamic because it is produced by *continuously changing spatio-temporal relations* (in contrast to scientific definitions of space that rely on principles of finitude). It is, therefore, a spatial or geometric figure that is generated by material and psychical relations.

This *contingency* of spatio-temporal relations means that it is an inherently equivocal figure, which resists reduction into either abstract material forms or unextended (i.e. immaterial) ideas. Instead, the plenum's irreducibility is also an expression of the complex *living* substance that underpins its existence – not as a finite quantified whole, but as a kind of 'aggregate' or 'composite'. For example, the plenum cannot be reduced to a definite single measurement of space, even at the limits of representation, i.e. the infinitely small (the 'infinitesimals') or the largest quantity (the 'immensum'). Rather, the plenum's unity, or 'wholeness', is a kind of 'approximation'; an 'accident', rather than a determined or pre-given 'beginning' or 'end'. As a result, this attention to a continuous *process* of differentiation promotes not only the material plenitude of the plenum, but also the irreducibility of its psychic activities.[1] That is, the plenum is a geometric figure that is inherently concerned with duration or 'life'. Furthermore, its potential for infinite differentiation enables it to express the psychic processes of life, which Leibniz identifies as memory or 'the soul'. The importance of this psychic differentiation promoted in the plenum is well described by Robert Latta. He explains:

> Leibniz overcomes [the difficulty of finitude] by regarding the universe, not as an infinite mass occupying all that there is to occupy, but as a continuity or infinite gradation of qualitative differences, each containing within itself the principle of its own changes. He substitutes for an extensive plenum of mass an intensive continuum of force or life . . .[2]

So, the plenum's potential for differentiation is made up of two internal kinds of psychic activity, which provide the basis for its powers of 'life'. As a result, its value as a geometric, representational figure or body is modified from being merely a lifeless and divisible geometric body or form. Instead, Leibniz sustains the connection between representational figures and the powers of *perception* and *appetite* (i.e. two modes in which the individual's sensibility or powers of the soul are manifest). Perception, Leibniz writes, is '[t]he passing condition which involves and represents a multiplicity in the unity.'[3] But it is also a principle of psychic change that is further distinguished (i.e. intensified) into a more direct force: *appetition,* the 'internal principle' that 'brings about the change or the passing from one perception to another.'[4] Desire (*l'appetit*) or appetite, Leibniz tells us, strives for 'the whole of perception' but does not attain it; however, in doing so it enables 'new' perceptions to be produced. Sense-perceptions, the imagination and desire are therefore vital powers of transformation and production in the plenum's potential for self-determination or agency.

Furthermore, Leibniz is careful to tell us that perception and desire are not reducible to *symbolic* explanations of 'mechanical cause' or to the formal appearance of the 'figures and motions' that they produce. Perception and emotions cannot be reduced to diagrammatic forms or mechanical representations. Rather, he argues, perception and appetite are internally differentiated activities that endure continuously, expressing the different states of awareness that constitute 'life', so that any given perception is always *a concatenation of its past and future states*. Leibniz writes: '[e]very present state of a simple substance is a natural consequence of its preceding state, in such a way that its present is big with its future.'[5] Thus, the plenum's contingency is substantiated in both its irreducibility as a material unity and by its psychic activities of perception and desire.

And so the school-run becomes a plenum of daily life, in which bikes, porridge, steps, door handles, pavements, traffic and the schoolroom all come together into a topology of space-time, linked by the psychic and material expressions and feelings of three children and their mother.

PLENUM II: INSIDE THE MUSEUM

Whilst being reminded of other images and spaces in which the contents of cabinets led into a series of interconnected spaces, they find themselves standing in front of cabinets of birds and animals: hornbills, foxes, pheasants, cranes, warblers, dormice, dogs, flamingos, puffins, apes, cormorants, guillemots, flying squirrels and catfish. In the lower gallery taxonomy has given way to cabinets that show the power of spatial design in the weapons of Dogon warriors, Yoruba masks and shrines to gods and goddesses of war and plenitude. Down a corridor, another door opens onto a series of glass chambers that contain musical instruments and other sonic chambers so that, standing in front of video screens, directly under accompanying microphones, they are taken into the worlds of a Belarusian wedding, a North European rock concert and a Nigerian funeral. They move back through the glass-and-marble atrium, back along the corridor and up the stairs, repeatedly having to bend close in to the wall to squint at the pond-life in the aquarium that runs up the staircase, down the corridor containing larger tanks, and through another set of doors that leads onto the balcony, overlooking the displays of performance and ritual in African cultures. Aside from this upper space are areas for 'hands-on' activities, storytelling, eating, drinking and windows out of which are glimpsed views of the garden and the refurbished glass-house into which coffee and cake can be carried. . .

From the school-run to the public space; private pleasures that unfold between the nineteenth-century natural-science and contemporary ethnographic collections in a museum lead into a discussion about the *internal relationships* between entities, spaces and events.

The plenum is first described in the *Monadology* as a 'completely filled space, where each part receives only the equivalent of its previous motion.'[6] It is, therefore, a unity that is constructed through a continuous process of differentiation, and, because Leibniz rejects the concept of matter that divides it into either a physical material or an immaterial vacuum, the plenum is a 'continuum' that is constituted by contradiction. In addition, the plenum's structure and potential is determined not by means of applying external causes (e.g. the application of form, force or idea), but results from the differentiation that exists between its internal *qualities*. It is therefore a spatial figure that resists being limited to a principle of general and idealised spatial relations; instead it is a figure that is derived from internal and dynamic relations.

It is also a concept which Leibniz returns to and rethinks during his career, reflecting its capacity as a concept that is inherently concerned with change. Looking into Leibniz's writings you will find that they provide both a rigorous examination of the development of the physical and mathematical sciences, and also constitute a kind of *textual plenum* in the way that they operate between different disciplines, representing a series of *internal* differentiations of the construction of substance, matter and the individual subject. As a result, we might say that his writings represent a highly individuated and heterogeneous project that is reflected in the inter-disciplinarity of contemporary architectural practice – its buildings, texts, writers, audiences and users.

Thus, both in its internal capacity and in the reconfiguration of its forms within Leibniz's writings, the plenum is attributed a number of different qualities, ranging from its importance in the production of dynamic movement, and its manifestation of the 'soul' in theological discussions to its scope as a topological figure. In addition, these qualities link it to a larger series of spatio-temporal concepts in Leibniz's writings, including figures such as the Monad, the net and, perhaps most well known in the context of architecture, the fold.[7] A continuum of differentiated figures is generated in the development from one figure to another; for example, the figure of the net suggests a metaphor that is constructed by virtue of its dynamic spatio-temporal relationship in exchange with other entities.

So, the plenum's dynamic relations are underpinned by heterogeneous forms of production; both in its internal and external relations (and in the extent to which Leibniz's writing on the plenum is itself a continual negotiation and invention of metaphysical, theological and physical principles).[8] It is, therefore, a concept that embodies the potential for 'difference' in philosophical constructions of spatio-temporal relations, and might therefore also inform architectural discussions.

As indicated in the introduction, Leibniz's definition of *substance* underpins the complexity of the plenum as both a material *and* psychic agency, and is therefore central to this discussion about the production of difference in embodied architectural relations.

Reflecting the seventeenth century's preoccupation with the definition of 'substance', Leibniz's writings contributed to a highly charged philosophical, scientific and theological debate that included opposing views about the physical world, such as the nature of 'infinity' and 'atomism' (i.e. the debate about whether the atom is itself an *infinite substance or a finite limit*).[9] In addition, the issue of substance directly informed contemporary discussions about the dualism of mind and body in Cartesian thinking. Leibniz's solution to this problematic issue was to propose a concept of substance that is inherently multiple or infinite *because it can be infinitely divided.*[10]

Thus, in the context of examining the nature of the individual subject or unity (for example, the relationship between the part and the whole), Leibniz's project is also significant because change is generated by *differential relations which are internal*; rather than being derived from the external and mechanical causes that Cartesian division relied upon. According to Leibniz's concept of substance, the *infinite division* of a unity into parts is an intensification of its internal powers because each internal part represents a different *degree of expression* of the whole.

In addition, the whole can be 'expressed' within a single part. Paradoxically, therefore, the principle of division in Leibniz's project enables the production of qualitative intensities, figures or embodied subjects *because* it promotes intension versus extension (rather than quantitative extensions).

The plenum therefore represents a figure that is generated from both Leibniz's rejection of the exclusive division that Cartesians placed between the mind and body and his promotion of a particularly intense form of division or limit, which enabled the production of an *intensive and yet infinite living* substance. Furthermore, his writings on the relationship between bodies, motion and rest demonstrate his rejection of the 'structures of perfect solids and perfect fluids'; for example, in the essay 'On Matter, Motion, Minima and the Continuum' of 1675 he observes that:

> matter has varying degrees of resistance to division, [and] a given body can respond to the actions of the plenum by differing internal divisions, manifested as elasticity . . . .[11]

In addition, unlike Descartes' formulation that the mind and body are distinct substances, Leibniz proposes that the soul (i.e. the *psyche* or unextended matter) is also an expression of a heterogeneous substance. Therefore, while the plenum's (or the individual subject's) psychic activities are distinct from its powers of extension they are not, however, exclusive or disconnected from each other, so that a *continuity* of material differentiation is sustained between its extended and unextended qualities.

So, Leibniz's insistence upon a concept of substance that is both material and immaterial disrupts the tendency to divide, exclusively, matter from form, body from feeling, internal time from external space. Seen in this light, the modern museum shifts from being an institution in which the visitor undertakes a difficult negotiation of codified knowledge, into a series of relationships which are generated, internally, by incremental changes between the spaces of the galleries, architecture, displays and artefacts, and the responses of the visitor. The plenum re-figures the public museum from a collection of zones of scientific division into a realm in which the desires, expressions, species, qualities, and the diversity of organic life and inorganic artefact are brought together into a continuum of place, event and imagination.

PLENUM III: DRAWING

> *Leaning on the table, the line is drawn out, moving from the minute, close-up adjustment of the angle of an internal wall to the upright stretch of the back and straightening of the arm in the lean-back from the table, which also serves as a pause and reflection of the overall section. On the adjoining table to her right, the telephone rings. She pushes away from the drawing, still sitting in her chair, and leans over to reach for it, relaxing quickly into the conversation: a plan for a night out at the Shanghai. Returning to the drawing she leans back over the planes and surfaces that are being laid down for the village on the coast, which has become a series of transversing cuts embedded into each other, disrupting the previous transparency of the paper onto which they are*

*being made. But in amongst these thoughts about the materials and
processes of drawing she is conscious, too, of her rising anxiety about the
'singing' table she will be sitting at later in the day, which may become a place
in which she is forced to become Elvis, Abba, Gloria Gaynor or worse. Soon,
however, the drawing will take its place on the window, next to the others,
filtering the light through pen, ink and cut paper, each space inhabited with
images, lines, planes and gestures that shift between dimensions depending
upon how close you are to them. They are drawings that carry a number of
sensibilities, techniques and procedures; that belong to her and another, latent
with the traces of conversations, debate, distraction, whistling, boredom,
anxiety, excitement, concentration, and always full of the knowledge that they
are unfinished.*[12]

A description of a drawing, full of the 'matters of life', anticipation, interruption,
pause and discontinuity. An image of a *technical plenum* in which the technical
qualities of its lines, planes and surfaces *also* express the aesthetic experience
of psychic change which embody the architect whilst she is drawing. Here, then,
in this place of 'drawn-out' knowledge, the idea, reason or form is generated,
not by a reductive or imposed technique, but by examples of 'technical'
procedures which are particular because they are imbued with emotional and
psychic expressions which constitute the activity of thinking and making in
architectural design.

In the previous section, the plenum was shown to be an infinitely
differentiating substance. But Leibniz's philosophical theory of intensive
substance is also evident in his contribution to mathematical and *technical*
theories of infinity, especially in his invention of Calculus. The importance of
the operation of 'limit' or 'division' in Calculus, for example, is evident in the
calibration of different geometric figures; so we find that the construction of
a curve is possible because Leibniz registers the minute and 'imperceptible'
differences in curvature that transform a straight line into a curve. (In contrast,
classical geometry generates different figures by means of applying an *external*
operation, such as the different Euclidian axioms required for drawing a circle or
parallel lines.)

But, frequently in contemporary architectural debates, the production of
real difference is often considered to be possible only by promoting our psychic,
sensory, political or cultural experiences of the world. Accordingly, these models
of difference tend to be based upon the exclusive opposition between *qualitative*
sense-based experiences and *quantitative* mathematics, technology, engineering
and physical sciences. Alternatively, if qualitative difference is generated in
technical or scientific procedures, methods or events, it may well be considered to
be unlikely or flawed. Discussions about whether geometry can generate different
qualitative expressions of space is one of the most contested zones in architectural
design, and is particularly focused in the claims made for non-Euclidian digital
drawing and modelling techniques. Sceptics, however, question how practitioners
of these 'new geometries' fail to register the extent to which their buildings uphold
dominant interests in form-making, at the expense of other, more contingent,
organic agents in architectural design and the building's use. Leibniz's writings,
however, provide an interesting theory of geometry, in which difference is central

to its powers of production; for example, in this brief discussion Leibniz's geometry is shown to be concerned with the production of *internal difference*, which is a fundamental challenge to the assumption that geometry is always *only* concerned with the production of disembodied, external and abstract space. By contrast, Leibniz's concern with the production of internally differentiated subjects or figures suggests a qualitatively different kind of geometry; that is, it is a 'science of magnitudes', which generates *qualitative difference* – not quantitative form (i.e. shape), as is normally suggested.

In this context, geometry becomes reconfigured as a technical embodiment of the *qualitatively different relations* that exist within and between spatial figures. The plenum is a paradoxical figure that expresses difference internally and externally at the same time, and Leibniz calls this geometric difference 'vice-diction' because two different states are produced *simultaneously*, but are not defined by the exclusion or opposition of one from the other.[13] Thus, Leibniz's theory of difference is based upon a principle of 'self-identity' in which matter and space are *non-similar* at any point in time. Furthermore, the production of an individual identity or geometric figure is not the result of geometric magnitude (i.e. the definition of a geometric figure based upon its shape or size), but is a registration of the difference between one individual subject and the next.

As a result a strikingly paradoxical and 'intensive' notion of division is promoted, which generates relations between wholes and parts that are *qualitatively* different rather than the notion of a purely mechanical or rational form of division, so that *geometric figures become expressions of particular differentials, relations, ratios* or '*reasons*'. Furthermore, this is a radical shift in the construction of knowledge or 'Reason' in the process, in which Reason is generated in the *particular* idea (i.e. a kind of 'self-reason') rather than in the general 'truth'.

Finally, then, in the act of drawing plans and sections for a group of coastal houses, the plenum registers the different psychic and physical processes that are embodied between paper, cuts, planes and architect. Together, the architectural drawing and the architect embody a complex geometric configuration which is technical, particular, aesthetic and expressive of qualitative 'Reason'.

CONCLUSION

As we have seen, plenums can express both the embodied spatial relations and the psychic experiences of the individual in architecture and the built environment. Furthermore, by extending these relations out into architectural contexts we find that the plenum provides connections between internally generated geometries and the perceiving, thinking architect and user.

Derived from Leibniz's writing on substance, the plenum is a continuously differentiating figure of 'perceiving' matter (or sensibility) that can inform both discussions about how to produce real difference in the built environment – its sites, methods of production and relations – and enable us to resist the tendency to base these relations upon on a series of formal or *inert* distinctions.

In architectural contexts, therefore, the plenum carries within it material and formal qualities – together with the psychic, perceptual and emotional qualities that construct the specificity of architecture and spatial events. It is a figure that is qualitative both in terms of the scope it provides for rethinking the relationship between matter and form, and also because it registers the *technical* and *embodied* 'reason' in the processes of designing architecture. Additionally, these material, structural and temporal constituents are also reflected in the differentiation of the individual subjects or users and their powers of reflection, perception and desire. So the reflexive relationship between the plenum's constituents generates a spatio-temporal figure that promotes both the material differences existing in the built environment *together* with the qualitative differences that are embodied in the experiences of the architect, engineer, user and the wider community.

1   > Differentiation emphasises the potential for the plenum to undergo constant change and therefore links it to theories of 'difference' in metaphysical and post-structuralist philosophy, in which the potential for continuous change may be biological, genetic or psychic. In addition, for Leibniz, it is also a continuous geometric differentiation.

2   > Robert Latta, *The Monadology and Other Philosophical Writings*, New York and London: Garland Publishing, 1985, p. 40. The notion of 'intensive force' draws attention to the potential for the plenum to be defined through its powers for transformation. Intensive transformations may therefore be found in the movement between different material states and psychological feelings.

3   > Gottfried Leibniz, *Discourse on Metaphysics, Correspondence with Arnauld, Monadology*, translated by G.R. Montgomery, La Salle, Illinois: Open Court Publishing Company, 1973, §14, p. 253.

4   > *Ibid.*

5   > *Ibid.*, §22, p. 256.

6   > *Ibid.*, §8, p. 252.

7   > Deleuze's discussion of the interstitial spaces in Leibniz's theory of the Baroque represents a gesture towards the actual plenum chambers that exist between floors and ceilings in the construction of a building. See Gilles Deleuze, *The Fold, Leibniz and the Baroque*, translated by Tom Conley, London: Athlone Press, 2001. Plenum chambers are also key constituents in combustion engines.

8   > Leibniz's theory of the plenum contrasts with preceding Cartesian theories of it, particularly in his emphasis on the importance of the plenum as a figure of movement and differential change *by degrees*, not kind. His writings on the plenum from the 1760s explore these theories of continuity and 'endeavour'; for example, in the essay 'On the cohesiveness of bodies' (1672), the potential for movement and change operates at a psychic and embodied level. Leibniz writes: 'If one body endeavours to move into the place of another, these two bodies are continuous [...] The proposition is of great importance, for from it follows the propagation of motions in a plenum, and that when one body is moved it endeavours to carry away all the other bodies with it, and that things in the world of however small a size can be sensed by the whole universe [...]'. See Richard Arthur (editor and translator), *The Labyrinth of the Continuum: Writings on the Continuum Problem, 1672–1686 by G. W. Leibniz, The Yale Leibniz Series,* New Haven and London: Yale University Press, 2001, p. 9. Later, in the *Monadology*, these corporeal conditions are further defined into the psychic qualities of continuity, i.e. the soul, perception and 'appetite'.

9   > In §1 of the *Monadology*, Leibniz calls the Monad a 'simple' substance 'without parts', and the following sections develop this instantiation of the Monad in relation to magnitude. It is expressed in the concepts 'aggregate' in §2; in §3 it is 'Atoms of Nature' that are 'neither extension, nor form, nor divisibility'; and 'indissoluble' or without beginning in §§4–5. In addition, in §3 Leibniz refers to the Monad as an 'element' drawing a parallel with Euclid's definition of a point when he writes that Monads are 'the Elements of things', positing an explicit relationship between the substance of the Monad and Euclid's term 'element' (Leibniz, *op. cit.*, p. 251). In addition, if we recall Euclid's first axiom in Book I of *The Elements*, he states that a 'point is that which has no part.' See Euclid, *The Thirteen Books of the Elements*, Volume I, edited by Thomas Heath, London: Dover Publications, 1956, p. 153. We also find the paradox of limit and infinity present in the notion of the point, the Monad and the plenum.

10   > Interestingly this is almost the reverse of the solution posed by the philosopher Spinoza, who also challenged the Cartesian argument that mind and body are two different substances through his principle of an *indivisible* substance. See Spinoza's *Ethics* (1677).

11 > R. Arthur, *op. cit.*, p. lxv.
12 > Thanks to Laura Allen.
13 > In contrast, arithmetic might be said to be quantitative insofar as it registers difference that is generated *successively*, tending towards exclusion, therefore, not the simultaneity or 'vice-diction' that spatial or geometric relations (i.e. ratio) might engender.

MARX MATTERS,
OR: AESTHETICS, TECHNOLOGY, AND
THE SPIRIT OF MATTER

JON GOODBUN >MARX MATTERS, OR: AESTHETICS, TECHNOLOGY, AND THE SPIRIT OF MATTER

6.1 >WaG Architecture, Department of Immersive Network Environments, Invisible University. A contribution to David Greene's ongoing LAWUN project.

'Locally Available World unseen Networks', better known by its acronym 'LAWUN', is a project that Archigram member David Greene has been working on for the last thirty years. It is work that seeks to project architecture away from matter, away from building towards pure network, pure event-information-space. Recent manifestations of the work have been based upon live performances and mobile phones. Older manifestations typically featured 'Electric Aborigines' – technologically extended nomads who would travel with their prosthetic environments. Fixed, permanent architecture would be reduced to 'a servicing frame in a field waiting to be used or built upon. Very concentrated. The nearest thing to a village or town or building that should be allowed.'[1] The real architecture here happens at the interface of the body and the ether of communication networks encompassing the planet.

Even whilst this work is very obviously indebted to mid-twentieth-century communications theorists such as Marshall McLuhan, it would seem to remain a most contemporary project. However, in many ways these same preoccupations suggest affinities that are much older. If the cathedral used the experience of one immaterial medium – *light* – in conjunction with matter to ask theological questions through architectural experience, isn't Greene just doing the same but with a six-fold increase in wavelength from light waves to radio waves? There is more at stake in such a question than might at first appear. Greene is not alone in working with what I argue are the 'spiritual forms' of invisible networks or fields. A pantheistic cosmology, which in its general form imagines the universe of matter to be interpenetrated with fields or networks of energy or spirit centred upon the active human body, is a surprisingly frequent image in contemporary global culture, and can be found in manifestations as varied as the 'Jedi force' in the *Star Wars* films to the dominance within contemporary management theory of what we might, following Slavoj Zizek, call 'Wall Street Buddhism'.[2] More than just a by-product of entertainment technology or a commodification of eastern religions, this pantheism has had a particularly productive and interesting history, drawing together in perhaps unexpected ways the philosophy of Karl Marx and the emergence of the discourse around space in architecture – a combination which I shall try to outline in this text. I will argue that both of these bodies of work emerged from 'Young Hegelian' philosophical circles, soaked in the mysticism of an 'orientalised' nineteenth-century German culture. Both discourses remain, in different ways, structurally pantheistic. For Marx it is a pantheism that describes the quasi-mystical properties of the commodity. In architecture, Hegel's Spirit has become, quite simply, Space.

In this sense one might say that Greene's immaterial LAWUN project is a properly nineteenth-century piece of work, a pure Hegelian architecture.

EMPATHY AND SPACE

The history of architecture is the history of the sense of space.[3]
August Schmarsow, 'The Essence of Architectural Creation'

Our sensuous bodies are the interface between the world of mind and the world of matter. We commonly talk of having five senses, more or less directly related to five specialised bodily organs, which pass information from the world to the brain.[4] To sense something is to receive impressions in the mind through the body. We also commonly refer to other senses or sensibilities, which are perhaps more obviously social and cultural 'organs' within the body.[5] So when Schmarsow notes that we have a 'sense of space', his observation is not one that we have any necessary difficulty with. To suggest that this sense changes over time might be more challenging, particularly if it is thought to imply that our bodies too are historically changing. However, Schmarsow's near contemporary Karl Marx developed a number of ideas about the historical production and social development of the human body and senses, and it is useful, I believe, to read these two thinkers together. Schmarsow's assertion that architecture is primarily *spatial* was perhaps the most innovative part of his statement.

Whilst for many today the assertion that architecture is spatial is a truism, at the time that Schmarsow was writing, it represented a significant development and contribution to architectural thinking, and an emerging form of 'Kunstwissenschaft'[6] known as 'Einfühlungs' or 'empathy' theory. This discourse was primarily a phenomenology, a way of understanding formal spatial experience and expression as a simultaneously kinaesthetic, visual and cognitive phenomenon. It might be broadly summarised as the proposition that the architectural inhabitant imagines or projects the spatial environment as a second skin, an external membrane to their body – *an interface or prosthesis* – through which one expands into, feels and wears the form or space occupied. The cognitive map or body-image that we carry around with us is constantly adapting to the environment that it is in: when holding a stick our body-image expands to include this tool, when driving a car it expands to enclose the vehicle. When in a building one expands into and *empathises* with it. Empathy theory describes space (and the objects contained by space) as an alienated, yet recoverable, organ of our individual and social bodies. It is the medium through which mind and matter connect, subject and object recombine.

The term 'empathy' was first coined by Robert Vischer in 1873, in a paper which extended his father's work on aesthetic theory. He was, however, just one of a number of German art theorists and perceptual psychologists who were developing similar ideas in the final decades of the nineteenth century.[7] In the first decades of the twentieth century these thinkers would be joined by artists and architects, who, following in particular the writings of Wilhelm Worringer and Sigfried Giedion, would find in empathy theory one basis for uncovering meaning within non-representational form. Some tendencies within architectural thinking in particular hoped to find in the discourse on space that emerged directly out of empathy theory the basis of a modern 'autonomous' and rational practice. Whilst such hopes may have been misplaced, as a contribution to historical, social and phenomenological spatial analysis the idea of empathy remains a very usable and necessary part of architectural thinking today, not least in order to better understand a significant mode of our own spatial abstraction, *our* sense of space: the network.

NETWORK SPATIALITY

The network is a structural figuration of space consciousness in modernity, one of the forms through which we currently imagine and reproduce our relations to society and the world – indeed, following Manuel Castells, we might say the network is *the* cultural form of global capitalist metropolitan modernity.[8] As an idea, a conceptual figure, the network has a history. It erupts almost from nowhere in the eighteenth century, and by the nineteenth century images of networks can be found structuring abstract scientific diagrams in physics, biology and chemistry as atomic structures, force fields and bodily circulation systems – and increasingly as concrete realities in the form of town and regional plans, and as transportation, communications and infrastructure systems. The figure or concept of the network has been very productive for us as a tool, as a piece of technology, partly because of the complex formal properties of the network figure: it is potentially endless, isotropic, heterotropic, dynamic, non-centred, centred, multi-centred; and these formal properties allow us to use it to describe and analyse and produce phenomena as varied as those listed above. Perhaps most significantly however, the network's importance as a socio-cultural *gestalt* is due to its correspondence with the dominant organisational forms within capitalist society: the production, circulation and exchange of capital and commodities. Quite simply, mental images of global networks are produced through the experience of the circulation of capital and commodities, and through communication patterns. For the experiencing modern metropolitan subject, lived everyday encounters with these network environments fundamentally and radically changed their understanding of themselves in relation to objects, environments and each other. These experiences are something to do with the way we produce our sense of space. In pre-industrial society, every object that an individual was likely to encounter would come from their immediate world, and would have a local history, meaning, use value and so on. For the individual in industrial society, the relationship through exchange to every other object on the market network is radically different in kind. The market network is experienced as an extension of the local environment, and as a transformation of the individual's sense of space. Developments within communications technologies, as noted by Marshall McLuhan and John McHale,[9] similarly intensify the experience of extensions of the local environment, more specifically as extensions of the individual themselves, and are equally radical in transforming the experience of, and sense of, space.

This shift in the sense of space, or, more accurately, this shift in the way that individuals produce cognitive maps describing their relations to their social and physical environments, can be clearly seen in architectural and artistic production. Whilst there are few major typological precedents to the network in pre-modern art and architecture, suddenly, by the early twentieth century, it is everywhere. We can feel the presence of infinite networks in the grids of Mondrian. We can *empathise* and project ourselves into dynamic networks in the force-field forms of the Futurists and Expressionists. We can plug ourselves into, and wear, the endless megastructural frameworks envisaged by post-war architects ranging from Constant to Soleri, Archigram to the Metabolists, Superstudio to Friedman.

In these network projects we find an architectural web that ultimately encompasses the planet, an interface to, a framework for, or a reification – a making visible and material – of the immaterial networks of modernity. And just as the initial experience of immaterial networks radically develops and extends through processes of alienation of the sensuous human body, these environmental interfaces continue to ask questions of subjectivity in modernity: the separation of subject and object as a dialectic of mind and matter.

According to Jonathan Hale, Fredric Jameson, in his essay 'Cognitive Mapping', sets out 'possibilities for a new kind of Marxist aesthetic'[10] – one which ideologically examines spatial sensibility, looking for what Louis Althusser has elsewhere described as, '[t]he Imaginary representation of the subject's relationship to his or her Real conditions of existence,'[11] through what Jameson describes as 'an extrapolation of [Kevin Lynch's] spatial analysis to the realm of social structure.'[12] There is some kind of correspondence between the forms of society, the forms of individual experience, and the forms of the metropolis, which itself provides the particular conditions in which the space of concrete experience (super-individual society) and the space of inner experience (individual subject) are mapped onto each other. Whilst it is clearly in precisely this mode that I propose the above discussion of network spatiality to be understood, there is, I think, more to be said in contribution to the project of a new Marxist aesthetics.

Whilst the network is a specific historical form of spatial sensibility, acting in different manifestations as both the 'real conditions of existence' and 'imaginary representations', it is also in some way the *ur* form of spatiality that makes visible the concept of space and renders viable the possibility of socio-spatial cognitive mapping. As such, it lies at the heart of Jameson's extension of Marxist aesthetics, although in order to realise to what extent this is the case, we need to return to the theological forms of nineteenth-century German philosophy.

HEGEL AND THEOSOPHY

> Germany is now the fertile soil of pantheism. This is the religion of our greatest thinkers, of our best artists . . . Pantheism is the open secret of Germany[13]
>
> Heinrich Heine, *History of Religion and Philosophy in Germany*

A particular form of pantheism was developed by the German philosopher Georg Hegel. In his model, matter is thought of as alienated spirit, as alienated God. When Hegel states that 'God is God only in so far as he knows himself. His self knowledge is, further, a self consciousness in man and man's knowledge of God, which proceeds to man's self knowledge in God',[14] he is describing a model where God/Spirit is realised through the matter of the universe (primarily via humanity and art) and becomes aware of itself as alienated spirit. It is not difficult to argue that Hegel's philosophical edifice is a highly organised and thought-through form of mysticism, and hermeticism in particular.[15] Hermeticists hold that God is completed by, and partly dependent upon, matter. For Hermetics, as for Hegel, humanity is part of God, and realises God through spiritual self-awareness and practice.

We can say with some confidence that there are conceptual forms in Hegel's thought that have significant structural similarities with mystic-oriental cosmologies. In addition to a universe pregnant with spirit striving towards self-consciousness, these organising forms would include the smooth and dynamic logical space of dialectics, and, most importantly, a subject/object continuum: a field-based model of projected consciousness or extended body relations in which these two poles (subject/object or body-mind/world) are not thought of as entirely separate and discrete – *I am here and that object over there is not me* – but rather as connected areas of intensity within networks of matter and spirit, fields of alienation. As we shall see, similar models would prove invaluable when turned towards spatial aesthetics.

GERMAN ORIENTALISM AND THE YOUNG HEGELIANS

The kinds of theosophical ideas that were so formative to Hegel were active across European culture throughout the nineteenth century – and particularly widespread in Germany, where pantheistic, animist, vitalist, Gnostic, romantic and Neoplatonic philosophies were, it seems, never far from the surface of intellectual debate. Simultaneously, field, wave and aetheric imaginings were productively animating scientific speculation, whilst spiritualistic beliefs – such as attempts to communicate with the dead – were also enjoying enormous popularity amongst the masses, and formed a significant proportion of the content of the emerging mass media.[16] Suzanne Marchand, Jennifer Jenkins and others have recently argued that this phenomenon must be understood as part of a particular historical cultural phenomenon: *German Orientalism*. Orientalist cosmologies found fertile ground in Germany, and increasingly through the nineteenth century and into the twentieth, academic orientalist discourses – primarily philology and archaeology – found themselves challenging the historical basis of both the Christian church and Classicism.

It is within this context that the Young Hegelians emerged as a grouping, centred on the University of Berlin. This group of radical philosophers argued for an extension and reformulation of the implications of the Hegelian project. They shared ground in calling for bourgeois reform of the German state, and attacking the Christian beliefs that they found underpinning the state. They argued instead for the *divinity of Humanity*, and emphasised 'history as the progressive union of god and man.'[17] Of this group, Ludwig Feuerbach, Karl Marx and Friedrich Theodor Vischer have had the most lasting import, and are of particular interest to us here.[18] All three of these writers, although often seeking to deal with the religious mysticism in Hegel by insisting that *man is God*, nonetheless always take on and develop oriental spiritual-conceptual *forms*, particularly those we might characterise as an *aesthetics of projective alienation*. These forms seem to provide them with some exceptionally productive methods for thinking about mankind and modernity.

It was Feuerbach who first directly attempted a materialist reworking of Hegel, and specifically strove to reverse the role played by religion in understanding mind and matter. In *The Essence of Christianity* (1841) he argued that rather than some universal spirit being present in and realised though man, it was rather man that created God and religion, as projections – as alienated forms – of himself.[19] The importance of Feuerbach's influence upon Marx is well documented – not least by Marx himself.[20] Less well documented – in fact almost completely uncommented upon within Marxian scholarship – is the influence of Friedrich Theodor Vischer, whose major work, *Aesthetics* (1846), we know was read and returned to by Marx at various times in his life.[21] For F.T. Vischer, aesthetics is important as he finds in it a more advanced stage of spiritual development than in religion, and it no doubt provides for him something similar to what Marx had just, in parallel, described as 'making the world philosophical'.[22] In the words of William J. Brazill, aesthetics for F.T. Vischer is:

> The overcoming of alienation, a progressive fusion of human consciousness with matter that was itself the meaning of history. Thus for Vischer aesthetics

was the key to human development, for *man fashions his own consciousness in historical forms so that he might know as an object the spirit inherent in himself.*[23]

This work by F.T. Vischer was, I argue, to provide a common basis for two revolutionary new discourses, those of Marx and the architectural-aesthetic concept of *Space-Empathy*. In both discourses, as with Hegel, an oriental cosmology is the essential underlying paradigm – a 'utopian' or pantheistic network model of subject/object relations. For different though related reasons, both Marx and the empathy theorists were interested in repositioning Hegel centrally over the human body.

EMPATHY, MARX AND AESTHETICS
When Hegel states that 'art spiritualizes, it animates the mere outward and material object with a form that expresses soul, feeling, spirit',[24] he means that we are able to read specific content out of abstract form through an intuitive understanding of its expressive force. However, if for Hegel the aesthetic object really is an expressed spirit, and for F.T. Vischer it was a rather more humanised matter, for his son Robert Vischer, who first coined the term 'Einfühlungs', it was more clearly 'that the soul was no longer innate in the object observed, as Hegel maintained, but it was rather a projection from the individual observer.'[25] Hegel's spirit had become space.

In *On the Optical Sense of Form* (1873), Robert Vischer builds upon an orientalist phenomenology and aesthetics taken from his father:

> This symbolising [by which he means perceived aesthetic meaning – J.G.] can be based on nothing other than the pantheistic urge for union with the world, which can by no means be limited to our more easily understood kinship with the human species but must, consciously or unconsciously, be directed towards the universe.[26]

However, he adds another orientalist model – that of the dynamic, vital and sensuous human body, which he places at the very centre of his father's pantheism. He synthesises this with a psychology taken from the proto-Freudian Karl Albert Scherner, whose work *The Life of the Dream* (1861) R. Vischer acknowledges, stating:

> Here it was shown how the body, in responding to certain stimuli in dreams, objectifies itself in spatial forms. Thus it unconsciously projects its own bodily form – and with this also the soul – into the form of an object. From this I derived the notion of Empathy.[27]

In this ambitious paper, R. Vischer outlines the major components of a sophisticated theory of architectural empathy,[28] and develops a socio-biological thesis on beauty through a series of descriptions of different types of formal empathy. These range from speculations about correspondences between material form and the physical biological structures of our senses and nerves – in statements such as: 'the horizontal line is pleasing because our eyes are positioned horizontally',[29] and even: 'light produces an agreeable vibration in the respective nerve group through the regular form of its wave movement'[30] – to general statements about the projective body in the aesthetic perception of matter: 'I can without difficulty place myself within its inner structure, at its centre of gravity. I can think my way into it, mediate its size with my own, stretch and expand, bend and confine myself to it.'[31] In a particularly interesting passage in relation to Marx, R. Vischer describes the particular type of empathy at work when we use tools:

> We invent working, driving, primordial figures, derived from the created world, figures who treat things as such simply as an appendage of themselves, very much as I feel a stick to be an extension of my arm and an increase of my power. This is a special sense of form [*Formgefühl*], which, like a foreign shoot grafted onto pure self-feeling, can be described as a continuation of it.[32]

For Marx, too, there is no 'natural' or 'normal' condition of humanity. He too sees the species as self consciously productive in the world. That is to say, it produces itself as species, it produces its world, and it produces its own self-consciousness. This consciousness is the opposite of matter, but also identical with it. This is because, for Marx, consciousness emerges out of productive material sensuous activity. He states: 'production produces not only an object for the individual, but also an individual for an object.'[33] Again, Marx notes, when reading F.T. Vischer's *Aesthetics*, that 'the beautiful exists only for consciousness . . . beauty is necessary in order that the spectator may merge with matter', and again 'that the enjoyment of the beautiful is immediate, and that it requires education would seem to be contradictory. But man becomes what he is and arrives at his own true nature only through education.' Quoting Schiller, Marx notes that 'beauty is simultaneously an object, and a subjective state. It is at once form, when we judge it, and also life when we feel it. It is at once our state of being and our creation.'[34]

When Marx asserts that 'man is affirmed in the objective world not only in the act of thinking, but with all his senses',[35] he is returning to an aesthetics of the human body as a way of developing Feuerbach's materialist critique of Hegel beyond the limits of both materialist and idealist philosophy.[36] The objectification of reality, the projection of man's subjective forces and abilities, is itself a material process for Marx. So when he states, 'All objects become for man objectifications of himself,' and 'The sense of an object for me goes only so far as my senses go,' he seems to be thinking in ways very close to Schmarsow when the latter writes 'the spatial construct is, so to speak, an emanation of the human being present, a projection from within the subject.'[37] Similarly, when Marx writes, 'the senses have their own history. Neither the object of art nor the subject capable of aesthetic experience comes of itself,' and again, 'The senses have become theoreticians in their immediate practice . . . The forming of the five senses is a labour of the entire history of the world down to the present,'[38] he seems to be laying the philosophical basis for why, as Schmarsow noted, there is a history of the sense of space. Equally, the empathy theorists are in effect engaged in the kind of intellectual work – a detailed historical study of our historical forms of space and body sensibility – that Marx seems to call for.

Marx is developing his thinking in order to establish the basis from which to write anew history, economics and philosophy – this time starting from the experience of the sensuous human body outwards, into its extensions and prosthetics in the form of society. These extensions of the body are produced and reproduced by technology, which takes on the aesthetic task of objectifying matter. Technology and art therefore play a similar aesthetic role here. Both mediate or bridge between subject and object, between consciousness and matter.

However, in the networks of global capitalism, aesthetically objectified matter has a particular historical form: the commodity – and it was in unravelling the animistic nature of the commodity that Hegel's orientalism would be so productive for Marx. The commodity is, for Marx, 'a very queer thing, abounding in metaphysical subtleties and theological niceties.'[39] It is, as Terry Eagleton notes:

> a kind of grisly caricature of the authentic artefact, at once reified to a grossly particular object and virulently anti material in form, densely corporeal and elusively spectral at the same time. The commodity for Marx is the site of some curious disturbance of the relations between sense and spirit, form and content, universal and particular: it is at once an object and not an object.[40]

Moreover, it is in the densely networked space of the metropolis that the fetishistic power of commodities is most powerfully conjured, as Michael W. Jennings notes:

> When they work together in networks, the commodities that arise under industrial capitalism 'talk to each other' shaping a totalizing . . . manmade environment that appears to be natural while remaining wholly illusory. Humans move through such networks of commodities as through a phantasmagoria, unable to exert control over themselves or over their environment.[41]

COGNITIVE MAPPING AND CRITICAL CYBERNETICS: A NEW 'KUNSTWISSENSCHAFT'

Whilst this paper seeks to promote the possibility of specific architectural knowledge gained through a phenomenology of the modern body in space, it is also categorical in its insistence that this possibility must itself be produced out of the experience and conception of our broader metropolitan environment. Although beyond the scope of this paper, it would be possible to trace the relationship between an understanding of network environments as simultaneously morphological, psycho-libidinal, socio-spatial and abstract-conceptual phenomena, and a philosophical elaboration of the concept of the metropolis. Such an exercise would extend to cover the different ways in which both Walter Benjamin and Henri Lefebvre take on the problematic of a spatial experience.[42] If this is one direction in which it seems valid to take Jameson's challenge, it is just as intriguing to ask whether we can once again develop, in terms of the ambition of actual content, the work of the nineteenth century *art-scientists*. Given new models from biology, the neurosciences and psychology we can perhaps review and update some of the aesthetic models discussed, and outline a new

Kunstwissenschaft: it is now increasingly possible to describe specifically what is happening in the *matter* of the mind and body, when producing and experiencing the spatial and movement memories described by Vischer and Schmarsow. We can begin to write a historical materialist account of the dialectical relationship between the production of space and the production of the brain. We can outline a study of brain structure and mind-consciousness in relationship to the imagining, production and experience of architecture.

Equally, we continue to find the spectres of pantheism even in the most materialist emergence models. Biologist Richard Dawkins has argued that environments built by organisms – such as the webs of spiders, the nests of birds, the dams of beavers, and so on – must be understood as phenotypic expressions of the genes of the organisms, in exactly the same way as fingers, hands and wings are understood to be. Dawkins himself has not promoted any reading of human building production as phenotypic, and although of course (following our own discussion!) human society and conceptual abstraction clearly make it problematic to try to transpose wholesale this model onto humans, it is equally unlikely that these processes are not at work at some level in human production. If there are spatial phenotypic expressions, proto-architectural impulses, genetically hardwired into the human organism, then the broad humanist 'archetypal architecture' question – the idea that there might be organisational forms of matter that we make in the world that, whilst not absolutely fixed or fundamental, are at a deep spatio-biological level 'part of us' – becomes crucial.

Furthermore, current models of brain development and cognitive theory emphasise the radical role that perceptual environments and interactions with matter have on the development of the human brain. Just as, for Dawkins, organisms interact with their environments, transforming them into phenotypic expressions of their genes, for cognitive theorists our spatial and social environments and practices literally develop and shape our minds. Whilst it is perfectly clear (as Jameson no doubt intuits) that some environments are more progressive than others in terms of promoting socio-psychic development, at present our knowledge about this resembles alchemy as much as any kind of spatial science. We might loosely describe work in this area as the 'cybernetic ecologies' tradition in architecture.[43] Cybernetic-ecological architects in this sense might include Aldo van Eyck, who has theorised the idea of architecture as *counterform*, a kind of physical environmental stamp whose imprint is at the neural and social levels, and Antonio Gaudí, whose communicative immersive environments cyberneticist Gordon Pask has described as 'the most cybernetic structures yet in existence.'[44]

Perhaps then what is at stake then in Jameson's demand for a new Marxist aesthetic, as much as a new *Kunstwissenschaft*, is a critical politicisation and expansion of cybernetics. Whilst grasping this totality remains a philosophical task, and although we may not currently be able to help but perpetuate the division of labour between material and spiritual work, we should note that 'the architectural' is in many ways uniquely positioned to at least reflect upon this problem. However, due to the nature of the material that needs to be dealt with – precisely because in its totality it is 'properly unrepresentable' – it will remain in part a discourse with theological form.

1   >David Greene, 'LAWUN Project No.2, The Invisible University' in *A Guide to Archigram 1961–74*, London: Academy, 1994, p. 365.

2   >At the Weimar Nietzsche Forum 2003, Slavoj Zizek described a condition of 'Wall St Buddhism' which I am extending here to include the broad drift in management theory today, wherein a neo-Taoist model has been adopted. Commerce is basically seen as a primary manifestation of the tao chi – the energy force of society.

3   >August Schmarsow, 'The Essence of Architectural Creation' in Harry Mallgrave and Eleftherios Ikonomou (eds.), *Empathy, Form, Space – Problems in German Aesthetics 1873–1893*, Santa Monica, California: Getty Centre, 1994, p. 296.

4   >Classically, these being sight, smell, taste, touch, hearing. J.J. Gibson has, however, suggested a different five-sensory system: the visual, auditory, taste-smell, haptic and basic orienting system.

5   >A sense of style, sense of rhythm, sense of movement, sense of timing and so on.

6   >'Kunstwissenschaft' literally translates as the 'science of art'.

7   >Significant contributions were made by a wide variety of thinkers who developed these, or very similar, notions. Most notably, Lipps added rigour to empathy theory's scientific grounding, tying it to Gestalt psychology. Schmarsow added the insight that it is *space* that we empathise with in architecture, and developed further ideas about the basis of this projective imagination emerging from within the memories and experiences of the body. Importantly, he noted that our *sense of space* changes: it has a history – an idea that Giedion, Riegl, Wölflin, Worringer and others were able to develop very productively. It is not always clear to what extent these thinkers were developing Vischer's early work or had independently converged upon these ideas via Hegel, the general air of 'oriental' thinking, and in particular new philosophical interpretations of orientalism, especially that of Nietzsche.

8   >See, for example, Manuel Castells (ed.), *The Network Society*, Cheltenham: Edward Elgar Publishing, 2004.

9   >For McLuhan, all technology and media (from clocks, satellites and computers to languages) act as extensions of our bodies, as new organs, as prosthesis, in a way that I argue is related to projection in empathy theory.

10   >Jonathan Hale, 'Cognitive mapping: NY vs Philadelphia', in Neil Leach (ed.), *The Hieroglyphics of Space – Reading and Experiencing the Modern Metropolis*, London: Routledge, 2002, p. 31.

11   >Louis Althusser quoted in Fredric Jameson, 'Cognitive Mapping', in C. Nelson and L. Grossberg (eds.), *Marxism and the Interpretation of Culture*, Chicago: University of Illinois Press, 1988, p. 353.

12   >Fredric Jameson, *op. cit.*, p. 353.

13   >Heinrich Heine, *History of Religion and Philosophy in Germany,* Queensland, Australia: James Cook University of North Queensland, 1982, p. 119.

14   >Cited in Warren Breckman, *Marx, the Young Hegelians and the Origins of Radical Social Theory,* Cambridge: Cambridge University Press, 1999, p. 23.

15   >Glenn Magee is one of several contemporary Hegel scholars who have recently argued that Hegel's work must be understood not simply as a contribution to the discipline of western philosophy but also as a contribution to the discourses of Hermetic and Gnostic theological traditions. See Glenn Magee, *Hegel and the Hermetic Tradition*, Ithaca, New York: Cornell University Press, 2001.

16   >The development of radio in particular, and new media and communications networks in general, is increasingly understood as dialectically related, both imaginatively and practically, to the growth and ideas of spiritualism. Marconi, in particular, invented radio in order to talk with spirits.

17   >William J. Brazill, *The Young Hegelians*, London: Yale University Press, 1970, p. 136.

18   >Other prominent Young Hegelians (also known as Left Hegelians, though they called themselves 'The Doctors' Club') included the brothers Bruno and Edgar Bauer, David Strauss, Friedrich Engels and Max Stirner.

19   >See Ludwig Feuerbach, *The Essence of Christianity* [1841], trans. Marian Evans, London: Trübner, 1881.

20   >Although we should remember that the *Thesis on Feuerbach* was published posthumously by Engels from Marx's notebooks.

21   >According to Mikhail Lifshitz, *The Philosophy of Art of Karl Marx* [1933], trans. Ralph B Winn, London: Pluto, 1973. Lifshitz notes on p. 83, for example, that Marx's notebooks from 1857–8 contain a detailed synopsis of F.T. Vischer's *Aesthetiks*.

22   >'To transform the world in the image of Hegelian philosophy would mean to make of man in existential reality the divinity that, as Marx saw it, Hegel had already made him in thought.' Robert C. Tucker, *Marx-Engels Reader* 2nd edition, New York, London: Norton, 1978, p. 9.

23   >William J. Brazill, *op. cit.*, p. 172.

24   >Georg Hegel quoted in Brazill, *op. cit.*, p. 172.

25   >Cornelius van de Ven, *Space in Architecture*, Assen, Netherlands: Van Gorcum, 1987, p. 80.

26   >Robert Vischer, 'On the Optical Sense of Form', in Harry Mallgrave and Eleftherios Ikonomou (eds.), *Empathy, Form, Space – Problems in German Aesthetics 1873–1893,* Santa Monica, California: Getty Centre, 1994, p. 109.

27   >Robert Vischer, *op. cit.*, p. 97.

28   >*Empathy* is best understood not as a translation of *Einfühlung*, but rather as the category defined by all the various *–fühlungs* (feelings) that Robert Vischer develops.

29   >Robert Vischer, *op. cit.*, p. 97.

30   >*Ibid.*, p. 96.

31   >*Ibid.*, p. 104.

32   >*Ibid.*, p. 111.

33   >Karl Marx quoted in Mikhail Lifshitz, *op. cit.*, p. 79.

34   >Karl Marx, *ibid.*, p. 83.

35   >Karl Marx, *ibid.*, p. 78.

36   >Marx was almost continuously reading aesthetic theory throughout his life, from a broad range of romantics (including seminars with Schlegel) through to Hegel as a young man in the 1830s and 40s, to a major study of proto-empathy theorist F.T. Vischer in the late 1850s.

37   >August Schmarsow, *op. cit.*, p. 294.

38   >Karl Marx in Robert C. Tucker, *op. cit.*, p. 87.

39   >Karl Marx, *ibid.*, p. 319.

40   >Terry Eagleton, *The Ideology of the Aesthetic*, Oxford: Basil Blackwell, 1990.

41   >Michael W. Jennings and Neil H. Donahue (eds.), *Invisible Cathedrals – The Expressionist Art History of Wilhelm Worringer*, Place of publication: Penn State University Press, 1995, p. 92.

42   >In this context, for an elaboration of the concept of metropolis with particular reference to Lefebvre, see David Cunningham, 'The Concept of the Metropolis' in *Radical Philosophy* 133 (Sept / Oct 2005), pp. 13–25, and with particular reference to Benjamin, see David Cunningham, 'The Phenomenology of Non-Dwelling', *Crossings* No. 7, 2005, pp. 137–61.

43   >I am working here with three broad definitions of cybernetics. 1: the use of epistemology (the limits to how we know what we know) to understand the constraints of any medium (technological, biological, or social) – Paul Pangaro. 2: The science of observing systems – Paul Pangaro. – Warren McCullock 3: An experimental epistemology concerned with the communication within an observer and between an observer and the environment.

44   >Gordon Pask, 'The Architectural relevance of cybermatics'. *Architectural Design*, 1969.

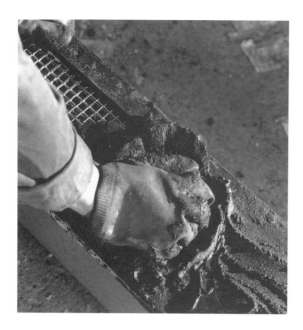

Moulding clay with hands
kneading the world

a clump of earth
a Taschenwelt

racing time, to be ahead of the hardening of the crust

Forming the crust
Swirling of sense and meaning

Adrift in a place, placed in a drift

The leap into a chamber afloat above the crust
The incubator

The invisible hand stirring the contents of the box

People meeting, disconnecting, joining, confronting each other

The power of music, Live 8 and the global metaspace

'Sing to the people!' – the message of Nelson Mandela to the planners –
'Otherwise they do not understand you'

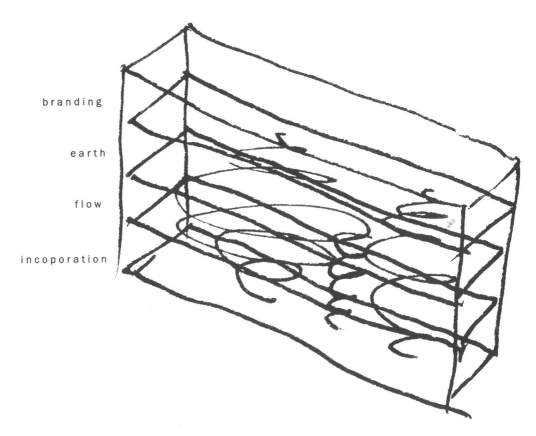

branding

earth

flow

incoporation

LONGING AND BELONGING: INCUBATORS

The Urban Gallery is a metaspace enabling the observation of flows and forces, but also a place in which to negotiate the intertwining between them, creating in effect new life forms, an incubator. The non-cities, liminal territories defined by threshold conditions, infrastructures, mountain ranges, seas, rather than population densities, are the homelands of the near future. By expressing these territories as incubators conditions of belonging and longing become visible through the intricate connectivity inside a metaspace, its architecture the topology of such non linear intertwining.[1]

Deeply embedded divisions: the seam of gold and the Apartheid legacy of separation

A Liminal Body

How to manage undermined earth and the swirling arsenic dust

Soweto, the new capital, go with the Africa Van
Moulding the skin, an experiment in texture

Seeing through the perforated thickness, skimming the thin cover

The assembly: blocks, panels, shells, spheres, caves

Observing the sky: the earth as foundation. Weight and Lightness, touching the heavens

Thickness and flight, the horizon embodied in 'Homerton X'

A loom is a multiple horizon, constantly weaving sky and ground, reality and aspirations of communities for Homerton, weaving the urban space, projecting an instrument into the city, the metaspace of interrelating projects, a coevolution of prototypes, twisting in time, twirling actors and agents.

The handling of the Loom: an Urban Gallery: Knowledge, stories first. Second: play, injecting potential – we call that 'organisational form of the prototype'. Telling the potential, games and scenarios, a community creates an identity: third. Fourth: Where to go when all this matures, like a ripe fruit on tree? When is it ripe? Pick the fruit gently so it does not bruise. Or, the Urban Gallery as incubator: form a nest, lay the egg, let it come out when ready.

The Open Source, a new agora of exchange, barter and deals; an evolving place, moulded by all those in the game.

The House of Participation, a search for new forms of governance.

Protopolitics as a goal for planning tools, inchoate things – who wants them? Where are we now? Who kneads us, who needs us?

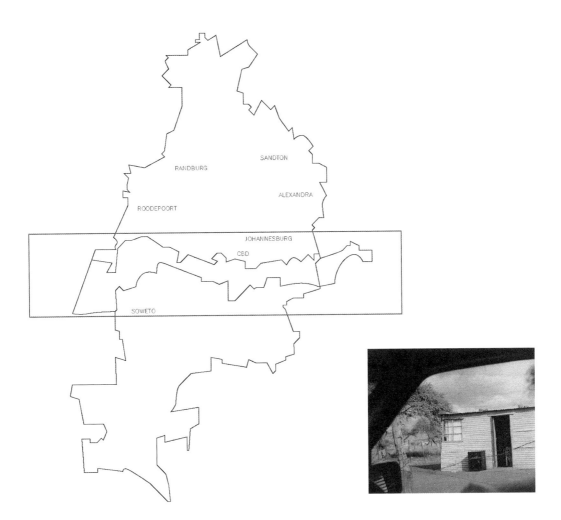

LONGING AND BELONGING: RUMOURS

With apartheid gone, and the mining companies turned property managers,
the void in the centre of Johannesburg, leftover land that was once the
place where the gold seam emerged at the surface, now toxic land
undermined by myriad tunnels and caves, is both the landmark symbolizing
the early mineral wealth that created the city and the legacy of
apartheid planning making barely erasable marks dividing different
sections of the population.[2]

LONGING AND BELONGING: THE AFRICA VAN

Soweto . . . is the home for black people, mainly poor, with no ability to
move house across the void that runs E W through Johannesburg . . . But
across the void come the minivans, carrying the people from Soweto to
their jobs in the North. Their stitching pattern is defining the
character of this void . . . In the fifties as part of the Apartheid
policies of segregation, black people were ordered to live in these
homelands. Pass laws meant a controlled passage of black people who
needed a job in the large cities. Women and children stayed in the
homelands, semi urban territories. Effectively the 'homeland' created a
false place of belonging, a real longing, and a pernicious condition of
people being a stranger, a migrant, in the cities and the rest of the
country.[3]

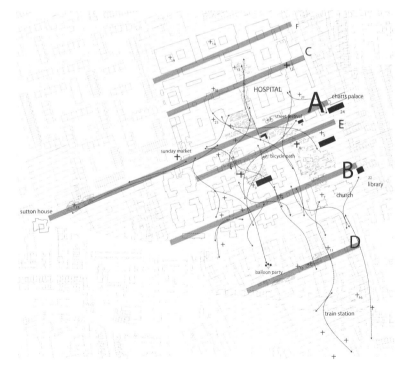

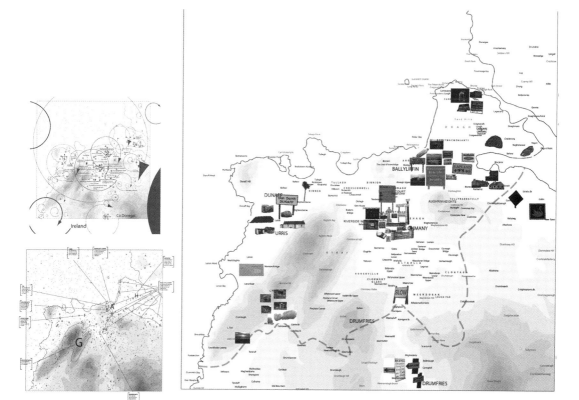

LONGING AND BELONGING: PROTOPOLITICS

The Clonmany Area is a parish with three small villages nestled between mountains and sea in the west of Inishowen, Ireland. The parish has no governance structure except the County Council whose remit stretches over a very much larger territory. The Clonmany Area Pilot Project group looked into the need for a cooperative mechanism for the thirty-eight groups that live in partial harmony and partial conflict. The Pilot Project for Clonmany forms the basis for the negotiation of joint projects, urban prototypes creating a proto-political space.[4]

A POST SCRIPT
There is a continuity between the work we did during the late eighties and the current work. Underlying it all is the main theme of the skin of the earth as a dynamic materiality, and the inhabited space: the second skin. This theme, stated at the beginning of *Urban Flotsam*, comes back in practically all projects, sometimes through the physical substance of matter, cement, clay; sometimes through the less physical materiality of human activities and urban processes, collective emotions and information exchange. Parallel to that theme runs the assumption that architectural artefacts are 'Taschenwelts', small worlds reflecting larger orders, and that the same Taschenwelt as a concept lies at the basis of the idea of the Urban Gallery, a planning methodology connected to the proposed practice of Urban Curation.

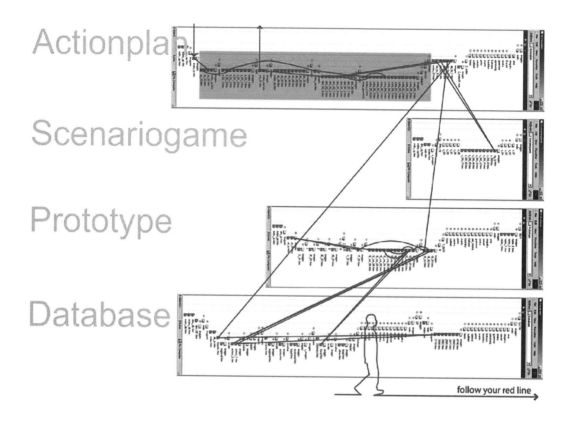

Actionplan

Scenariogame

Prototype

Database

follow your red line

+₁   Hospital gardens

+₂   street market

+₃   HMP pavillion

+₄   cafe

+₅   pond

+₆   nursery

+₇   community centre

+₈   club

+₉   educational farm

+₁₀ playground

+₁₁ youth club

+₁₂ winter garden

+₁₃ Hospital access

+₁₄ garden and children's playroom

+₁₅ bikers kiosk

+₁₆ kiosk and bakery

+₁₇ art painting walls

+₁₈ elderly entertainment room

+₁₉ toy library

+₂₁ Hospital's visitor parking

+₂₂ library exhibition room

+₂₃ Hospital cafeteria

There are nuances in the treatment of this theme. We are currently developing a prototype for a double monocoque roof element for a pavilion in Homerton, Hackney, in East London. This prototype is a fusion between the topological exercises with grids and swirling flotsam that we started to use during the Skin of the Earth project in Moscow in 1989, and have used since then for several projects such as the Osaka Stepping Stones – basically treating the study of the dynamics of the skin of the earth as a game – and exercises in the expressive and structural properties in cement that we started with the Apeiron project in Fort Asperen in 1988, and continued in the Skin of the Earth project. The prototype for Homerton will be cast as a single piece in a complex mould and then suspended in a steel cubic frame, forming a floating roof element. This suspended cut-out of a materialised horizon (referring back to the undulating horizon formed by the surface of water, or of moving flotsam) is a model we are testing on different scales: the hand-held scale of the small model; the educational model, constructed by students in the London Metropolitan University; the actual prototype, to be erected in Homerton; the low-energy prototype house; and the basic type of an urban block in the Madrid competition for the combined law courts of Spain: *Encruciado e Circuito*. The prototype in Homerton is part of a feasibility study, 'Homerton X', of which we were co-authors. The idea of that study was to create the basic form for a dynamic masterplan. Since the main stakeholders have difficulty communicating, or in any case proceeding with the plan, we are working with Hackney Marsh Partnership to create a catalyst of change in the form of a fragment for a pavilion – as a focus of local cultural programming.

The largest scale of operations, in the form of the Urban Gallery, is increasingly linked to large-scale chunks of the earth – natural Liminal Bodies – where we work with associative networks to create negotiation spaces for prototypes. The situations where the Urban Gallery is being applied, or where preparations are in progress, are: The Transoceanic Corridor in South America between Valparaíso in Chile and Buenos Aires in Argentina; the planned railway infrastructure between Minas Gerais and Vitória on Brazil's Atlantic Coast (in the form of a consultancy role); the Thames Gateway, east of London; and 'Sector E' in the Netherlands, between Rotterdam Mainport and the Rhine-Ruhr Metropolis.

1   > Raoul Bunschoten, 'Homelands' in *Oase,* Rotterdam: 010 Publishers, 2005, p. 88.
2   > *Ibid.*
3   > *Ibid.*
4   > Raoul Bunschoten and Gary Doherty, 'Protopolitics: a case study in territory and identity' in *Architectural Association of Ireland Journal*, March 2005, p. 30.

It is a beauty that comes from order found, not order given, as if its permanent harmony existed precariously in a transient and unpredictable world.

Joshua Taylor on the 'Matter Paintings' of Antoni Tàpies[1]

There is a sense of delight about the roughness of the concrete at La Tourette (figure 8.1). Yet perhaps delight is too passive a word to describe the condition, as it is closer to revelry. There is the sense that Le Corbusier is revelling in the rawness of the casting. One can still sense the very plasticity, the viscosity of the concrete in its prior state as it seeps unevenly down the formwork; a condition captured in stasis as an embodiment of experience and a memory of its other nature.

Concrete is more often used in an illusionary way, detailed and executed with precision to ensure a surface that bears no association with either the material or the process. But this is an approach which effaces the very nature of the material itself. By contrast, the way in which the inherent duality of concrete is celebrated throughout La Tourette, and in other projects by Le Corbusier, through its apparent

8.1 >La Tourette
Monastery detail of east
facade surface.

imprecision suggests a love of both the tectonics of the material and the hand of the maker. In its expressiveness it is similar to Richard Serra's attitude when he speaks of his own work and working process: 'I began to wonder how I could use paint merely as material, as an industrial found object; I did not want to use it to make something else, to create an illusion.'[2] As both sculptor and painter, Serra has worked intimately with many materials and can well understand the evocative presence material can have in an artefact, and yet how elusive this condition may be to achieve. The reality of material and its role in the presence of the artefact are qualities common to both architecture and painting. Yet both practices can equally succumb to the illusion of the narrative or to a theorized positioning which can subvert or disavow material consequences in favour of other preoccupations – agendas that are often based on an intellectualization of the content of the painting, or the building, by its author with or without reference to the culture in which they act or the material with which they make.

Though not mutually exclusive, there remains a certain tension between a regard for material and the creation of illusion – a tension, one could argue, concerning the understanding of order and the control of meaning. Joshua Taylor, as quoted above by John Yau, speaks of a precariousness based on order found, rather than order given in relation to material paintings. He alludes to the compelling sense of fragility they manifest regarding the nature of life, and describes, in effect, a condition of imprecision rather than precision, of openness rather than control, which could influence the emotive power of a material artefact. This position suggests that a relinquishing of control, as it relates to processes and the abandoning of influence over final interpretations, could be the means to create this quality of transient fragility, by placing the reading of the artefact beyond the simplicity of the narrative – imbuing it instead with an evocative ambiguity in terms of both its material rendering and its ultimate meaning.

Such an abandonment of control in search of the fragile or elusive image is, however, hardly how one has come to think of Le Corbusier. When considered across his career he is more typically known for his lack of interest in material, or indeed any process-based issues in form making, attaching importance instead to 'the concept of the architectonic plan, as opposed to the particular conditions of its material realization,' as Stanislaus von Moos has argued.[3] Certainly this is the attitude one comes to understand from Le Corbusier if he is taken at his word. His expressed interest in the tectonic quality of building never related to expressive potential but rather to the liberation provided by the exploration of space, form and light. From his earliest words on the subject, in an essay on the decorative arts, Le Corbusier appeals to the 'Law of Ripolin', or whitewash, to rid space and form of its clutter and irrational decoration in the hope of attaining a healthier environment, or to achieve the elimination of the equivocal.[4] This attitude to the making of space is clearly seen in his earliest works, such as the Villa La Roche. Regardless of the materials or means of construction, which often took the form of a concrete frame infilled with rough blockwork, the works are consistently rendered to exclude any display of structure, tectonic logic or material presence. Le Corbusier insisted that to exploit the tectonic nature of building as an expressive tool was a naive position as architecture was a plastic art, one focused on the unity of the idea rather than the minutiae of its making.

Much has been made of Le Corbusier's apparent shift away from this position from the 1930s onwards, and of the deviation towards a more poetic use of both traditional and new materials in his architectural compositions. Both von Moos and, more particularly, Christopher Green in his essay 'Architect as Artist' have made interesting correlations between Le Corbusier's painting and his architecture as it relates to this transformation process. Certainly Le Corbusier himself was explicit enough about the importance of his painting to his thinking within the realm of architecture, understanding the two as sympathetic studies. But as Green suggests, 'When he called his art the "secret" of his architecture it was not about formal analogies, but about the activities of making art and designing buildings . . . it was about processes and a very creative engagement with things understood in a very particular way.'[5] Moving beyond the formal analogies traditionally alluded to, the critical relationship to examine could be between the understanding of paint as material and the appreciation of building as material artefact, extending to a consideration of the act of painting and the act of building. For it may be the architect's very distance from the process that leads to the common treatment of material as an instrument of graphic effect in the service of other agendas rather than an expression of material consequence. Perhaps through his intimate engagement with the material and process of painting, Le Corbusier developed an increasing regard for material expression in his building work as both an embodiment of material presence and a measure of process.

INTIMATE ENGAGEMENT: MATERIAL, PROCESS AND CHANCE

The consideration of this critical lineage in the thinking of Le Corbusier becomes clearer when viewed through the medium of painting, and more importantly through the thinking of painters. The tension between illusion, whatever its inspiration, and material has historical lineage among both the artists as well as architects of the modernist period who struggled to relieve themselves of the constraints of style, or, more specifically in the case of painters, of narrative. Mark Rothko once said of this: 'There was never any question in plastic art, in poetry, in music of representing anything. It is a matter of making something beautiful, moving or dramatic – this is by no means the same thing.'[6] The evolution in Rothko's work in particular is telling of a desire on the part of the artist to absolve himself of explicit narrative in search of intimacy and timelessness, and the achievement of a reciprocal relationship between painting and viewer.

Rothko's struggle against the controlling vision of narrative was manifest in several phases of his work, but it was the final murals which began to hint at the power of the material as significant in the creation of meaning. The sheer scale of the work, its manifest denial to explain itself and the amorphous quality of colour values and relationships succeed in generating what Rothko describes as an intimacy and humanity. Emotions are engendered within his viewers, rather than intellectual thought or understanding, as a result of more than simply scale or intense ambiguity – for the very nature of Rothko's use of paint had its influence on the allusive reading and associations stimulated by his work. As Ellsworth Kelly once said, the 'paint application is also crucial . . . with Rothko, you feel the way he caresses the canvas.'[7] This intimate handling of the material, the sense of the presence of the maker in the artefact, had considerable consequence on the evocative power of the work and perhaps, by association, its emotional accessibility.

Similarly this quality of evocation is present in the black oil tracings of Pierre Soulages, images which contain reference to nothing beyond the tracery of his paint brush. This startling simplicity of material and process has the capacity to draw the viewer ever deeper into its black depths as the reading of these paintings subtly shifts in relation to the viewer's position, achieving an intimate and reciprocal relationship reminiscent of Rothko's work. Yet Soulages draws his inspiration more clearly and directly from the materials of painting. Though consistent in eschewing any figurative reference in his work from the start, Soulages became aware that the tracery of the brushwork itself was contributing to the tonal variation he was attempting to achieve, as he describes:

> I noticed I was giving it different values by means of the traces. So I went one stage further and started doing paintings with nothing but the same black paint. And the result was quite different, because it was the substance, the texture – by means of contrasting reliefs and the brushstrokes – which gave this single black colour its tonal values.[8]

Soulages goes on to describe the relevance of the material properties in this process: 'If you use an emulsion paint, such as a resin-based emulsion, the surface contracts once the water has evaporated. Oil, on the other hand, sets, just like cement, and keeps all traces absolutely intact.'[9] The evocative power Soulages attains in his paintings is dependent both on a precise use of process and a knowledge of material, to achieve an image as elusive as it is compelling.

But this precise understanding and manipulation of materials is extended much further in Serra's work, to the manifestation of chance in the process of making. As Serra describes in the context of his recent *Line Drawings*:

> The drawings are created using a stylus on the reverse side of the paper that is laid over a pool of melted paintstick. No direct drawing is done on the front of the paper. I don't see the drawing I am making until the paper is pulled off the floor and turned over . . . I have used various means over the years to avoid known solutions. In this series of line drawings the process is more important to me than analyzing and placing a line in relation to other lines.[10]

Serra's argument for the introduction of the incidental or contingent is seemingly a pursuit of the unknown, something that would place the final image beyond the limits of his conscious imagination. This approach stands in contrast to the work of either Soulages or Rothko, both of whom retain control of the process in pursuit of a precise rendering of an equivocal image. Serra's work achieves a different form of resonance, with process-based traces that embrace the apparent potency of imprecision. The argument for chance or contingency seems to be an attempt to remove the last vestiges of intellectualization from the work, in order to broaden the possibilities of what can be read from the final image and to achieve a more equivocal meaning.

This power of equivocation, the capacity of painting to inspire different readings and evoke the unconscious imagination, is a theme throughout the work of the painter Jean Dubuffet. And the introduction of the unknown and uncontrollable for Dubuffet lay in both the manipulation of the material and the

8.2 >Jean Dubuffet, *La Table Nue* (1957). Oil on canvas, 0.98m x 1.30m.

process. Like Serra, Dubuffet's manifest interest was not only in the nature of paint but the question of chance in the process. Dubuffet's peculiar understanding of the nature of paint and its disposition – 'In the sense one speaks of the disposition of an animal'[11] – informed his experiments with this medium, which were, as Peter Selz has suggested, both 'purposeful and rational in permitting, indeed, in stimulating the action of the irrational elements of accident and chance.'[12] Dubuffet's early work consisted of trials and experiments with the constituent elements of paint, resulting in irregular textures and images such as his *Table Nue* (figure 8.2). These are hasty paintings in fact, painted quickly with material formulated to dry abruptly, unevenly, unpredictably, resulting in an apparent clumsiness and creating, according to Dubuffet, a tension of uncertainty which 'forces the imagination . . . to function more vigorously.'[13]

Dubuffet often used this image of a table in his paintings, but painted it in an ambiguous fashion resulting in an indefinite quality which enables the viewer to impress upon it their own thoughts – as Dubuffet describes:

> Any place in this world is peopled by a swarm of facts, and not only those which belong to the life of the [table] itself, but also, mixing with them, others which inhabit the thought of man, and which he impresses on the table by looking at it.[14]

Unlike other matter-based painters, Dubuffet was not exploring the materiality of paint for its own sake; neither was he attempting to evoke any quality of this material. But through an intimate knowledge of its properties, particularly the speed with which it dries and how the acceleration of this process has consequences on the final surface of the image, he was able to find a means to capture an elusive sense of ambiguity through the use of imprecision.

This preoccupation with the exploitation of the accidental, based on material properties as well as the process of painting, is suggestive. The power of art has been described as lying in its ability to produce empathy in the viewer, or in other words the enabling of emotional projection. John Yau, in discussing 'matter paintings', suggests that, '[a]rt that does not acknowledge time, contingency, and incompleteness, is a fantasy.'[15] This idea gives voice to the realities of process, rarely acknowledged in art or architecture, and informs the pursuits of artists such as Soulages, Serra or Dubuffet – for the traces left by process could be understood as an embodiment of time, while its imprecisions reflect contingency. The ensuing incompleteness of the final image allows the viewer's imagination access into the work through the lack of finality or conclusion. This is a contradictory position to the conclusiveness more often pursued in art and architecture.

Still, a painter's immediate relationship to the material and process means he or she is, to some degree, compelled to fabricate the element of chance in creating indeterminate images, thus undermining the objective to eliminate their own authorship. Robert Rauschenberg dismissed the manufacture of the accidental in such a controlled process, saying: 'You can't use chance in painting without turning out an intellectual piece. You can use it in time, because then you can change time.'[16] It is this element of time, in addition to the nature of the process, which enables architects to appropriate chance in their work more sympathetically – for architects do not, as a rule, make, but rather speculate about making and leave the act of making to others. In architecture chance is not a choice but an unavoidable reality due to the process of translation in the hands of others.

Unfortunately the potential of this erratic process in the making of architecture is rarely valued by its authors. Indeed the more typical attitude is one of control, despite the obvious fact that control is as much an illusion in architecture as chance may be in painting. The desire to control persists not simply in the making of space but also in the handling of material to achieve precisely predetermined results, which accept nothing of the random or the indeterminate in the final artefact. Tadao Ando is an obvious reference here, known for his meticulous work in concrete – precise to be sure, but detailed and executed to ensure a surface which embodies little of the character of either the material or the process. In effect Ando reduces the concrete to serve the narrative, for, despite his careful and conscious rendering of light, he is singular in his objective to ensure a prescribed reading.

TRANSMISSIBLE THINKING: SHIFTS IN SCALE

The rough workmanship of La Tourette stands in opposition to any attitude of careful precision and control. In its expressiveness it suggests an attitude akin to Serra's, or perhaps more significantly to Dubuffet's when describing the disposition of paint. La Tourette arrives unexpectedly within the larger portfolio of Le Corbusier's work and is indicative of a shift away from the disregard and disdain for equivocation, chance and material considerations which are clearly manifest both in his earlier writings and built work – a position as clearly apparent in his architectural endeavours in the pure white villas as in his contemporaneous experimentation with painting. But if the painting and architecture is considered through the lens of material, process and chance rather than through formal similarities, a different reading of Le Corbusier's development is revealed.

In the mid-1920s, while Villa La Roche was being built, Le Corbusier wrote to his client Madame Meyer on the subject of accident and chance:

> We dreamed of making you a house which would be smooth and plain like a well proportioned chest and which would not be marred by multiple accidents which create a picturesque element that is both artificial and illusory, which do not ring true beneath the light, and which only add to the surrounding tumult.[17]

His earliest paintings decisively demonstrate this distaste of chance and accident. *La Cheminée,* claimed by Le Corbusier to be his first painting, was preceded by careful drawing studies (figure 8.3) to define the final image and control the outcome, such that the painting is barely distinguishable from the earlier studies despite the difference in medium and process.

Subsequent paintings of the early 1920s continue this preoccupation with deliberate planning and careful control of the image and of the material itself. Paintings from the 1920s, such as *Nature Morte en Violin Rouge* or *Guitare Verticale* (figure 8.4), exhibit similarities in both composition and material consequences. Although the paintings are clearly evolving – branching out from the earlier representational work towards more experimentation with composition – the paint

8.3 >Jeanneret, *La Cheminée* (1918). Study in pencil on paper.

8.4a >Jeanneret, *Guitare Verticale* (1920) (second version 1920). Oil on canvas, 1.00m x 0.81m.

8.4b >*Guitare Verticale,* detail of paint surface.

as material artefact remains limited in its role to the simple arrangement of colour and indication of depth. Even the brushwork is carefully excluded from contributing to the image.

This muteness persists through the 1920s, even into the latter half of the decade when, as Green notes, there is a fundamental re-assessment of imagery reflected in the paintings, a focus on the natural and irregular in form, and experimentation with composition.[18] While 'irregular' imagery had been appearing in Le Corbusier's paintings since the late 1920s and even into the early 1930s, the paint itself remains silent or is just beginning to deviate from the clarity of edge condition between fields of colour so obvious in his earliest works. It is only later that the appreciation of the irregular within the context of the material itself becomes evident, from images such as *La Pêcheuse d'Huîtres* (1935) (figure 8.5). We can see here not simply the play of form, colour or composition, but experimentation with the deformation of the paint surface for compositional effect. There is an obvious departure from the control of all accident and chance with careful pre-planning to a position where the processes of painting – application of thickness, addition of texture, ambiguity of edge, and subsequent mutation of the material through scarring – begins to inform the final composition.

The 1930s and 40s, a period of limited building, proved to be significant for Le Corbusier's experiments in painting, and had impact both on his small house commissions and his published polemics. His first major commission after this period of re-evaluation, was the Unité d'Habitation in Marseilles. Originally planned in steel, the project was ultimately carried out in concrete, and subjected

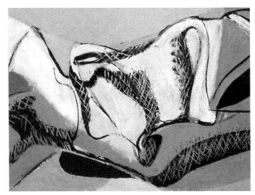

8.5a >Le Corbusier,
La Pêcheuse d'Huitres
(1935). Oil on canvas,
1.30m x 0.97m.

8.5b >*La Pêcheuse
d'Huitres,* detail of
deformation of paint
surface.

to what was considered very poor craftsmanship. When challenged by his critics on the poor craft of the rough boardformed concrete, Le Corbusier defended the irregularity of the surface by appealing to the beauty of contrast:

> I have decided to make beauty by contrast. I will find its complement and establish a play between crudity and finesse, between the dull and the intense, between precision and accident. I will make people think and reflect and, perhaps as Dubuffet would have it, make their imaginations function more vigorously.[19]

Experimentation in Le Corbusier's paintings just prior to this impressive disclosure on the virtue of the imprecise is telling. Paintings of the early 1940s such as *Cirque Horizontal* (1942) or *Divinité Baroque* (1943) (figure 8.6) are exceptionally rough in terms of brushwork and are, interestingly, beginning to experiment with a juxtaposition of texture and line that is evocative of Dubuffet's work. This is a process-based experimentation in composition, which explores superimposition and the contingent in the image. It can equally be read as a study in contrast, not simply of field to line but between the unformed and the formal, between the accidental and the precise – thus linking the act of painting and the appreciation of imprecision at the Unité.

The later work at La Tourette (figure 8.7) represents an extension of this thinking, eschewing regularity in the boardformed concrete surface in favour of a more eccentric and evocative texture. But it is a surface generated primarily by the process of making rather than evidence of original authorship, for the irregular protrusions along the edge of the chapel which are critical to its ambiguous reading – a half-understood allusion to forces not obvious to the viewer – are simply the inevitable marks left behind by the underlying prestressing cables used to reinforce the irregularly loaded chapel roof. The prestressing, in this case, has been rendered in such a way as to imply a conscious appropriation of structural forces. Perhaps this is indicative more of a seizing of opportunity than a favouring of chance, but it suggests an increasing acceptance of chance as the unplanned consequences of the prestressing were so obviously appropriated into a project, allowing the outcome to be influenced in unexpected ways.

8.6 >Le Corbusier,
Divinité Baroque (1943).
Oil on wood panel, 0.33m
x 0.21m.

8.7 >La Tourette
Monastery — elaboration
of prestresssing rods on
chapel facade.

From Le Corbusier's early design sketches to Xenakis' later design drawings it is clear that a coherent unity in conception was desired not simply in form but also in the material expression of the project through carefully designed boardmark patterns, but little of this intention regarding surface detail was to survive intact. While the 'unity' of the architectural idea and resulting form of La Tourette remained coherent throughout the process of design and construction, the singularity of the reading, particularly in terms of surface, was adulterated by the process of building. When Sud Est Travaux assumed control of the project, instituting a wide range of changes to reduce the cost, processes such as prestressing the frame and precasting of singular elements such as the light canons were to leave behind indelible marks. The prestressing scars, consciously appropriated into the chapel image, exist in the earlier monastery buildings in cruder and less authoritative ways, yet are nonetheless critical to the ultimate reading of the building. The impact of this secondary system of thinking and of this secondary line work overlaid on the original conception had an impact throughout the building, from the shifting depths of some, otherwise regularly calibrated, cross-beams to erratic and singular incisions on the underside of others (figure 8.8), and the regular yet inexplicable marks of prestressed rod ends apparent across all façades – all serving to undermine the planned rhythm of the façade. These systematic intrusions subtly alter the reading of the final form by damaging the precise image in inexplicable ways, creating ambiguities which are only to be resolved by imaginative projections on the part of the inhabitant.

8.8 >La Tourette
Monastery - courtyard
facade detail.

CONCLUSIONS

'Nothing is transmissible but thought' was the title of Le Corbusier's last essay, and it alludes to the importance throughout his career of an involvement beyond traditional architectural endeavour, which was essential to his thinking about architecture proper. It seems clear that his increasing appreciation of the spontaneous and the irrational in his art and architecture was interdependent. He was interested in the act of making, not with precision through exploring material properties or expression but in the marks of process. It appears that Le Corbusier was touched by the idea of the hand of man leaving its imprint – an imperfect tracery on the perfect idea, reminiscent of Soulages' traces and Dubuffet's vigorous imaginings and perhaps, as Yau might suggest, understood as a measure of time, contingency and incompleteness.

To describe this process as a shift in preoccupations is less accurate than to conclude that his initial premise regarding synthetic unity underwent a deepening and broadening – the maturing of a prior position. To the end, the celebration of the tectonic, be it in detail or compositional elaboration, was excluded from his work, for although the projects in Marseilles and at La Tourette appear more suggestive of a material presence through imprecision, the truth is that their fabrication is not significantly different from the early villas. In both of these later projects the concrete was used as structural frame, with the remainder of the building infilled in a variety of materials – including blockwork, precast units and, in the case of the Unité, steel – only to be subsequently rendered into a unity with cementitious materials in a manner not so very different from the white villas of the 1920s. The exploitation of the inherent properties or disposition of the material was, as in the paintings, never deeper than surface effect.

What was clear instead was an increasing regard for the sensual possibilities of material, which could heighten the rendering of the experience of the space and the meaning of the artefact. Perhaps this is a more mature position, which understands architecture as a synthetic and unified art of making space that is nevertheless material based. The evolution of an attitude toward the process of making and its unpredictable consequences on the final artefact may have been the significant shift, as there appears to be an increasing latitude regarding the consequences of chance interventions on the final reading of the work.

Hence the unexpected surfaces of the party walls at the balconies of the Unité (in fact only blockwork with a casting of cement on their surface) that deviate from the apparently intended regularity of the planar surface because of an unexpected deformation in the formwork on the first pour, which left irregular markings on their surfaces. Rather than reject the work on inspection, Le Corbusier is said to have insisted on the continued use of the damaged formwork throughout the project.[20] This is an even more telling testament to a reconsideration of the accidental than the boardformed concrete work at the base of the building – as it manifests a conviction regarding the relevance and promise of the unpredictable consequences of process in the making of the project.

Although he was not fully responsive to the inherent potential of material either as painter or architect, Le Corbusier's work did develop in depth and range specifically due to the unrivalled immediacy and lessons of his painting. There is a kinetic-based learning in the intimate handling of material and the processes associated with it, which has the capacity to stimulate and inform the subconscious, through which the intuition can carry lessons learned to another field of endeavour – thus broadening the understanding of the potential of architectural unity.

1 >Joshua Taylor as quoted by John Yau in 'A New Context for the "Matter Paintings" of Antoni Tàpies', www.seacex.com/documentos/tapies_06_contexto.pdf, accessed 28 August 2004.
2 >Interview by Alfred Pacquement in Richard Serra, *Writings Interviews,* Chicago, London: The University of Chicago Press, 1994, p. 158.
3 >Stanislaus von Moos, 'Le Corbusier as Painter' in *Oppositions*, No. 19, Winter Spring 1980, p. 101.
4 >Le Corbusier, 'Argument' in *The Decorative Art of Today*, translated by James Dunnett, London: The Architectural Press, 1987, p. xxvi.
5 >Christopher Green, 'The Architect as Artist' in Raeburn and Wilson (eds.), *Le Corbusier: Architect of the Century*, London: Arts Council of Britain, 1987, p. 111.
6 >Jacob Baal-Teshuva, *Mark Rothko: Pictures as Drama*, Köln: Taschen, 2003, p. 26.
7 >Baal-Teshuva, *op. cit.*, p. 47.
8 >Michael Peppiatt, 'An Interview with Pierre Soulages with Michael Peppiatt', *Art International*, No. 3–4, 1980, http://www.pierresoulages.com/pages/psecrits/peppiattUS.html, accessed 28 August 2004.
9 >*Ibid.*
10 >Richard Serra, *Line Drawings*, New York: Gagosian Gallery (ex. cat.), 2002.
11 >Jean Dubuffet, 'Landscaped Tables, Landscapes of the Mind, Stones of Philosophy' in Peter Selz, *The Work of Jean Dubuffet*, New York: The Museum of Modern Art, 1962, p. 63.
12 >Peter Selz, 'Jean Dubuffet: The Recent Work' in Selz, *op. cit.*, p. 163.
13 >Jean Dubuffet, 'Memoir on the Development of My Work from 1952' in Selz, *op. cit.*, pp. 78–9.
14 >Jean Dubuffet in Selz, *op. cit.*, p. 72.
15 >John Yau, *op. cit.*
16 >Barbara Rose, *An Interview with Robert Rauschenberg,* New York: Vintage Books, 1987, p. 64, as cited in Peter Gena, 'Cage & Rauschenberg: Purposeful Purposelessness Meets Found Order', 1992, www.artic.edu/2pgena/cageMCA.html, accessed 26 August 2004.
17 >Maurice Besset, *Le Corbusier*, London: The Architectural Press, 1987, p. 94.
18 >Christopher Green, *op. cit.*, p. 111.
19 >Le Corbusier, 'L'Unité d'Habitation at Marseilles' in *Le Corbusier 1946–1952 Oeuvre Complète Vol. 5*, Zurich: Les Editions d'Architecture, 1953, p. 19.
20 >Based on anecdotal evidence from long-time inhabitants of the *Unité* on a site visit in October 2003.

SCOTT POOLE >PUMPING UP: DIGITAL STEROIDS AND THE
DESIGN STUDIO

SPEED

At the beginning of their studies in architecture is there a student who does not
want to be more artistically effective, intellectually agile, and just flat out fast? It is
in their nature to want to be immediately brilliant.

Near the height of the controversy regarding the use of steroids in Major
League Baseball, Tony Kornheiser, a sports reporter for the Washington Post
facetiously confessed to taking steroids in order to become 'bigger, stronger and
faster on the keyboard'. 'You should see me type now', he wrote, 'I'm unbelievably
fast, yet precise at the same time. I'm the Eric Clapton of the laptop. I can type all
of Moby Dick in 14 minutes. I can type faster than Evelyn Wood can read it.' He
goes on to say,

> I couldn't believe how powerful the steroids made my words. Suddenly I
> could throw in a word like 'enigma' without ever worrying what it actually
> meant. My vocabulary expanded exponentially. I used to be a three-syllable
> guy at most. But under the influence of steroids I could bat out four-syllable
> words like – well, like 'exponentially' and five-syllable words like
> 'onomatopoeia' . . . Steroids gave me all sorts of confidence.[1]

Beginners are impetuous. They sense that quickness is something of value in the
arts and they are essentially correct in this assumption. What beginners typically
lack, however, is the ability to distinguish between quickness and haste, between
the capacity to move swiftly with skill and precision and the impulse to act on the
spur of the moment without accuracy, attention to detail, or the background of
thought and experience that speeds intuition. Understandably, beginners are
confused. How can they act quickly in artistic situations when the urge to act fast
so often leads to outcomes that reveal their innocence and inexperience? How can
they get going and act without delay when disciplined thinking seems to slow
them down so much?

SLOWNESS AND SUBSTANCE

Naturally, someone who has just started to learn something difficult is attracted to
the possibility of a short cut to virtuosity, often overlooking the vital role that
material, technique, and time play in the conception and making of a work of art.

'Long years spent in the studio,' writes James Elkins, 'can make a person into
a treasury of nearly incommunicable knowledge about the powderliness of pastels,
or the woody feel of different marbles, or the infinitesimally different iridescences
of ceramic glazes.'[2] In his compelling description of Rembrandt's self-portrait,
Elkins acknowledges that it is an accurate visual description of the face of an
aging man. But it is also, according to Elkins, 'a self-portrait of paint. The oils are
out in force, like the uglinous oozing waters of a swamp bottom.' He goes on to
say, 'The thoughts that crowd in on me . . . are thoughts about *qualities.* I feel
viscid. My body is snared in glues and emulsions, and I feel the pull of them on my
thoughts. I want to wash my face.'[3]

Similarly, the concrete of Louis I. Kahn's Kimbell Art Museum speaks about
itself, the architect's imagination, and a refined sensibility to material that is
acquired over time.[4] It is not a generalized concrete, the concrete of city sidewalks
and anonymous floor slabs, but an expression of the qualities, properties, and

9.1 >Louis I. Kahn, detail – exterior wall of the Kimbell Art Museum.

potentials of a specific material with a specific surface tension and a particular greyness.

Concrete is watery, sloppy, thick and heavy. On the otherwise smooth exterior of the Kimbell Museum, thin abrasive lines mark joints where the concrete slurry has oozed out and petrified between narrow spaces in the precisely configured formwork. Near these joints, shallow cylindrical voids capped with lead locate where the formwork has been held in place, revealing traces of the construction process.[5] Surprisingly, the concrete surfaces, inside and out, more closely resemble the waxy essence of flowers, the mottled surface of a painting, or the fluorescence of silica than they do the dull grey of gravel (figure 9.1).

Early in his career, Kahn explained that his approach to drawing involved finding a vital essence beyond the appearance of things. 'I try in all my sketching not to be entirely subservient to my subject, but I have respect for it, and regard it as something tangible – alive,' he wrote.[6] It is hardly unexpected then, that he would have little regard for the bland and lifeless quality of standard concrete. Instead, he imagined for the Kimbell Museum a surface colour that resembled *moth wings*,[7] suggesting not only a particular hue but a feeling of lightness. Kahn's desire to achieve this precise quality involved, among other things, adding volcanic ash to the concrete mix[8] and searching throughout Texas and Louisiana for a particular colour of sand.[9]

Materials, especially commonplace materials like concrete, do not let go of their secrets quickly or cheaply. As the Kimbell Museum developed from design to construction, considerable delays and misunderstandings occurred between Kahn and his collaborating architect Preston Geren, who had a difficult time understanding Kahn's time-consuming approach – one that involved experimentation with untried methods and a continual interplay between initial design drawings and construction documents as the building evolved.[10]

Likewise, for Peter Zumthor, architecture is slow.[11] He spent years developing and refining the technical skills that enable him to draw out the elemental force of materials with precision. Famously, at Vals, he intertwined place with a particular substance, establishing what he terms a 'primordial reaction to the rock mountain.'[12] The ancient, sensual qualities of stone quarried a short walk away from the thermal baths evoke the permanence of a place remote in time, even though the form is decidedly modern (figure 9.2). This feeling is enhanced by the moistness of the interior atmosphere, the dim light, and the murmur of water – qualities experienced over time. 'Sense emerges,' Zumthor writes, 'when I succeed in bringing out the specific meaning of certain materials in my buildings, meanings that can only be perceived in just this way in this one building.'[13]

In contemporary architecture there is an abundance of experimentation with new and interesting materials, but material virtuosity is rare and the combination of material intelligence and conceptual refinement even more uncommon. In his book *Building Skins*, Christian Schittich writes: 'The joy in experimentation finds expression in countless innovations. However the material use isn't always successfully integrated into the overall concept.' 'Too often,' he continues, 'what results is mere decoration of skins that are separated from the building, more empty shell than skin.' He concludes by saying, 'drawing attention at any cost seems to be the engine that drives many such innovations, for our fast-paced world clamours ceaselessly for novelty.'[14]

9.2 >Peter Zumthor,
spring grotto, Thermal
Baths at Vals,
Switzerland.

TEMPO AND PERCEPTION

In the world of virtual reality, slowness is a relic of an exasperating past. In the dynamic, hyper-digitized, cyberceptive world, speed and novelty are supreme. Information is exchanged at dizzying rates, and the stream of words, sounds, and images that we create, and are exposed to, seem to multiply exponentially. To cope with the increasing acceleration of information, new forms of technology promise to alter the way we perceive our surroundings. According to Roy Ascott, 'Cyberception not only implies a new body and a new consciousness but a redefinition of how we might live together in the inner space between the virtual and the real.'[15]

Life lived in the actual world, however, has certain constants: our inner world and the outer world are linked by way of a simple mathematical relationship – the rate at which we live affects the quality of our sensations. There is a limit, affected by speed, concentration, and attention, beyond which sense impressions no longer take hold. 'If by some sudden magic,' wrote Gyorgy Kepes, 'we were to live a million times more rapidly than we do, in surroundings that retained their present pace, the coming and going of day and night, the slowest movements of a sleeping child, would become a blur, a texture too smooth to be grasped by the senses.'[16]

Our grasp of the world involves bringing an uninterrupted flow of memories and sense impressions into focus by controlling our perception of time. We set the tempo that enables clarity and definition; that gives priority and intensity to certain moments. We decide when time will flow swift and steady and when it will become viscous and sticky.

The tempo of our lives can also be linked with our ability to retain what we perceive. In his novel *Slowness*, Milan Kundera develops a basic existential equation explaining the relationship between retention and perception. 'There is a secret bond between slowness and memory, between speed and forgetting,' he writes, '. . . the degree of slowness is directly proportional to the intensity of memory; the degree of speed is directly proportional to the intensity of forgetting.'[17]

The urgent task of the teacher is to put students in a position to grasp this secret bond between slowness and memory, between long attention and lasting impression, before they become seduced by the general euphoria of virtual reality, promises of enhanced velocity, and illusions of automatic virtuosity.

DURABLE KNOWLEDGE

Even beginners who have spent a short time working with colour understand that it is an incredibly unstable phenomenon, always changing relative to its bordering or surrounding colour. A basic lesson with colour involves observing the effect of a dark background and a light background on two identically coloured objects. In this controlled situation the changes are obvious: the identical objects appear darker on a light background and lighter on a dark background. That the information required for possessing this knowledge was right in front of one's eyes yet escaped notice begins to provoke speculation about what else, embedded in the world, one is looking at yet failing to see.[18]

Through this exercise a significant modification of consciousness occurs: objects begin to have a dual nature – at once things that can be seen and touched in the material world, and also sources of perceptual change. In effect the student acquires what the artist Robert Irwin calls, 'an extended way of looking at the world.' 'Once you gain it,' he continues, 'you carry it with you and you live in an enriched world.'[19]

This new awareness, relatively easy to grasp, is hard to forget. Donald Judd called this type of knowledge 'durable', implying that a clear awareness of facts learned through attentive study has a certain resilient, long-lasting, and sturdy character. 'Color as knowledge is very durable,' he writes, 'I find it difficult, maybe impossible, to forget.'[20]

Similarly, the memory of making and depicting an actual physical object by hand is hard to forget. It is also a kind of durable knowledge because it involves changes in perception and a specific awareness of facts that one only arrives at through intense observation and constructive effort.

In the following one-week exercise, for example, beginning students construct and then draw a plaster sphere. The exercise begins with the casting of a plaster cube, then the transformation of the cube by turning it on the open end of a PVC pipe. A considerable effort is involved in the initial formation and subsequent transformation of the sphere, including the construction of the mould, the preparation of a place to pour, the mix of plaster and water, the meticulous cleaning of the workplace, waiting for the plaster to set, removing the mould, and finally the tedious task of turning a rectangular solid into a spherical shape.

Making the sphere takes more time than anticipated. Each step in the sequence of events dilates time, and every lapse of concentration causes mistakes that multiply time. Initially the slow pace is frustrating, but this experience in constructive concentration leads to unexpected enrichments of later work. Mixing the plaster with their hands, feeling the heat of the curing process, and turning the sphere over and over makes the students immediately more attentive to the value of sensory information – in addition to giving them a new respect for the term 'first-hand experience'. The lasting sensible impression of this process helps the student to grasp the fact that this and other constructive acts involve a complex sequence of events that gradually take place over time (figure 9.3).

With the sphere in hand, the student then constructs a drawing. Working backward from the standard practice of making drawings conceived in advance of concrete objects gives the student an edge in observation. They are already aware that the object they have made has certain qualities. They know where flaws exist and why they are there. Air, for example, is often trapped beneath the surface of the plaster. When they depict the object, students often show this and other imperfections. They do this not merely because the flaw is visible, but because their sphere is no longer a conceptual object. Inevitably it retains traces of the process of construction that remain at the forefront of their consciousness (figure 9.4).

The memory of this constructive process extends perception. It slows the student down and allows them to develop a patient and persistent approach to a series of actions. When they draw the shadow of the sphere, for example, they have already acquired a heightened awareness of material and an enhanced sense

9.3 >Hand–turned
plaster sphere with
material removed during
fabrication.

9.4 >Student notebook –
written observation and
graphic depictions of the
sphere.

of touch that makes them more attentive to the texture of the paper, the quality of the lead, and the pressure of their hand. Each consideration takes time, and none can be acquired in a hurry.

When they begin to construct this drawing the students already know too much to preconceive the result. They know, from close examination, that the shadow of the sphere is something more than a uniformly dark space on the surface close to an object. And they know from experience that the relationships involved in the construction of an object are often too complex to understand in advance. For example, choosing where to position the sphere on the rectangular sheet of paper, deciding whether the shadow will be cast to the right or the left, even settling on what hardness of lead to use, involves actions based on judgments that are often reassessed as new information emerges. So they act in order to have enough information to begin again.

'Our efficiency,' the architect Renzo Piano writes, 'implies the complexity of doing and doing again.'[21] This paradoxical efficiency, searching without the expectation of immediate success, allows specific aspects of the problem to gradually unfold and the difficult task of finding meaningful interrelationships to begin.

THE PROMISE OF DIGITAL TECHNOLOGY

Advances in the virtual dimension promise to have a resounding impact on architects and architecture. 'Technologies of simulation,' according to media authority Derrick de Kerckhove, '. . . are becoming so flexible, affordable and user-friendly that they eliminate the need for the slow and difficult steps in drafting and modeling.' He goes on to say, 'They allow faster processing and rendering, hence a closer approximation to thinking. Imagining and imaging almost become one.'[22] The old-fashioned 'efficiency' of slowly building a constructive imagination through repeated acts of drawing and making has mercifully come to a close. Or has it? Have advanced digital technologies and computational quickness fundamentally changed how we learn to give shape to the content of our imagination?

Without doubt, simulation technology has altered the speed at which designers conceive and produce images. One obvious advantage of digital

9.5 >Aluminium in the process of fabrication on a CNC milling machine.

9.6 >Digital image of object modelled in the Rhinoceros NURBS modelling program.

technology is the exchange of information between members of a team, who can now send files across a room or around the world. That advantage is somewhat diminished by the fact that drawings often look complete at every stage of development, leading to the actual construction of embryonic ideas. Similarly, rapid prototyping devices allow a designer to quickly fabricate and make adjustments to three-dimensional objects. Again, these objects tend to look complete from the outset, rarely giving the designer any insight into how the object might actually be constructed at a large scale.

Along with these technological advances there is the promise of advances in the appearance and substance of architecture. Certainly, the physical simulation of mental images is at an all time high. A 3-D printer, for example, can make intricate models of computer renderings. An object that has just come to mind can be held in the hand a few hours later. Casting such objects in the past would have taken advanced skill and painstaking effort. Now complex objects can be fabricated in almost no time at all. A designer can have an idea at breakfast and an object in their hand before lunch. And, best of all, between breakfast and lunch one can be producing other digital simulations because the designer does not even need to be present while the object is being made.

A CNC milling machine, for instance, can turn a block of metal into a sensuous shape in the course of an afternoon (figure 9.5). The CNC machine, however, unlike the 3-D printer, requires the expertise of a technician who installs the cutting tool, configures the blocking to immobilize the object during the cutting, and makes adjustments to the tools and blocking during the process. As a result, the designer may fabricate an alluring object yet remain detached from the constructive forces that ultimately enable the fabrication.

While three-dimensional software programs and rapid prototyping devices produce remarkable shapes, those shapes have less to do with finding limits – an essential aspect of art, architecture and design – than with working within the *pre-established limits* of the software designer's imagination (figure 9.6).

THE PROBLEM WITH SIMULATION TECHNOLOGY

Does the speed of processing and rendering bring us closer to thinking, or, more precisely, the kind of constructive thinking required of the architect? Proponents of simulation technology typically imply that the rate of image production and consumption is directly proportional to the intensity of imagination. In other words, our imagination will increase in force as we increase the speed at which we make and process images.

One could also make the case that our voracious consumption of images contributes to an impoverished imagination. It might be anachronistic to return to Leonardo da Vinci, but he too subscribed to the idea that imagery and imagination have a direct proportional relationship. In his advice to painters he asks them to consider a new device for stimulating the mind. 'Although it may appear trivial and almost ludicrous', Leonardo nevertheless advises painters to isolate their concentration to improve their imagination – long looking at a wall spotted with stains, for example.[23]

Rapid simulation of mental images detached from the veracity of matter and the means of production can have an illusory effect on the imagination and foster

9.7 >Digital image of object designed in the Rhinoceros NURBS modelling program.

9.8 >Detail of corner – constructed of rubber bands and nails.

constructive *naïveté*. When the real conditions of everyday life are suspended there is no limit to formal preconception. Everything appears possible.

The resistance of material, however, limits what can be realized. Constantin Brancusi's numerous broken birds, for instance, were initially the result of forcing stone to do something that was not in its nature. His eventual success with this brittle material is less an argument for preconceived form than it is a reason to support the interplay between the imagination of the artist and the nature of a particular material. As Brancusi himself said, 'Matter should not be used merely to suit the purpose of the artist, it must not be subjected to a preconceived idea and to a preconceived form. Matter itself must suggest subject and form; both must come from within matter and not be forced upon it from without.'[24] For Brancusi, the ability to bring out the being in matter happened slowly. As Ann Temkin points out, it was years before he succeeded in making the veining of the marble a force in his sculpture.[25]

Rapid prototyping devices offer an illusion of instant sophistication. Students, especially beginners, easily become enamoured with how quickly their thoughts become solidified as objects. In no time at all the reality of matter, its nature and nuance, become inconsequential and formal results become the object of their attention (figure 9.7). This overemphasis on quick reproduction is counterproductive to a student's intellectual and artistic growth. It encourages a premature confidence that, among other things, lacks constructive depth and substance.

Similarly, the synthetic smoothness of computer-generated images can slow the development of constructive thought by creating a false sense of technical resolution. Rather than search for criteria and limits, for the disciplinary resistance essential to cultivating a vigorous constructive imagination, too much creative energy tends to be focused on the illustration of image-driven ideas. Not surprisingly, the objects and buildings often represented by these images would, more appropriately, be formed in moulds as a whole rather than built up of parts. In this context it is also not surprising that the word 'seamless' has gained increasing popularity in the art, architectural and design press in recent years. But is it not precisely in the construction of seams, in the joining of one thing and another, that architecture gains much of its fullness and force (figure 9.8)?

According to the contemporary Italian architect and critic Vittorio Gregotti, 'Architects of image, who see their design task in terms of providing a few general sketches, have become conspicuously common in recent years. This has been particularly true in the United States, where architects can rely on an advanced system of support . . .' 'The most obvious aspects of this phenomenon,' he asserts, 'represent a departure from our discipline's technical heritage, or at least an impoverishment of this heritage.'[26]

THE TASK OF THE TEACHER

Tools, in themselves, do not magically open our outlook on life. Advanced digital techniques and enhanced computational speed, while remarkable, do not inevitably bring about a heightened awareness of the world or elevated artistic thought. On the contrary, as the architect Juhani Pallasmaa observes, 'Pure utility and rationality, or even the most advanced technologies, cannot grant entry into the artistic realm. The realm of art is approached through metaphysical, existential, and poetic concerns.'[27]

Architecture is more than an image-driven appearance. It is an inherently constructive act, bound simultaneously to the flux of life *and* the permanence of human nature. The perennial task of the teacher is to put students in a position to structure the existential difficulties embedded in these polarities, not to pretend they do not exist.

ACCELERATING CONSCIOUSNESS AND BODILY IDENTIFICATION

In his Nobel Lecture, the poet Joseph Brodsky reflected on the particular way that writing verse quickened the intensity of one's mind and enhanced one's grasp of the world: 'The one who writes a poem writes it above all because verse writing is an extraordinary accelerator of consciousness, of thinking, of comprehending the universe . . .'[28]

Making architecture, like writing verse, is incredibly slow work because its material form is intertwined with basic questions of being human. It develops, for the most part, through quiet reflection, with actions that move at the speed of lead. Paradoxically, it is not velocity but the ability to accustom oneself to working slowly within density that intensifies consciousness – especially at the beginning of one's education in architecture and design. Subtle links between the mind and the multiplicity of the world are internalized by the hand, and move to the forefront of the student's consciousness. Information that was once considered insignificant – even trivial – becomes a vital part of an expanding perceptual horizon.

Gradually the architect within the student begins to understand the significance of their bodily identification with their work and its potential for meaningful exchange with others. 'A great musician plays himself rather than the instrument,' writes Pallasmaa in *The Eyes of the Skin*. He goes on to say, 'As the work interacts with the body of the observer, the experience mirrors the bodily sensations of the maker. Consequently, architecture is communication from the body of the architect directly to the body of the person who encounters the work, perhaps centuries later.'[29]

TWO STORIES ABOUT TEN YEARS

In conclusion, consider these two stories about ten years. The first is the story of Chuang-Tzu, told by Italo Calvino at the conclusion of his chapter on 'Quickness' in his book *Six Memos for the Next Millennium*.

> Among Chuang-Tzu's many skills, he was an expert draftsman. The king asked him to draw a crab. Chuang-Tzu replied that he needed five years, a country house, and twelve servants. Five years later the drawing was still not begun. 'I need another five years,' said Chuang-Tzu. The king granted them. At the end of these ten years, Chuang-Tzu took up his brush and, in an instant, with a single-stroke, he drew a crab, the most perfect crab ever seen.[30]

The other story was told during the first week of my architectural education. According to the story, there was a former dean of the school having his office painted. One morning, before class, he was examining the work of the previous day and observed that the line between the wall and ceiling wavered enough to be noticeable. Irritated that the quality of the work was under scrutiny, one of the painters remarked that he had ten years' experience. The dean corrected him saying, 'No, you have one year of experience, ten times.'

The two stories make the same point. Speed takes time. The immediacy of intuition is not likely to be found in a naive approach to software commands, market-driven images, and novelty. Rather it is something one earns by one's own efforts to cultivate an imagination enlarged by the qualities of matter and disciplined by constructive skills – an imagination grounded in human values and focused on the enrichment of our lives.

The exercises illustrated are the work of second-year architecture students in the School of Architecture + Design at Virginia Tech.

Images of student work in order of appearance: Erin Moon – hand turned plaster sphere; Tyson Hosmer – study of sphere; Jill Guertin – aluminium object in the process of fabrication on a CNC milling machine; Jill Guertin – digital image of object modelled in the Rhinoceros NURBS modelling program; Maria J. Villacreces – digital image of object designed in the Rhinoceros NURBS modelling program; Peter Davies – detail of corner joint constructed of rubber bands and nails.

1   > Tony Kornheiser, 'Steroids Are Getting Me All Pumped Up', *The Washington Post*, May 31, 2002, p. D1.
2   > James Elkins, *What Painting Is*, New York: Routledge, 2000, p. 22.
3   > *Ibid.*, pp. 114–15.
4   > By 1969, Kahn had been working with concrete for at least thirty years.
5   > Kenneth Frampton, *Studies in Tectonic Culture: The Poetics of Construction in Nineteenth and Twentieth Century Architecture*, Cambridge, Massachusetts: The MIT Press, 1995, p. 241.
6   > David B. Brownlee, 'Adventures of Unexplored Places', in *Louis I. Kahn: In the Realm of Architecture*, New York: Rizzoli International Publications, Inc., 1991, p. 23.
7   > In the early 1970s, Louis Kahn gave a lecture at Radford University in Southwest Virginia. At a certain point in the lecture he was speaking of his desire for a specific surface quality at the Kimbell Art Museum, saying that *he desired a surface that had the colour of* – and he hesitated for an uncomfortably long time, eventually closing his eyes. Some of the audience actually thought he had fallen asleep. Then he lifted his head, after this unusually long pause and said – *'Moth wings!'* From conversations with Professors Jaan Holt and Bill Galloway, Virginia Tech.
8   > Kenneth Frampton, *op. cit.*, p. 242.
9   > Kahn was trying match the concrete of the Salk Institute and searched throughout east Texas and Louisiana to find the right colour sand, eventually having to crush stone to complete the project. From a conversation with Professor Lawrence Speck, University of Texas.
10   > Accademia di Architettura, *The Construction of the Kimbell Art Museum*, Milan: Skira Editore, 1997, p. 114.
11   > Peter Zumthor, 'I am Working on the Substance, I am not working on the Form', *oris Magazine for Architecture and Culture*, Volume VI, Number 27, 2004, p. 18.
12   > *Ibid.*, p. 11.
13   > Peter Zumthor, 'A Way of Looking at Things' in *Thinking Architecture*, Basel: Birkhäuser, 1998, p. 10.
14   > Christian Schittich, 'Shell, Skin, Materials', in *Building Skins*, Basel: Birkhäuser, 2001, p. 18.
15   > Roy Ascott, *The Architecture of Cyberception*, cited in Derrick de Kerckhove, *The Architecture of Intelligence*, Basel: Birkhäuser, 2001, p. 3.
16   > Gyorgy Kepes, 'Introduction' in Gyorgy Kepes (ed.), *The Nature of Art in Motion*, New York: George Braziller, 1965, p. i.
17   > Milan Kundera, *Slowness*, New York: HarperCollins, 1995, p. 39, quoted in B. Tsien and T. Williams, 'Slowness', *2G International Review of Architecture*, *N.9,* Barcelona: Editorial Gustavo Gili SA, 1997, pp. 130–7.

18   >Or, as Ludwig Wittgenstein so aptly put it, 'God grant the philosopher insight into what lies in front of everyone's eyes.' L. Wittgenstein and G. H. Von Wright (eds.) *Culture and Value*, Chicago: The University of Chicago Press, 1980, p. 63e.
19   >Robert Irwin in Leonard Feinstein (ed.), *The Beauty of Questions* (Video), 1997.
20   >Donald Judd, 'Some aspects of color in general and red and black in particular', *Daidalos* #51, Berlin: Bertelsmann Fachzeitschriften GmbH, 1994, p. 46. In this essay, Judd uses a different example – afterimage: 'In Part VII Albers says to paste a red circle and a white circle on a black sheet of paper and then stare at the red circle. Then, look at the white circle: it is green or blue-green, the complementary of red.'
21   >Renzo Piano, 'The Building Workshop' in Edward Robbins, *Why Architects Draw*, Cambridge, Massachusetts: The MIT Press, 1994, p. 128. 'Gallileo Galilei said something like provandi e riprovandi, trying and trying again. It is a sort of basic philosophy of experimental work.'
22   >Derrick de Kerckhove, *op.cit.*, p. 52.
23   >Edward MacCurdy (ed.), *The Notebooks of Leonardo da Vinci*, New York: Garden City Publishing Co. Inc., 1941, p. 873.
24   >Friedrich Teja Bach, 'Brancusi: The Reality of Sculpture' in Ann Temkin (ed.), *Constantin Brancusi, 1876–1957*, Philadelphia: Philadelphia Museum of Art, 1995, pp. 23–4. 'Matter,' he (Brancusi) declared, 'must continue its natural life when modified by the hand of the sculptor . . .' According to Carola Giedion-Welcker, Brancusi 'knew he must keep continuous watch over the material, that he could give in to it indulgently, then, suddenly he must get the best of it.' See also: Carmen Giménez and Matthew Gale (eds.), 'Selected aphorisms' in *Contantin Brancusi: The Essence of Things*, London: Tate Publishing, 2004, p. 133: 'Art generates ideas, it doesn't represent them – which means that a true work of art comes into being intuitively, without preconceived motives, because it is the motive and there can be no accounting for it a priori'.
25   >Ann Temkin (ed.), *op. cit.*, pp. 170, 174–5. In his early birds (*Yellow Bird*, 1919, for example), the veining resulting from a pre-existing fault in the marble is unaligned; in later works (e.g. *Bird*, 1923–47) the veining becomes an integral part of the sculpture.
26   >Vittorio Gregotti, *Inside Architecture*, Boston: The MIT Press, 1996, pp. 98–9.
27   >Juhani Pallasmaa, 'Immateriality and Transparency' (2003), from a collection of essays: Peter MacKeith (ed.), *Encounters,* Hämeenlinna: Rakennustieto Oy, 2005, p. 203: 'While I acknowledge the interdependence of science, technology, and architecture, the disciplines are also inherently different. This opposition needs to be pointed out – although here I hope that my point will be not be misunderstood. I am not underestimating the significance of technology, I merely argue that the artistic dimension of architecture arises from other concerns and another mental ground. This reflects the fundamental difference between ends and means.'
28   >Joseph Brodsky, 'An Uncommon Visage' (1987), from his collection of essays, *On Grief and Reason*, New York: Farrar Strauss Giroux, 1995, p. 58: 'Having experienced this acceleration once, one is no longer capable of abandoning the chance to repeat this experience; one falls into dependency on this process, the way others fall into dependency on drugs or alcohol. One who finds himself in this sort of dependency on language is, I suppose, what they call a poet.'
29   >Juhani Pallasmaa, *The Eyes of the Skin,* Chichester, Wiley-Academy, 2005, pp. 66–7.
30   >Italo Calvino, *Six Memos for the Next Millennium*, New York: Random House, 1988, p. 54.

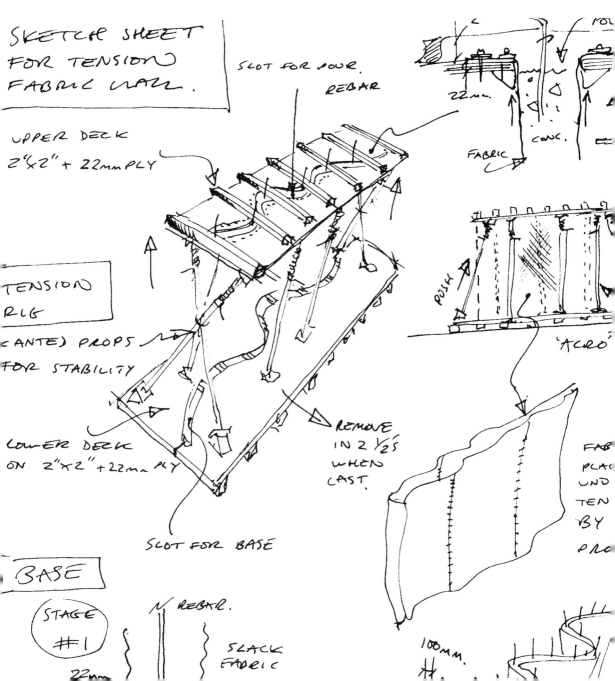

SKETCH SHEET FOR TENSION FABRIC WALL.

SLOT FOR YOUR. REBAR

UPPER DECK 2"x2" + 22mm PLY

22mm.

CONC.

FABRIC

TENSION RIG

(ANTE) PROPS FOR STABILITY

PUSH

'ACRO'

LOWER DECK ON 2"x2" +22mm PLY

REMOVE IN 2 1/2S WHEN CAST.

SLOT FOR BASE

FAB PLAC UND TEN BY PRO

BASE

STAGE #1

REBAR.

SLACK FABRIC

100MM.

22mm

ALAN CHANDLER >A PHILOSOPHY OF ENGAGEMENT: DEVELOPING A STRATEGIC ABILITY THROUGH DIRECT ENGAGEMENT WITH MATERIAL, PROCESS AND COLLECTIVE ACTION

If architectural education is a preparation for professional life, how does the educational structure of the teaching institution reflect that professional life and prepare students to 'think like an architect'? As one of the five educational criteria imposed by the profession in the United Kingdom, 'technical competence' is embedded within architectural educational requirements and must be demonstrated by every single degree and diploma student. Material matters, therefore, whether we like it or not. The issue, then, is how do we, as design teachers in schools of architecture, understand the role of technical teaching and learning within the context of the overall student experience? Can the role of strategic thinking be developed and utilised to embed technical thought within architectural thought, against the contemporary grain of separation, fragmentation and predictability?

In *The Nature and Art of Workmanship*, David Pye makes a distinction between the 'workmanship of risk' over the 'workmanship of certainty'. He clarifies the role of the individual maker with regard to either being involved with the determination of the result, or being placed outside of a pre-determined process. He asks us to look at means and ends. Clearly the 'workmanship of risk' reflects the ambiguities surrounding the actuality of architectural practice: 'In the workmanship of risk, the result of every operation during production is determined by the workman as he works and its outcome depends wholly or largely on his care, judgement and dexterity.'[1]

With the majority of architectural production focused on one-off buildings for particular users and locations, it is key to address the issues surrounding bespoke production; of equipping architects to exercise judgement and dexterity both at the design and production stages of building. The issue for education is to equip students to actively manage the practice of risk, to evaluate gain with respect to hazard and to define a means of operating that enhances the potential within any given situation. But how can one teach the management of risk when, increasingly, the framework of teaching itself is becoming risk averse? For example, most schools of architecture in the United Kingdom provide only model-making facilities, and workshops are considered both a risk to health and safety and a drain on the estates budget. Such schools are forced to treat materiality as notional and beyond everyday education; something to add on to form.

Materials are crucial to the development of a form language, yet so easily become a substitute for a form language. In schools and in practice, the application of larch planking, pre-patinated copper cladding or planar fitted glass is considered sufficient in terms of significance for the composition of a façade. Adam Caruso has lamented an 'ideas deficit' in contemporary architecture.[2] This deficit could be manifest in the increasingly 'scientific' approach to the conception of architecture: the drastic limiting of variables within the design process which edits out wide-ranging and often problematic aspects of architectural production in order to manage risk more effectively. It is ironic that the newest fields of architectural research – algorithmic modelling and digital form generation – borrow most emphatically the scientific process, editing out the complexities of scale, visual culture, material performance over time, redundancy, adaptation and renewal, and the consequences of devolved ownership. In this case, materiality is notionally mapped onto digital form, with the resulting architecture accurately conveying material as appliqué, subservient to a 'connoisseurship of form'. Yet this issue with digital architecture is simply a heightened form of a distinct tendency throughout the profession towards 'a-materiality'.[3]

The notion of an 'ideas deficit' present at the scale of building corresponds unnervingly to an assessment at the scale of urbanism of the current work of the UK profession by Jon Rouse, formerly of the Commission for Architecture and the Built Environment. He commented that the majority of urban schemes he has considered since the inception of CABE fall into two categories.[4] The first is the 'generic framework', which fails to demonstrate the critical means by which the analysis becomes a proposition. The second, opposing (but equally flawed) category is one of 'shape shifting', as he puts it, which deftly avoids the difficult reality of site and society by developing an unsubstantiated vision. If the contemporary means of dealing with material is split between banal accumulation and unrealisable presentation, is the contemporary architecture student destined to be either a quantity surveyor or an artist? It is useful at this point to consider the predominant strategies with which schools of architecture in the United Kingdom organise students' experience of materials; the tendency within schools is twofold.

SCENARIO 1: TECHNICAL EDUCATION AS ONE OF FIVE REGULATORY REQUIREMENTS

In Britain, technical studies can be considered as one among the five module criteria required by the Royal Institute of British Architects (RIBA) and the Architects' Registration Board (ARB). Lectures can then be devised in order to impart a sound knowledge of the damp-proof course and other delights. The task of subjecting technical familiarity to the intricacies of integrated design within the student's conceptual project is therefore avoided, and the relationship between design and technology is one of lip service, involving the repetition of industry-standard construction details. This falling back on the known, on the previously digested, occurs because the idea of being able to deliver a comprehensive technical education at a contemporary school of architecture is too intimidating. Technology is too diverse and shifting, too highly energised to take control of. In this scenario, technology and materiality become a set of generalised facts and principles that are examined discretely, in parallel with 'design'. Osmosis is assumed to occur between artificially separated areas of knowledge across a modular void. In attempting to tick all of the boxes, this safety-first strategy can inadvertently introduce uncertainty, and an inability of the student to deliver properly integrated propositions – falling back instead on merely 'generic frameworks', to use Rouse's term. In avoiding risk in architecture, one risks avoiding architecture itself.

SCENARIO 2: COMPLIANCE

Within both education and practice, form is becoming the pre-eminent subject for investigation. How far is form, in and of itself, an issue? Is form the final condition of architectural analysis? If form is thought about in these terms alone, then technical studies is an inconvenience, and it is necessary to devise a 'bolt-on' to our primary passions which will, if we are lucky, keep the regulatory 'dogs' at bay and allow us to range freely through immateriality. This compliance strategy tests the student's ability to post-rationalise to the limits, with, one suspects, a few spectacular successes and rather more spectacular failures. The re-imagining of architecture can easily imply the student proposition which falls from the sky with little or no consideration of social, economic or environmental context; in other words, compliance is a process of education in Rouse's 'shape shifting'.

ANY OTHER IDEAS?: STRATEGIES OF ENGAGEMENT

These 'true life' scenarios are part of the problem of the architect's role – either the architect as a safe pair of hands, technically equipped with limited means of deployment; or the architect as 'imagineer', serving commercial pressures by envisioning schemes which then pass over to management contracting, leaving the difficult business of resolution to others.

The RIBA/ARB joint criteria for validation attempt to ensure, through the prolific use of the term 'integrated', that the problems outlined above are avoided. However, in placing technology as an equal fifth of the requirements that both student and school have to deal with, it is hard to see anything other than a generalist model being put forward for practice. The five criteria actively help to produce the two scenarios I have sketched, and inadvertently perpetuate the situation described above by Rouse. The time needed to value the specific, to conduct the deep investigation required for a genuinely relevant architectural response, is short, with the process of thought and judgement buried within more easily measurable outcomes.

We need to define the relationship of idea to proposition more clearly in order to be more accurate about the role of, and the need for, a technical strategy. We need to value and measure processes of thought and judgement, as well as output and result. As Christopher Alexander has put it, 'The institutional powers of architect and builder – the power of design and the power of construction – must be wedded in a single process.'[5]

By definition, an idea in the mind's eye is ideal. As such, it is unattainable through description. It is mediated even as it is expressed. That mediation – the drawing – is the vehicle for construction, and is the device by which both the idea and the result are judged. Drawing has a pivotal role in communication in practice, the media and in school, yet is, by definition, hypothetical and inevitably incomplete. How far do the limitations of description affect the idea? Does description compromise the result?

The answer is yes, so if 'shape shifting' is to be avoided as an end in itself how can the description become informed by experiences which positively contribute to the trajectory of the idea? When description becomes projected into materiality, an understanding of the limits of the material combinations under scrutiny adds value to the idea and extends its potential. Technology is, in the words of Pye, 'the study and extension of technique'.[6] Technique is the knowledge of how to make purposefully, using raw materials. To undertake a meaningful technical study, therefore, the act of drawing needs to be informed by an experience and understanding of materials, and a mature understanding of the limitations of description. The technical study becomes an intermediary between the portfolio and the building site. Although prone to influence by both material naivety and the inaccuracy of ideas it can be, when successful, the vehicle for the acquisition of material experience and the precise articulation of ideas.

It could be said that rules have never prevented poetry. Rather, they either provoke it or support it in every case. Similarly, the technical study is a potential bridge between investigation and proposition. Perhaps material necessity is not in opposition to spatial or formal necessity, and an investigation into form language need not be exclusive or immaterial.

STRATEGIES OF ENGAGEMENT: THE TECHNICAL STRATEGY

Peter Salter developed the technical strategy into a very specific teaching framework while he was unit master and technical tutor at the Architectural Association (AA) in London during the late 1980s and early 90s. The emphasis of Salter's strategy was to broaden, and provide a wide range of technical and technological options with which the students could develop their work. Salter once referred to the technical study as a terrier, snapping at the heels of the student project.[7] I see this image as characterising the beginning of a project, demanding clarity and requiring that the intentions are precisely articulated in order to generate technically relevant decisions both now and later.

Within Salter's Diploma Unit at the AA, the 'Touchstone' project required a built piece from students which was able, through its material and constructive presence, to make explicit qualities of the place or situation which inspired it, but which was itself new and authentic in its conception. This developed into an exploration of 'the weather in the space', a challenge to students to find an understanding of more than the visual in architecture, and to strive for propositions which enveloped a complete sensory experience of a space – meaning that the smell of wet concrete, the haze of dust in sunlight or the humidity of a retaining wall was to be dealt with as integral to the work.

When Salter moved to the University of East London (UEL) in 1996, the strategy became wrapped up in a rather pithier notion of an 'economy of means'. It is a legacy of Salter's headship at UEL, where I now run technical studies, not to be satisfied with the rhetorical potential of a material but to require it to do more. 'Economy of means' is a hardworking theory; it is the practice of experience, of making significance from the insignificant, of achieving substantial results through material prudence. This notion of 'careful deployment' need not be restricted to materials. If one accepts that irrelevant knowledge hampers speed of thought, then we need to develop in students an ability to focus sharply and promptly on the issue at hand, and to engage the potential within material structure to help do that – in other words, to develop a matching 'economy of thought'. This is where the student clarifies the 'how' in relation to the 'why', and where the teaching institution focuses energy and inventiveness to maximise the effectiveness of limited resources. The task, the circumstance and the potential of material structure need to be placed into a questioning and critical relationship in order to achieve a relevant originality. As such, the most important tool for technical teaching is the 'strategy'.

A technical strategy needs to be an expression of the student's attitude, and is a tool for the investigation and interrogation of ideas. A conceptual assembly of both pre-existing and original areas of knowledge, the strategy is not the reiteration of a series of givens; it is, rather, the method of navigation chosen by the student that identifies and traverses a range of restrictions in a way which generates propositional moves. This process of technical teaching attempts to deliver as close a professional relationship as possible for the student, emphasising the value of constraint as the impetus for lateral thought.

STRATEGIES OF ENGAGEMENT: THE NEGOTIATED ITEM

Degree and Diploma-year students at UEL are required to produce a detailed resolution of their strategic ambitions in the form of a so-called 'negotiated item'. A purely conceptual solution is seldom satisfactory, and the relationship between technology, process and material performance can easily become diagrammatic. Therefore, at UEL, the area of detail to be developed by the student is clarified – 'negotiated' – with the staff to achieve maximum relevance. It is bespoke, and as such appropriateness and inventiveness are paramount. In order that they really understand the detail, the students are asked to build it at 1:1 scale. Without building, how can you learn to build?

An example of a negotiated item from 2005 is Claudia Dutson's brick project in Old Street, London. An interest in contemporary, non-orthogonal geometries was challenged by the recognition that the inner-city context of Old Street demanded that the language of load-bearing brick be respected. The technical limitations of solid masonry construction were recognised and dealt with by setting the thermal lining of the interior within the static brick shell, giving thermal and acoustic shelter whilst generating semi-outdoor promenades to bind together a varied mixed-use programme. Key to the resolution of the building was the development of a brick that could wrap around the non-orthogonal corners of the building at a 120-degree angle. This element allowed the whole to come together (figure 10.1).

10.1 >Student project at Old Street, London.

analysis

The bricks have the corner line marked on them, from this point a 'wedge' of brick is cut out allowing the two pieces to be stuck back together to form the 'twisted' brick.

To work out what the bricks would need to do in order to take the corner, studies in card and clay were

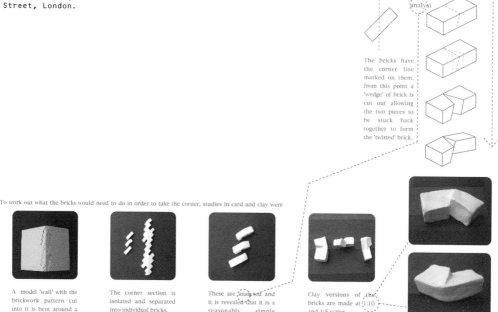

A model 'wall' with the brickwork pattern cut into it is bent around a

The corner section is isolated and separated into individual bricks.

These are analysed and it is revealed that it is a reasonably simple manouvre.

Clay versions of the bricks are made at 1:10 and 1:5 scales.

Physical and conceptual significance is made manifest in a construction detail. Emphasis on the history of the project's ideas is held within the final proposition, and, by implication – through predicting the long-term viability of the design – in how the future life of the proposal will unfold. Weathering, maintenance and adaptability all inform the proposition. This requires an innate and explicit material experience to guide the development of original thinking and of an authentic material language.

Architects are walking libraries of all the material connections and spatial options they have encountered. In creating a 'conceptual assembly' of strategic technical concerns, the purpose of the technical strategy is to fabricate a phenomena which is elusively termed 'experience' for the student, a substantial and diverse material history they can carry with them and build upon. The context within which the student operates – in school and beyond – is a means of self development. Clarifying the sources of ideas clarifies the motivation of the individual.

STRATEGIES OF ENGAGEMENT: THE WORKSHOP

It is the prime purpose of technical studies to generate essential experience of material structures in order to develop the students' abilities to comprehend and reinvest that experience on their own terms. One of the specific 'experiences' for students is the technical workshop, which introduces structural and material challenges that require both analytical and pragmatic working methods to create 1:1 evidence of that process. The experience gained within the workshop allows the student – and, later, the architect – to approach the definition of a technical strategy with greater sensitivity and confidence.

Technical workshops are in themselves architecturally ambiguous events. Real events in real time, they are 'constructed situations'. The line and the drawing which marshal the construction into order normally precede the making of structures with material. In the workshop this is not so, and the line loses its pre-eminence. Drawings simply become notations of actions: exploratory tools to investigate how something fits, where it is placed, or a sequence of actions. Workshops rely on both verbal and tactile strategies to generate the constructed situation between participants and their task. What advantage does this give? Primarily, the development of material resolution through making confronts the student with the inertia and sloth of material substance. The student cannot assume that the mastery of matter is the responsibility of others. In the very conception of a design, the qualities and properties of materials must be grasped and understood in order to make. Lines are the intermediaries between 'thought' and 'making', and their significance as substitute for matter needs to be understood. Architects seldom build their own work, but to begin an immersion into the act of building is the only means by which their line can become relevant and purposeful.

Workshops require a clear strategy and tactics to succeed within a timeframe, so they need precise definition and clarity of purpose. However, the energy and contribution of the participants must be accommodated, their unique individual contributions harnessed into the collective effort. If the outcome of the constructed situation is too tightly defined, the lack of engagement is palpable and the process becomes a mechanical labour rather than a collective endeavour. The participants have to be allowed to develop an intuitive understanding of the issues of the situation, to become confident through direct engagement with the material process, to be empowered to adjust and alter that process as it happens. This requires the workshop to develop a forum for discussion and exchange, with knowledge shared in order to stimulate propositions: an architecture of approximation.

The workshops which are illustrated here preceded the debates at the 'Material Matters' conference, where the question of direct engagement was a central idea.[8] They allowed equilibrium to be struck between the conception of material and its deployment. The tendency to conceptualise material – to discuss its 'truth' and to critique its expression – is, in and of itself, a very partial activity. Depending entirely upon how the material is worked, expression, significance and status can vary enormously. Concrete, for example, is expressive only when its primary quality – that of being liquid – has been lost. The pleasure of concrete lies in its ability to retain a history of its former state, of bringing opposing qualities of fluidity and solidity together in a process akin to the appreciation of figurative sculpture in the rendering of soft human form in stone. It is the method by which the material is acted upon that largely determines its significance, not the material itself.

The 'Wall' workshop was set up precisely to explore a system within which both economic and expressive parameters are understood and tested.[9] The

10.2 >A drawing as an action closer to comic book than art gallery, it is thinking through process visually.

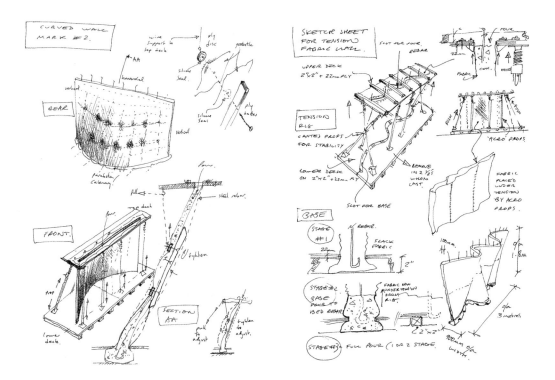

technical issue of restraint, using fabric against the hydrostatic pressure of concrete, was the focus of experimentation, allowing flexibility with regard to spacing restraints and, therefore, the local thickness of the concrete. This gave the ability to create the form of the Wall as it was being made, whilst employing a 'tensegrity' field to resist pressure rather than relying on valuable, but usually expendable, sheet material (figures 10.2–10.5).

The nature of the workshop piece or 'architectural prototype' is that it can act as an anticipation of the end of a process of thought. Simultaneously, it is an enactment of that process. The power of a prototype lies in its ability to embody a field of ideas, and in the means of testing the interrelationship of those ideas in a single moment. A prototype accelerates the proposition. The task for the 'Wall' workshop was to conceive of a prototype construction process which was both a practical and repeatable technique, yet which, within its own operation, allowed for and encouraged the constructors to actively manipulate that process. Variables such as the exact placement of restraints, their size and degree of constriction could be manipulated even as the concrete was poured, questioning the need for the extensive pre-determination required of conventional concrete work. The casting technique of the Wall showed how unpredictable – even incoherent – detail can emerge from a coherent technique. This subversive intention was at the heart of the Wall exercise, and formed a critique of industrialised building processes by dealing with the very aspect of construction that causes most difficulty: risk.

The conclusion of the 'Wall' workshop is not only a four-tonne piece of concrete. As with any constructed event, the actions generated by the process itself are immaterial and relate to the potential for future action rather than the fabrication of static conclusions. The Wall is a document that requires reading in order to define what the next move needs to be. This is a means of building in order to generate research activity, counter to accepted academic processes whereby the act of fabrication is the predictable demonstration of previously defined outcomes. It has the advantage of opening up new directions for

10.3 >Detail of the sweating of excess water giving stronger concrete with enhanced surface detail.

10.4 >Utilising acro-props as found objects to exert resistant force against hydrostatic pressure.

10.5 >The formwork struck.

investigation that are not predictable from the starting point of ignorance. The role of the prototype – built not with regulation, but with dexterity – is to accelerate and expand the process of decision making. It is the constructed conversation prior to the writing of the production specification, which others labour with.

Participation in the technical workshop or 'constructed event' enables a shift in perception and possession for the participant. Ownership of the process, of decision making and of risk evaluation, needs to become collective and genuine, and the instigator of the workshop has to be prepared to cede responsibility and credit for the final result. The myth of the architect as creator and arbiter of space still lingers in our culture of salesmanship, but is untenable in the culture of the workshop.

In conclusion, the practice of prototyping is a proper domain for architectural research. Constructive processes and material inertia need to be thought of not as impediments to formal invention, but rather as active participants in innovation. As educators and as architects the compulsion should be to build, learn and build again; a mode of operation at odds with traditional (non-architectural, yet dominant) research practice. Conventionally, a discrete series of operations would be defined which, through systematic and linear processes, became understood and evaluated according to pre-set criteria. Informed with a limited but effective body of intuition and understanding, building at 1:1 scale provides a broad platform from which significant areas of study – materiality, process, technique – can be tested simultaneously. It is only after the prototype is built that the linear model of analysis becomes vital in refining the opportunities that the full-scale making has generated. The prototype tests the interaction of materials and events, not merely their constituent parts. In constructing a prototype, one discovers how to build.

Grateful thanks to: The Don and Low Company, Allan Haines, Julia Hartmann, Katie Lloyd Thomas, Remo Pedreschi, Jim Ross, Signy Svalastoga, Mark West and the students who collaborated in the building of the Wall.

1   >David Pye, *The Nature and Art of Workmanship*, London: Cambridge University Press, 1968, p. 24.
2   >Adam Caruso, 'Analysis' in *Building Design*, 17 June 2005, p. 11.
3   >The term 'a-material' refers to a condition of architecture which is intentionally without material substance, in order that the consequences of materiality (weight, physical properties, scale, economy, endurance under use) are subsumed beneath the desire for visual form without physical limitation. It is not 'anti-material', a condition which has distinct intentionality, rather it is a state of non-engagement.
4   >Jon Rouse, Interview in *Building Design*, 9 January 2004, p. 8.
5   >Christopher Alexander, *The Production of Houses*, New York: Oxford University Press, 1985, p. 70.
6   >David Pye, *op. cit.*, p. 22.
7   >Peter Salter, *Intuition and Process*, London: AA Publications, 1988, p. 14.
8   >'Material Matters: Materiality in Contemporary Architectural Practice and Theory' was held between 29 March and 3 April 2004 at the School of Architecture and the Visual Arts at the University of East London.
9   >The 'Wall' was the built result of a workshop 'FABRIC = MASS + FORM' run by myself and Remo Pedreschi at 'Material Matters', which was devised in order to explore the use of engineered geotextile as a formwork for casting concrete walls, minimising the material used as formwork, and exploring variable hydrostatic geometry. For more detail about the workshop, see Alan Chandler, 'A Philosophy of Engagement' in ARQ, Volume 8 3/4, 2006, pp. 204–14.

126

FABRIC = MASS + FORM >ALAN CHANDLER (UNIVERSITY OF
EAST LONDON)

The interest in fabric formwork is in its deployment in a building process, which is faster than conventional formwork. Fabric formwork is inherently more sustainable due to the minimising of both concrete and shuttering, and, more radically, allows the constructor to intervene in the process of casting even as the cast is taking place.

The adjustable nature of the rig we created develops the potential for *in situ* wall construction to utilize tensile elements rather than compression members to contain, and only partly control, the liquid mass. By using tension to counterbalance the outward pressure of the liquid mass, equilibrium is sought and its effects expressed in form, no longer subjugating the inherent liquid nature of the concrete.

Our strategy was to build at 1:1 scale, in order to clarify finer-scale research projects which can then follow and enhance the project's conclusions. Without building, how can you learn how to build?

11.1

11.1 >FABRIC = MASS + FORM.

11.2 >FABRIC = MASS + FORM.

11.3 >FABRIC = MASS + FORM.

11.4 >FABRIC = MASS + FORM.

11.2

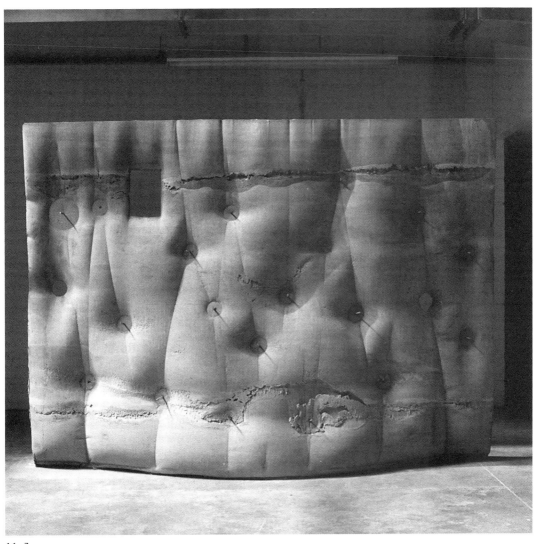

11.3

11.4

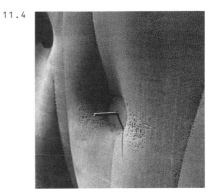

BODY BUILDING >RAPHAEL LEE AND ALAN CHANDLER
(UNIVERSITY OF EAST LONDON)

This workshop was devised to satisfy two distinct experiences of materiality and scale: firstly, to create a sculptural form in clay and, secondly, to take this form as a maquette for a larger concrete shell structure. In order to define the scale of this structure, it was decided that it should be large enough to provide a sheltered working space outside the wood workshop.

In the midst of a truly exciting week for the school of architecture, something characteristically crazy was taking shape round the back of the building. After a day of accelerated classical sculpting, the group threw themselves gung-ho into the business of building, driven by the spirit of Rodin or Bartholdi to recreate the ideal of natural beauty on a massive scale. The structural anomaly of Eladio Dieste's delicate canopies combined with the symbolic potency of a Statue of Liberty. It is little surprise that this ambitious project proved a substantial challenge, and despite the feeling of solidarity amongst the group, and from passers-by who pitched in wherever they could, it became a genuine struggle against the powerful forces of Nature: wind, rain and gravity. The result: a strange blobby folly, a monument to the prehistoric dwelling and testimony to the process of creation. A new Balzac.

11.5–11.7

11.5 >Body Building.

11.6 >Body Building.

11.7 >Body Building.

11.8 >Body Building.   11.8

BODY & MATTER: MATERIALITY AND THE SENSES >NADIA
MOUNAJJED, PEPI CHOURMOUZIADOU, STEPHEN WALKER
(UNIVERSITY OF SHEFFIELD)

In this project, we explored body sensibilities as a measure of the materiality
of the space. We focused on two undervalued senses: touch and smell. During the
passage through three different spaces, we gradually reduced a person's ability
to rely on their sense of vision, in an attempt to reveal the invisible beauty of the
other realities of space. The installation became a journey through the senses.

In the first space, a frame structure formed a cocoon consisting of semi-
transparent surfaces treated to achieve different textures and atmospheres.
The visitor was still in control of their senses, but as they moved deeper into the
installation the priority of vision was disrupted. Three objects – with their scents,
texture and light – became landmarks in the obscurity of the space, inviting the
person to explore further through touch and smell. Finally, the visitor walked into
complete darkness. By relinquishing control, the visitor who travelled far enough
was rewarded by having their vision restored.

We realized how feelings of insecurity are strongly associated with being in
control of our senses. Vision proved to be the primary sense, since a person feels
confident as long as they can visually perceive and define space. Sound and touch
follow, both significant tools for identifying aspects and characteristics of a space.
Physical boundaries and dimensions are delineated through bodily contact,
reverberation or echo.

11.9 >Body & Matter:
Materiality and the
senses.   11.9

HEIDI SVENNINGSEN AND CATHY HAWLEY >SENSE
(MUF ARCHITECTURE/ART)

11.10, 11.11

The workshop . . . presented photographic evidence of the new building's first peculiarities and quirks. The message wasn't that the new building is wonderful, but that it is subjective, as unique, vital and open to interpretation as Holbrook.

David Knight

In this new building taking up space can equal making a mess, in fact the new UEL 'rules for walls' prevented the students from making marks. We were allowed to break the rules, and used the building fabric as canvas for thinking about decoration, damage, detail, sensibility, where we want to be and what we want where we are.

PRINTING ON THE NEW WHITE WALLS WAS A PLEASURE
Students and staff around the school drew their daydreams for us, uncovering longings for money, sun, sex, mountains, sea, love, beauty and other escapes. Quick sketches became linocuts and then semi-permanent prints. Illustrations of places where everybody would rather be, of places considered worth being in, combined as all-over pattern. Taking up space can equal making spaces?

NOTES FROM WORKSHOP: WHAT MAKES SENSE IN A SCHOOL OF ARCHITECTURE?
Hand-made, imperfect, flaws, mechanical, hierarchies, marking, permanence, where you sit and what you see, the 'value of labour upon material' (Ruskin), lost meaning, up close, point of view, neutrality, partiality, grotesque, beautiful, pleasure, recognition, daydreaming, covered/revealed, control/randomness, symbolism.

11.10   >SENSE.

11.11   >SENSE.

11.12   >SENSE.

11.13   >SENSE.   11.12

11.13

ANALOGUE COMPUTING – ORGANIZING MATTER INTO
PATTERNS: BUILDING A ROPE COMPUTER >RICHARD
DIFFORD, JON GOODBUN, CORDULA WEISSER
(POLYTECHNIC RESEARCH STUDIO)

11.14

The Polytechnic workshop built an architectural computer out of rope, pulleys and
weights. We made a dynamic cybernetic feedback system, which organized matter
into patterns in space. There is a long, if at times marginal, history of architecture
which considers its productions, operations, descriptions and consumptions as
organized and patterned matter in space (exemplified most obviously by Antoni
Gaudí and Frei Otto). Through such mechanisms, richly subtle and complex
solutions can emerge. Such devices may draw upon the internal logic of geometry
or the mechanics of a physical system, but in so doing they can also potentially
imbue the design with qualities over and above the issue of the practical resolution
of a structural problem. The suggestion that a loaded rope or chain could be used
to experimentally determine the appropriate form for an arch or dome is usually
attributed to the seventeenth-century scientist, and architect, Robert Hooke.
Another of Hooke's interests may suggest a similar application of his preference
for a mechanical solution: the sash window. Drawing upon the components of
the sash mechanism, together with devices such as those illustrated in a recent
publication by German engineers Erwin Heinle and Jörg Schlaich, we dynamically
(self-) organized matter in space.

11.15

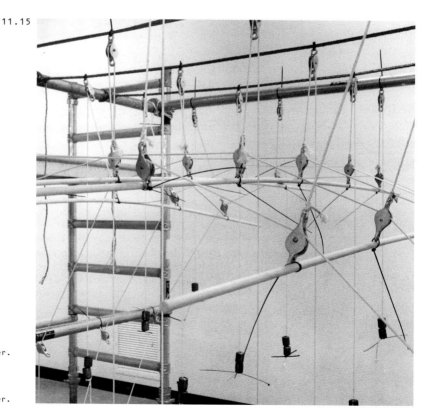

11.14   >Analogue
Computing – Organizing
Matter into Patterns:
Building a Rope Computer.

11.15   >Analogue
Computing – Organizing
Matter into Patterns:
Building a Rope Computer.

Deleuze developed two concepts – the optical and the acoustic sign – that refer
to how sight and sound interact. This workshop set out to explore 'water's visual
and audible importance in conveying rhythm.'[2] By working with water – and
its reflections and mirroring images – and with sound, the workshop explored
temporality through experiments and observations. This raised fundamental
issues about the relationship of space to time. Using recording devices (sound
and light), the participants observed and recorded. Then they used these to set the
agenda for the design. One of the most successful groups within the workshop
discovered accidentally, during the design process, a material that they did not
know about and which generated, through its material qualities and structure,
just the kind of sound and light they wanted to work with. Thus, the workshop
participants began to understand the importance for design not just of materials
but also of research.

2   >Gilles Deleuze, *Cinema 1: The Movement Image*, London: The Athlone Press, 1986, pp.
77–8.

11.16 >Water: Deleuze's
notions of optical and
acoustic signs.

BUILDING A DRAWING >STEPHANIE BRANDT, CONSTANCE LAU
(BARTLETT SCHOOL OF ARCHITECTURE)

11.17

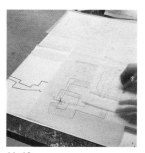

11.18

'Words are such powerful things, and when they correspond to visual impressions . . . they may reasonably stand as proof'[1]

Robin Evans, 'Translations from Drawing to Building'

The workshop was driven by discussions about the interface between abstract concept and its physical appearance, theory and practice, writing and design. We began with the exploration of one given material, a book, individually chosen by each student for its own qualities and in relation to the brief – aiming to question, challenge and manipulate this prefabrication.

The purpose and the basic question was whether the process of compiling architecture into a book has limited the understanding and appreciation of these (architectural) ideas in their pure, initial and (most importantly) intended form. Perhaps a different method of [re] presenting architecture is required?

As an alternative to 'Translations from Drawing to Building', we started to engage with the process of 'Building a Drawing', hoping to create an awareness of the ambiguous nature of architecture through the process of shifting its reading and understanding as matter. The resulting work – every individual interpretation – suggested we see architecture not just as mere physical matter.

11.17   >Building a
Drawing.

11.18   >Building a
Drawing.

1   >Robin Evans, 'Translations from Drawing to Building', *AA Files* number 12, 1986, p. 1.

11.19

One Box
12 Materials from Switzerland
12 People
One Table
3 Days
A New Product

Day 1: 12 Raw Materials
Cork, beeswax, wood, rubber, glass, hemp, stone, bitumen, metal, clay, flax and
leather. Each participant chose one of the raw materials, which were presented
in their purest and most natural way, and studied their different qualities and
attributes. Lines, patterns, surfaces, textures, masses, weight, temperature,
sound, smell and light were patiently observed as if for the first time.

Day 2: Finding New Recipes
As one of the main materials used in the building industry today, we have chosen
concrete as the base material for the project as it allows special forms of a good
size to be created economically in a short time. The participants invented and
tested new recipes, applying the different qualities studied previously. Some
added other materials to the concrete, manipulated the mould or treated the cast
object superficially.

Day 3: 12 New Products
Wild and sensitive, dry and artificial, wet and shiny, oily and rough, transparent
and dark, fragile and light.
　　　The final products were exhibited together with the raw materials and a
written recipe on one big table.

11.19　>Import/
Export.

11.20　>Import/
Export.　　　　11.20

11.21

Kinya arrived with Naoki, the master plasterer, and seven Japanese students to meet 23 culturally diverse University of East London students and friends. The first day we split into three groups with the idea of making three small pieces, each demonstrating different techniques used by Naoki – but as the groups worked on small clay models, a larger, more ambitious, project emerged which linked the interests of all. A desire for a comfortable place – in contrast to the stark campus of UEL – became the driving force, and the making of a small tea house was decided on.

Each group was allocated a task: one to make the rammed earth walls; one to create the lime-rendered hazel roof; and another to build the fire, barbecue and chimney from adobe bricks. Midway through the week, the groups merged and became one, each person helping where needed.

The peculiarity of the site, backing onto the A13 road, helped define the alcove shape of the tea house, dug into the earth, facing south, enclosing to block out the noise.

11.21 >The Mud
Workshop.

11.22 >The Mud
Workshop.   11.22

11.23

11.24

11.25

11.23 >The Mud Workshop.

11.24 >The Mud Workshop.

11.25 >The Mud Workshop.

11.26

11.27

11.26   >The Mud Workshop.

11.27   >The Mud Workshop.

SURFACE STRUCTURES IN THE DIGITAL AGE: STUDIES IN FERROCEMENT

MARTIN BECHTHOLD >SURFACE STRUCTURES IN THE
DIGITAL AGE: STUDIES IN FERROCEMENT

SHELLS, BLOBS AND CAD/CAM

How are digital design and manufacturing technologies impacting on our choice
and use of materials? What are the opportunities for design if we re-think
traditional design and fabrication processes? This paper investigates the custom
design and fabrication of surface structures in the quest for a new tectonic
approach enabled by digital design and manufacturing (CAD/CAM) techniques.
Two new design and fabrication processes for folded plate and shell structures are
presented in order to research use of CAD/CAM for complex and individualized
architectural designs. Both proposals present innovative uses of ferrocement, a
cementitious composite material (figure 12.1).

Until recently CAD was mostly employed to do what could have been done
by hand – producing largely two-dimensional representations of architectural
designs. Improvements in productivity through digital versus analog methods
are still debatable, depending on when and how exactly digital design tools
intervene. It was the emergence of powerful surface and solid modelling tools
that, by facilitating the modelling of spatially complex three-dimensional shapes,
affected our design thinking more profoundly. Sophisticated renderings of curved
and complexly shaped buildings and components populate the architectural
magazines, and digital production techniques are listed as their means of
fabrication, suggesting that these 'impossible' shapes can now be produced
simply at the push of the button. Nothing, of course, could be further from the
truth.

In the eyes of many, Computer-Aided Manufacturing (CAM) techniques
are closely associated with complexly shaped building designs, as present, for
example, in the work of Frank O. Gehry, Bernhard Franken or Kas Osterhuis. Work
by other designers continues in a similar formal direction, albeit often originating
in different design approaches. While the many innovative aspects of this type of
work remain undisputed, it is also clear that architects tend to overlook CAM's
admittedly less exciting applications for fabricating more normative architectural
components and elements. These applications include a broad range of Computer-
Numerical Control (CNC) techniques employed on a variety of scales, including
structural steel and timber fabrication, windows and cladding panels as well as
smaller architectural products, to name just a few. For some systems – such as,
for example, timber or steel frames – there are parametric design and detailing
environments, based on a 3-D model, that support the traditional shop drawing
process but also enable fabricators to generate machine instructions based on the
same 3-D design model. Here the efficiencies afforded through CAD/CAM remain
almost entirely on the fabricator's side, and data migration from the designer to
the fabricator is difficult at best.[1]

The current interest in CAD/CAM in relation to 'blobby' complex shapes may
be a transitional phenomenon. But it undoubtedly has the benefit of making us
question a design paradigm that originated in the laws of high-volume industrial
production and their economies-of-scale effects: the repetition of identical
architectural elements and components as a primary cost saver in architectural
construction. Unique, complexly shaped envelopes and components challenge
designers and fabricators alike, since traditional modes of representation and
fabrication are no longer applicable. These forms rarely permit repeated use of
identical components, and thus present a dilemma. While the creativity of

12.1   >Parametric design
study of an undulating
structural surface,
designed in a class
taught by the author.

individual construction solutions is often remarkable, the greater issue of interest here is the degree to which the production of highly varied architectural elements can move the profession towards a new mode of individualized production in architecture. Can CAD/CAM technology reduce the need for the repetition of standard elements in order to be cost effective?

A first step towards such individualized fabrication is a flexible digital modelling approach, best implemented in parametric digital modelling. Parametric design methods are enabled through dimensionally-driven design development tools such as SolidWorks, Catia, ProENGINEER and others. These are software environments that differ radically from traditional surface modelling and drafting tools, since all elements of the three-dimensional model are controlled by dimensions, constraints, interrelated equations and macros. The designer defines behaviours rather than fixed dimensions, an approach that radically differs from traditional design methods. In a façade model, for example, the spacing of windows could be defined not only as a certain percentage of the total wall length, but scripts can add more windows as the wall length exceeds a certain amount. Once these kinds of object-oriented models are set up, the designer can output variations in a short time by simply altering certain model parameters. Provided the model has been set up intelligently – and the time involved here should not be underestimated – the overall model will rebuild according to the newly input design parameter.

A parametric design model only facilitates individualized fabrication if the production setup allows for the resulting variations to be produced efficiently. The question thus remains of whether digital fabrication techniques can enable the production of custom elements at a similar cost compared to standardized elements. In order to move towards a more efficient customization in architectural construction we need to question the very processes by which we fabricate architectural design. Process redesign is inevitable if new digital fabrication techniques are expected to broaden design scope. In the quest for a new design paradigm based on digital design and production, this paper investigates new fabrication processes for rigid load-bearing surface structures – roof shells.

WHAT IS A SHELL?

Shells are material-efficient structural systems that generate load-carrying capacity due to their folded or curved geometry. Shells are extremely thin compared to their span – modern shells can be 7–10 cm thick for spans of up to 20 metres and more. This efficiency is only possible since the surface itself is structurally active. Loads are carried by means of so-called membrane stresses. These in-plane stresses act in multiple directions simultaneously, and they are vastly more effective than the bending stresses that dominate in conventional structures. Shells often superficially resemble the complexly shaped blob forms generated by digitally well-versed architects. But the curvatures and folds of these blobs makes most of them unsuitable as load-bearing surfaces. Instead they are usually built using conventional structural systems such as frames, beams and columns. Shells, amidst the interest in these new geometries, remain almost forgotten.

In order to better illustrate the characteristics of shells, it is useful to look at some built examples. In the first half of the twentieth century, concrete shells were

12.2 >Torroja's daring
roof design for the
Zarzuela racetrack.

the most economical means to cover spans in the order of up to 50 and more
metres. The labour-intensive construction of the necessary timber formwork was
justified by the extreme thinness of the single and double curved surfaces, saving
thus precious and costly material. The work of Eduardo Torroja in Spain, Felix
Candela in Mexico and Pier Luigi Nervi in Italy epitomizes the aesthetics of the
early shell builders. Their designs were mostly based on simple geometric shapes.
These forms were comparatively easy to design, analyse and build.

Among the most significant shell structures from this period are Torroja's
cantilevering roof for the horse racetrack at Zarzuela near Madrid, completed in
1935, as well as Candela's Bacardi Factory in Mexico City, completed in 1960.
Torroja's design was first verified by building and testing a full-size prototype. The
soaring, thin concrete surface frames the view of the racetrack and echoes the
softly rolling hills in the background (figure 12.2). The shells remain in good
condition even though their maintenance was long neglected.[2] Candela's range
of shell structures for the Bacardi factory's production and storage facilities are
graceful, dignified spaces. The tiled hyperbolic paraboloid (HP) umbrellas shown
allow daylight to stream along the textured concrete roof shells, filtering the strong
sunlight (figure 12.3). Both of those projects demonstrate that repetition of
identical shell segments was already a dominating principle in early shell design.

Later approaches to shell design often abandoned the constraint to a simple
geometric shape such as the HP shape. Instead, complex shapes were generated
in physical model experiments with hanging fabrics, pneumatic membranes, or
using other techniques. Here, the principle is that the loads and forces in the
model experiment 'automatically' generate a structurally efficient shape. These
shapes can be very efficient as long as the types of loads in the full-size project are
similar to those present in the form-finding experiment. The work of Heinz Isler in

12.3 >The tilted HP
umbrella shells of
Candela's Bacardi storage
space is based on a
series of hyperbolic
paraboloid shapes.

12.4 >Isler's shell for the Deitingen gas station was derived from the shape of a hanging fabric. The same formwork could be used for both shells.

12.5 >The folded-plate structure for this church in Neuss, Germany, modulates the space and controls daylight.

Switzerland remains a leading exemplar of this approach (figure 12.4). Isler was among the first to elevate experimental form-finding to a scientific level in the 1950s and has, since then, designed and built several hundred concrete shells. His designs follow similar families of shapes. Large gluelam timber beams form the primary formwork elements, covered with a layer of thin wooden boards and rigid insulation board that connects permanently to the concrete. Isler's designs remain economical mostly because the expensive timber beams are re-used from project to project – thus forcing a repetition of shapes that can compromise the design.

A similar approach to curved shell roofs is exemplified by folded-plate systems. These shell-like structures generate stiffness through the folding of flat plates, as documented in the work of Pier Luigi Nervi. The aesthetic potential for this technique is well illustrated by the church design of architect F. Schaller and structural engineer S. Polónyi in Neuss, Germany (figure 12.5). Here, an arrangement of 7 cm-thick concrete plates forms a calm and meditative church space. In general, as with shells, the interest in these systems faded in the 1970s, although steel folded-plate systems recently attracted attention through the Yokohama Ferry Terminal project by Foreign Office Architects. Spaceframes and other steel structures have largely replaced shells and folded plate systems as structural solutions for many medium to long spans.

Today, only Heinz Isler remains active as a shell builder in Switzerland. But shells are now being reconsidered by designers who use animation tools, algorithmic programs and other computational design techniques to explore complex shapes. These approaches push the limits of architectural design and production further than would have been feasible without robust computational

12.6 >Folded plate prototype.

design and digital fabrication techniques. The time has come to re-visit shells, experiment with new shapes and parametric design variations, and exploit their structural efficiency in the context of sustainable, material and energy-saving design principles.

FERROCEMENT

This paper argues that digital fabrication techniques can empower design if we re-visit materials and re-conceive their related fabrication processes by incorporating digital fabrication principles. Ferrocement is an exemplary case of a versatile material that can be shaped easily, but due to its labour-intensive construction techniques, the lack of applicable codes and general unawareness of architects and engineers, it is hardly used any more in construction. In combination with parametric digital design tools and digital manufacturing techniques, ferrocement can become a material that resolves some of the problems present in the construction of complexly shaped structural surfaces. In the following sections origami techniques in ferrocement and a new design and fabrication process for ferrocement sandwich shells are presented in some detail (figure 12.6).

The invention of reinforced concrete started with a rowing boat, built by J.-L. Lambot in 1848. In addition to regularly spaced metal bars, this boat was reinforced with a thin metal mesh. Mesh reinforcement quickly ceased to have any significant impact on the development of concrete, and the technology was practically forgotten until Pier Luigi Nervi began to use it in the design and fabrication of boats, roof shells and other structures immediately after World War II in Italy. Today ferrocement is again practically forgotten as a building material in western developed countries.[3]

Ferrocement is a mesh-reinforced cementitious composite with material properties that are quite different from traditional steel-bar reinforced concrete. The dense reinforcement patterns significantly reduce the widths of cracks in the cement/sand matrix, and a very thin cover of the reinforcement is normally sufficient to prevent corrosion. The typical depth of ferrocement components ranges between 10 and 50 mm, but thinner parts have been fabricated as well.

The thin reinforcing steel mesh facilitates the production of curved, and even doubly curved, ferrocement components. The mesh layers can be easily shaped to the required form without elaborate tools. One of the traditional construction methods – the 'armature method' – even enables builders to construct complexly shaped ferrocement boat hulls or other elements without resorting to a rigid formwork. First, pipes and bars are bent to describe the three-dimensional shape. These elements are connected into a three-dimensional framework. Next, multiple mesh layers are stretched over the network of rigid steel members and tied together. The densely spaced mesh is then plastered by hand. Depending on the number of mesh layers needed, the tying of the mesh can be very time consuming and tedious.

Ferrocement offers a number of opportunities that are not currently exploited. The material enables embedment of objects such as water pipes for heating or cooling elements. Such panels could serve as interior partitions or even furniture, helping to manage the microclimate for the occupants in addition to other climate-control strategies. Ferrocement can be folded along pre-determined lines that are left without matrix during fabrication. The thin, continuing mesh

12.7 >Proposal for
a folded-plate roof
structure.

provides structural continuity and acts effectively as a hinge during the folding process. The ability for the traditional armature construction technique to build complexly shaped ferrocement components without a rigid formwork can be transformed into a cost-effective construction technique for curved structural roof shells by using shotcreting techniques for the application of the cement matrix instead of hand-plastering. Ferrocement can be produced by laminating alternating layers of matrix and mesh over rigid forms – and here the opportunity for colour variations between layers offers an additional mode of design exploration. Furthermore, the material itself can be easily customized to suit specific needs. Fibre-reinforced cement mixes, advanced composites and self-stressing techniques are only some of the possibilities that remain to be fully explored in terms of their design potential.

In the following sections, two concepts for ferrocement construction of structural surfaces are described in more detail: Origami Techniques and Ferrocement Sandwich Shells.

ORIGAMI TECHNIQUES IN FERROCEMENT

The idea of folding thin ferrocement sheets was first developed in a paper, and later a patent application, by Rob Wheen from the University of Sydney.[4] The work presented here quantifies and develops the initial idea, and tests the process through the fabrication of a prototype.

The general concept of folded ferrocement involves fabricating flat components with continuous mesh reinforcement, but leaving fold lines free of matrix to enable a hinging action along these lines when folding the component into its final shape. These hinges are plastered after the component has been folded and is secured in its final position. Potential advantages of folded ferrocement are the relative ease and low cost of producing flat ferrocement parts and the associated good quality of such components. For larger elements, transportation to site as flat components is advantageous as they can be nested easily on a truck bed.

Possible applications range from outdoor furniture such as benches, chairs and tables to landscaping elements like retaining walls, and architectural elements such as façades or structural folded-plate roofs (figure 12.7). Large applications favour folding on site; for smaller applications such as furniture it is likely to be more cost effective to fold before transportation to the final site. The main questions that needed to be answered include the process and control of the folding operation and the impact of the hinge design on the performance of a folded ferrocement component.

12.8 >Parametric model
used to study folding
sequences. Modifying the
dimensions of the model
manipulates the shape of
the system. The formwork
needed to pour the flat
plate shapes can be
generated on a variety
of CNC tools, including
lasers and routers.

PROCESS OBJECTIVE

Both on-site construction and prefabrication were common when concrete folded-plate systems were still commonly used prior to the 1970s. Typical designs repeatedly used the same plate size in order to reduce the cost of the formwork. Now the ease of producing 2-D patterns and moulds using Computer-Numerically-Controlled (CNC) technology suggests the development of a folding process such that parametric variations are inherently possible and not substantially restricted by severe cost implications. By freeing designers from the need for repetition, design scope can be broadened (figure 12.8).

FOLDING OPERATION

The study of folding mechanisms was first pursued with a small physical scale model, while at the same time analysing folding sequences with parametric assembly models in a Design Development Environment. The objective was to explore supporting mechanisms that would allow the folding not just of one, but of many types of folded-plate designs, thus enabling the parametric variations discussed earlier. A simple folded system was used to study the movement sequences and necessary support mechanisms to control the position of the plates in all stages. The study resulted in the design of a simple support jig and mechanical system to initiate the folding process.

This model was then tested through a larger prototype that represented the same folded-plate design. Here, the flat pattern of the formwork was derived from the parametric model and cut on a CNC laser cutter. The fold lines, with a width of 20 mm, were present as bosses in the otherwise flat form. The fabrication involved the lamination of three layers of matrix and two mesh layers. The bottom layer of matrix was left to cure slightly before the first mesh layer was applied. A square, galvanized steel mesh with 6 mm mesh size was used. At the folds a single mesh layer continued, while the second mesh was trimmed back. After letting the flat component cure for several days the part was moved onto the folding jig. The resistance of the joints required a significant effort to fold the component. During the folding process it could be observed that cement portions on the underside fell off, since the mesh had the tendency to bend in a continuous curve over a distance that exceeded the width of the hinging joint. After the prototype had been folded to the correct position it was temporarily fixed in the supporting jig and the folds were plastered with matrix[5] (figure 12.6).

HINGE DESIGN

The folding of the prototype had shown that the hinges strongly resisted the folding operation. This resistance of the hinge can be influenced by the number of mesh layers present, or by choosing a different mesh material at the hinge. Some of the more promising materials include high-strength polyethylene fibre or glass fibre. These are strong in tension, yet easily bendable, thus making for an ideal mesh to bridge over the hinge. Due to their comparatively high cost, however, it is advisable to use these synthetic fibre mats only locally along the hinges, and to supply the remainder of the plate with a more cost-effective metal mesh.

A deflection simulation of several prototypical folded-plate roof structures showed that the overall deflection of the structure is not affected by reduced stiffness at the hinge. The simulation was carried out using computational Finite-Element Analysis.[6] Only the free edges of the folded plate systems show a significant increase in deflections if the hinge is softened. Here, transverse stiffeners may be necessary to compensate for the more pronounced deformations.

DESIGN EXPERIMENT

In order to develop the process further it is useful to consider a different folded-plate design. This more complex scheme also represents the advantages of parametric variations in the plate configurations. Through the design study of this system, further insights are expected as far as structural aspects and construction details are concerned.

A cantilevering roof canopy was modelled in a parametric design environment. Thereby, a single digital design object was created, and individual configurations of this single object in an assembly file generated the overall scheme as a linear array of cantilevering folded plates. A Finite-Element Analysis provided insights on the required plate thickness and degree of reinforcement. The particular geometry of the scheme makes the subdivision of each cantilevering element into several sub-elements necessary – these being the cantilever itself, the inserted transversal stiffeners and the vertical cantilevering column. Different types of joints were developed to enable a connection on site of the folded sub-systems. On-site connections are possible via inserted steel plates that should be welded onto the reinforcement. A similar connection provides the necessary link to the foundations (figure 12.9). The variations in the individual shapes can be easily accomplished through CNC-cutting of the particular patterns or moulds necessary for the production of each part. These moulds can be made from virtually any wood-based material. In a larger production mode one can also imagine CNC-cut adjustable mould templates, directly controlled by the parametric digital model.

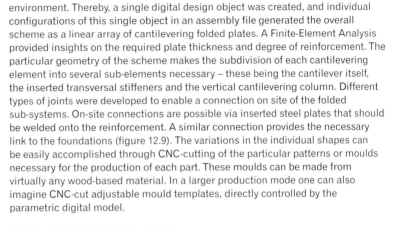

12.9 >Scale model of the cantilevering canopy: in the digital model each canopy segment was derived from a single generic parametric design object.

FERROCEMENT SANDWICH SHELLS

The ability of ferrocement to be easily shaped into single and double-curved shapes is an opportunity for the construction of complexly shaped concrete roof shells. These structural surfaces are generally expensive to construct since they need to be poured over a rigid formwork, usually made out of wood. The traditional armature method of ferrocement construction suggests that complex ferrocement shapes can be built without moulds. Dimensional accuracy, however, is difficult to achieve in this process. The supporting steel pipes and reinforcement bars tend to deviate from the designed shape – deviations that in a shell could easily result in excessive deflections and cracks. Further inaccuracies are introduced through deflections of the pipe framework during plastering.

A NEW PROCESS: PERMANENT FERROCEMENT FORMWORK

Instead of using a solid, and thus inevitably relatively thick, cross-section for curved structural surfaces the research proposes splitting the surface into two thinner components that are connected in a shear-resistant manner. By fabricating only the bottom surface in ferrocement and by using this surface as a permanent formwork to pour the upper layer of conventional concrete in place, the structural requirements for the ferrocement layer are reduced. As the load transfer in this layer is reduced, so is the number of mesh layers that need to be tied. The thin ferrocement layer – prefabricated efficiently off-site – serves both as a means of construction and as a structural layer in the finished shell (figure 12.10).

12.10 >Cross-section through a structural shell sandwich: the lower layer consists of pre-fabricated ferrocement. Concrete-embedded ribs create a shear-resistant connection to the upper, primary structural concrete layer that is poured on site.

This new process is based on prefabrication, and it requires that larger roof shells be subdivided into transportable segments. By modelling the shell and its segments in a parametric design environment, the geometry and thickness of the segments can be associated with the master shell model. Changes in the master geometry can propagate down to the individual segments. A triangulated network of steel ribs is modelled for each segment, a step facilitated by modelling macros that were developed during the research. A flat 2-D pattern for each rib can be easily derived from the 3-D model, and the rib shapes can be nested and CNC-cut

12.11 >Process Diagram:
a, b) Shell subdivided
into 7 segments,
principal reinforcement;
c) Shell segment modelled
with network of ribs;
d, e) Steel rods and mesh
are applied over the
ribs; f) Shotcreting
application completes
the prefabrication of the
permanent formwork.

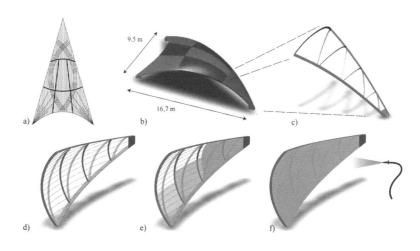

9.5 m

16,7 m

a)

b)

c)

d)

e)

f)

12.12 >On-site assembly
of the shell segments
requires only simple
temporary supporting
systems to hold the
ferrocement panels in
place while the upper
concrete layer is curing.

12.13 >These and many
other shell designs
can be constructed as
ferrocement sandwich
shells. Applications
other than roof shells
are equally possible.

from plate steel on a plasma cutter. The slots and tabs of the ribs allow accurate positioning during the welding process. The frame of curved steel flats replaces the inaccurately bent pipes in the traditional armature process (figure 12.11).

The rib network needs to be covered with thin steel rods. These can be placed in and welded to rib notches that, again, are embedded as macros in the parametric design model. When plasma-cutting the steel ribs, these notches are automatically included – without noticeably impacting on cutting costs. An assembly of mesh and glass-fibre fabric forms the surface onto which the cement-based matrix can be either sprayed or manually plastered, depending on the setup. After the ferrocement has cured, the interstitial space between the ribs is filled with foam insulation. The finished panels are transported to site, where they are assembled on a temporary supporting structure. After welding the edge ribs together, the primary reinforcement bars of the upper sandwich layer are put in place and the concrete can be poured. Since the reinforcement bars continue across segment joints they provide additional stiffness and structurally join the panels to a continuous shell surface (figure 12.12).

The proposed construction process borrows from traditional construction techniques, but largely eliminates the time-consuming tying of mesh layers. Digital fabrication techniques for the ribs improve the accuracy of the system, and the sandwich cross-section of the shell increases its overall stiffness as well as improving the thermal resistance of the roof envelope (figure 12.13).

CONCLUSIONS

This paper investigates new digitally-driven fabrication processes for ferrocement folded plates and shells in an effort to better understand attitudes towards materials and processes in the age of digital design and production techniques. As thin structural materials, load-bearing ferrocement surfaces necessarily need to be either folded or curved, preferably doubly-curved, to obtain the kinds of load-bearing capacity that is suitable for architectural applications. Both geometries are

12.14 >Proposal for an exhibition space by Jason Oliviera. The scheme was designed for a class taught by the author.

difficult to obtain using traditional construction techniques, and new digitally-based design and fabrication methods are proposed. The characteristics of these new processes are based on prefabrication in order to maximize productivity. These processes no longer penalize the individualization of components, thus reducing the need for repetition in the production of architectural surface structures and similar applications. The work shows that, if considered in conjunction with state-of-the-art digital design and manufacturing technology, opportunities arise that broaden our design scope (figure 12.14).

Ferrocement sandwich construction techniques also could be used to fabricate complex shapes other than pure shells. Such free and sculptural shapes can be easily generated by digital modelling tools and computational design techniques, but are challenging to build. Structurally they are not normally as efficient as a pure shell, because much of the load transfer is accomplished through bending instead of membrane stresses. For those sculptural applications, the depth of the steel ribs would have to be adjusted and sized to carry the majority of bending moments. The ferrocement-and-concrete sandwich would serve as a structurally active infill surface. Folded-plate construction can also serve to produce smaller components such as outdoor furniture, folded retaining walls, or façade cladding.

The re-introduction of shell and folded-plate structures into our design vocabulary would mark the welcome return to a more rigorous design thinking in this day and age of seemingly random digital forms. Shells necessitate a close collaboration between architect and engineer right from the early design phases. Today's powerful computational tools and CNC fabrication techniques can greatly facilitate the designing and building of surface structures. Using shells to minimize the amount of material needed to span medium distances can contribute to overall design sustainability. New reinforcement materials such as, for example, carbon-fibre grids have already been used in the cement-based coats of existing concrete structures. Exciting new possibilities lie ahead for surface structures. And ferrocement – or should we say cementitious composites – may yet turn out to be more a material of the future than one of the past.

ACKNOWLEDGEMENTS
Research Assistants: Justin Lee (Origami Techniques in Ferrocement)
Jason Halaby (Ferrocement Sandwich Shells)

1   > For more detailed information on CAD/CAM see: Schodek, Bechthold *et al.*, *Digital Design and Manufacturing. Applications in Architecture and Design*, Hoboken, New Jersey: John Wiley and Sons, 2004.
2   > The racetrack, as well as all remaining work by E. Torroja, is listed as a national monument in Spain. After an extensive restoration the track is now open again for races.
3   > Ferrocement continues to be used in Asia, especially in countries with comparatively high material-to-labour cost ratios. Chinese boat builders, for example, continue to work with ferrocement in the construction of barges of various types.
4   > Rob Wheen, 'Concepts of Origami in Structural Concrete' in *Civil Engineering Transactions*, The Institution of Engineers, Australia, 1980, pp. 108–11.
5   > Due to the lack of transversal stiffeners, the structural capacity of the prototype is limited.
6   > Finite Element Analysis is a computational method of structural analysis that is based on subdividing a structure into discrete or 'finite' elements. Supports, loads and material characteristics can be specified for this mesh. The output primarily includes deflections and stresses.

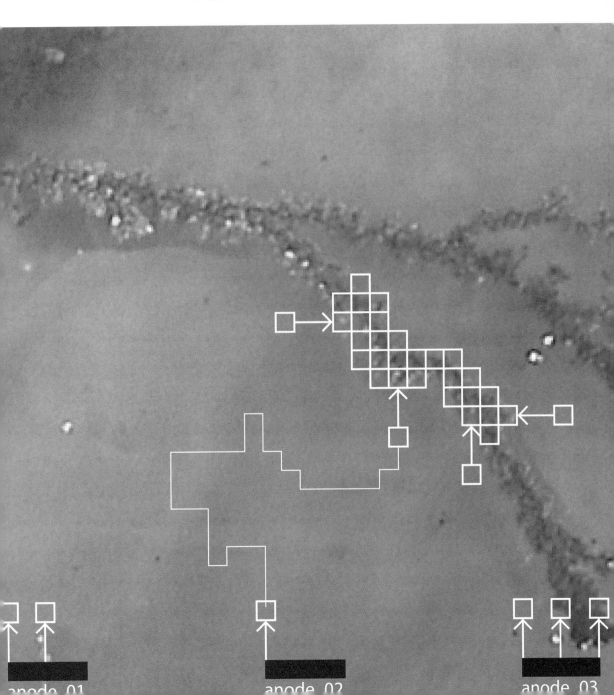

PABLO MIRANDA CARRANZA >OUT OF CONTROL: THE MEDIA OF
ARCHITECTURE, CYBERNETICS AND DESIGN

Architects who studied during the 1990s may very well have been the last to learn
with rulers, set-squares or compasses as the main tools for designing architecture.
Since then they have had to deal first with the introduction of the computer in
architectural practice, and then with its almost total dominance as the main
means of producing architecture. While the CAD industry markets new tools that
promise increasing creative ease and power for the new architects/users, stressing
their enabling capabilities – never their constraining and disabling ones – the well
established relationship of architects with their media has changed drastically in
the last two decades. Besides unconditional acceptance and consumption of these
new 'tools', or otherwise an obstinate Luddism – praiseworthy, perhaps, in its
critical resistance but not all that practical in the face of contemporary CAD
dominance – there is a need to look at the longer-term effects of the use of
computation in architecture and at the relation between architects and their
technologies.

The following paper is part of an attempt to explore this relation of
architecture and computing media, and consists of two parts. The first part
examines some of the consequences for architecture of computers, understood
as cybernetic devices involving feedback and complex causal relations, and
their identification with the automation of purpose. The second part covers an
experimental perspective machine based on cybernetician Gordon Pask's work on
electrochemical computers. The experiments carried out by Pask during the late
1950s were remarkable for a great number of reasons, but the interest here
concentrates on their emphasis on the material substrate of computation as the
embodiment of those circular relations identified by cybernetics. Pask's artefacts
also exemplified the principle of analogy and the layering of metaphors that
characterises computers. The account such a device gives of the dominant
technology employed for producing drawings highlights the substantial difference
with traditional drafting, and reveals the relative degree of absurdity involved in
the computer drawing.

The intention of both parts is to try and put forward an understanding of
computation not as a remedy, prosthesis or extension to drawing, but as a medium
distinctly different from graphic depiction with a potential to affect radically the
making and understanding of architecture – a discipline traditionally closely linked
to the technologies of projection developed during the Renaissance.

THE CRAFT OF DESIGN
Marshall McLuhan defined the relation of media and self as the working of a
'servomechanism': an adaptation of the self to its own technological extensions
to form a closed system, in which the recognition of these extensions becomes
impossible.[1] It is interesting to think about architecture's relationship to its media
according to this simile inspired by cybernetics. 'Craft' could be formulated in this
context as the alterations and adjustments of a body to the technologies involved
in the processes of producing architecture. These adaptations and adjustments
often escape recognition because of their integration with the technologies they
relate to.

The early craft of the mason and other craftsman consisted of alterations
and changes coupled to the direct manipulation of materials. In a schematic
history of such cybernetic relations, their craft gave way to that of the master

builder, which depended on the command and organisation of skills and resources in the construction process. During the Italian Renaissance, the craft of the architect started taking form as the relation with the projective technologies implied in the representation of future constructions through plans, elevations, sections and other geometric artefacts. It was the command and craft of drawing which set the genus of architects apart from the building trades and, according to Adrian Forty, it was drawing's connection with geometry in the newly discovered science of perspective that gave architecture a means to associate itself with abstract thought – giving it the status of intellectual, rather than manual labour.[2]

The word 'design', from the Italian 'disegno' or 'drawing', is, since its introduction in the Renaissance, not only the technique which intercedes between the designer and his or her work, but it also condenses geometrical form, judgement and purpose into a single concept. The concept of design in architecture articulated the relationship between the new persona of the architect – as the origin of purpose and judgement, and, therefore, the author – and the building, which became the means for measuring and judging his or her talent. In his essential contribution to setting up design as the mediating entity between the new system of architect, builders, patrons and users, Alberti conceived the notion of 'concinnitas'. 'Concinnitas', 'aptness for' or 'adaptation for a purpose' and, inspired by the classical tradition of oratory and Cicero's rhetoric in particular, Alberti adopted it from the Latin 'concinnus' – 'skillfully put together or joined'. Thus design was structured as an organic account similar to that of verbal delivery,[3] a development which associated architecture with the liberal arts by establishing design as a rational discursive process, and as the logical organisation of materials.

The promotion of architecture to an intellectual activity through its association with oratory and science, and the emergence of the architect as 'creator', are not the only evidence of the influence of Neoplatonic concepts at that time. Through an almost literal implementation of the archetypical Platonic allegory of the cave, the mechanisms of projection inscribe Platonic discourse into the technologies and media of architecture. In this implementation of the myth, the architect becomes the demiurgic figure who, simply through occupying a point in an ideal space and gaining insight by detachment from the plane of sensual projection, is able to translate and project ideas on to chaos. The introduction of projection produced a displacement of the locus of craft. If before the Renaissance craft had been placed on the surface itself – on the 'chaos' that was organised by inherited heuristics and the working of the hand, and by the senses in Platonic terms – during the period this craft's site moved to another surface, that of the 'higher' one of an intermediate plane on to, and from which, ideas are projected. The craft that developed implied an architecture that is organised as the control and authority over the production, not of buildings but of architectural ideas and their representation embodied in the technologies of projection. This is the form in which architecture, with the inevitable modifications of five centuries of use and evolution, has reached us today. Despite substantial changes in the technology employed, the architect's craft is still placed on the mediating plane of the drawing, over which he or she has apparent command.

THE COMPUTER DRAWING

According to McLuhan, 'the process of upset resulting from a new distribution of skills is accompanied by much culture lag in which people feel compelled to look at new situations as if they were old ones.'[4] Since the introduction in 1979 of the Xerox 8010 – the first marketed computer with a Graphic User Interface (GUI) – we experience computers in an oblique way, through their capacity to imitate familiar tools and situations such as a radio, a typewriter, a video-editing table, a desktop and so on. Walter Benjamin had already noticed that 'mechanical equipment has penetrated so deeply into reality that its pure aspect freed from the foreign substance of equipment is the result of a special procedure . . . [shooting and montage in the case of cinema]. The equipment-free aspect of reality here has become the height of artifice.'[5] Along with other twentieth-century media, electronic computation has developed according to similar premises.

The stratification of more 'natural' metaphors as a way of improving usability began even in the very early development of digital technology. In his attempts to increase the ease of computer usage, John von Neumann proposed 'short codes', programming languages that would run on the basic logic designs he had already differentiated from the underlying physical processes.[6] This was also the beginning of a systematic concealment of hardware by software, electronic signifiers by interfaces between formal and everyday languages[7] – a process ultimately necessary in order to market the computer to a wider public: initially scientists, researchers and academics who could get acquainted with those computer languages, and then to the general public through the use of GUIs.

The computer has assimilated the architectural drawing in the same way that it has many other tasks and activities at work and at home. It isn't therefore strange, in relation to the history of this assimilation, that the first civil GUI Sketchpad, developed by Ivan Sutherland at MIT in 1963, was also the first Computer Aided Design (CAD) program. Drawing on the screen became from this point on just a useful metaphor, a simulation of the craft and process on which much of the discipline of architecture is based. Benjamin has also written that 'the ability to master certain tasks in a state of distraction proves that their solution has become a matter of habit.'[8] It was indeed through the use of habitual situations and metaphors in the GUIs that the commodified computer could be mass-marketed. It was also the means for marketing CAD to a profession based on the execution of processes and tasks 'in a state of distraction'.

From the 1960s to the 80s, that is, from the years of pioneering development of CAD to the decade in which it started being commercially introduced into architectural practices, computation and architectural drawing underwent a similar process of assimilation of one into the other: the drawing as a metaphor to be extended to other uses, and computation slowly creeping under the drawing's surface. If the way of introducing the computer as a useful appliance was to employ the trick of the habit, the essence of the GUI, the habitual technique for the last four centuries in architecture had been to draw. The initial process of electrification of the drafting board, which took place in the late 1960s and early 70s through digitalising tables, optic pens and other physical interfaces, gave way to the grafting of the drawing into the computer screen, and the transformation of the drawing into its computerised simulation.

From Ivan Sutherland's Sketchpad to the Virtual Reality Cave, the computational simulation of drawing and projection was characterised by the paradox of introducing the computer in architecture without actually introducing computation. Design through geometric representation, not through computation, remained at the centre of the architectural production process; the conservation of the drawing left the logic, rhetoric and myths of a way of yielding architecture based in the technological revolution of the Renaissance mostly unchallenged.

Deriving geometry through traditional drawing and doing it through computation, as in current modelling packages, are two radically different operations. Architecture has developed a practice of evaluating geometry in designs that is consistent with the techniques for producing it; at the moment we still evaluate computer-generated geometries through the criteria of drawn geometries. As a result we often praise the complexity of computer-drawn forms according to the virtuosic technique required to draw them manually.

The general tendency among many progressive practices developed around the 1990s has been to explore and use the computer as a tool, but its effect on a discipline heavily structured around the media of production has seldom been addressed. This purely instrumental use of the computer has too often resulted in the production of intricate geometries through whatever new digital instruments become available, which are justified only by their mere possibility. Without the evaluation criteria the new conditions may require, such geometries are still treated and valued in relation to traditional architectural representations, praising the capabilities of the machine to produce difficult drawings and at the same time inadvertently surrendering the understanding of the processes behind them.

Architects believe that they are still drawing, when the fact is that drawing has disappeared to become simply an interface of computation. If until recently architects were responsible for the technologies of architectural production, today's digital tools and techniques have been authored, as for example in the case of Bezier splines or Blinn shading, by engineers, mathematicians and hackers. In mistaking the creative work of the tool producer with that of the user-architect, the profession runs the risk of developing a discipline based on the consumption of the latest algorithmic technique or graphic software package and of having to keep pace with the developments of software fashion for designs to have 'the latest' geometrical flavour.

Architecture as a discipline seems to be rather oblivious to the logics and discourses of its new technologies, under which it is already operating. This blind spot is produced by habit and is the one McLuhan has identified in the myth of Narcissus, who is unable to recognise himself in his technological extensions. In the connection between architecture and electronic computation, it is this blind spot that is in acute need of study. The medium creates its ends, as much as an end creates its medium. We should perhaps wonder how this new medium affects the goals, purposes and judgment of architecture.

CYBERNETIC LOGICS: TELEOLOGY AND FEEDBACK

Many of the technologies and principles of contemporary computers were developed as part of cybernetics in the two decades following World War II. In effect, cybernetics recognised and unified concepts which had been put forward in the late eighteenth and first half of the nineteenth century, and were central to their scientific, economic, industrial and technological developments. These included Adam Smith's liberalist principles of the self-regulation of markets, John Stuart Mill's proposition of emergent properties, and particularly Charles Darwin's theory of evolution, as well as some of the technological developments associated with industrialisation such as automation and mass production. These concepts gave rise to systems with certain degrees of autonomy and decision-making capacity. In his essay sent to Darwin, the English naturalist Russell Wallace describes the struggle for existence through an illustrative simile:

> The action of this principle [the struggle for existence] is exactly like that of the steam engine, which checks and corrects any irregularities almost before they become evident; and in like manner no unbalanced deficiency in the animal kingdom can ever reach any conspicuous magnitude, because it would make itself felt at the very first step, by rendering existence difficult and extinction almost sure to follow.[9]

According to Gregory Bateson, Wallace was effectively proposing here the first cybernetic model, by comparing natural selection with the self-regulating circular train of causal events of the steam governor.[10]

Heinz von Foerster, cybernetician and editor of the transactions of the Macy Conferences, highlights circular causality as a unifying term of cybernetics:

> A concept, now closely allied to information theory, is the notion of circular causal processes. A state reproducing itself, like an organism, or a social system in equilibrium, or a physicochemical aggregate in a steady state, defied analysis until the simple notion of one dimensional cause-and-effect chains was replaced by the two-dimensional notion of a circular process.[11]

Paradoxically, these ideas were suggested for the first time at a point in the nineteenth century when the liberal humanist subject had become one of the elemental units of politics, economy and culture. They were the first symptoms of a current condition that Katherine Hayles has defined as 'post-human',[12] which is characterised by the breakdown of that same liberal subject, and is a result of the substitution of the individual self as source of control and decisions by the post-war identification with cybernetic mechanisms. In this 'post-human' situation the designer as a human author identifiable with the source of the purpose of designs has been literally taken out of the equation – out of the feedback loop – and substituted instead by a series of circular causal relations and iterative accumulations of corrections and accidents. In this substitution the distinctions between natural and artificial cease to exist when it comes to the origins and reasons of objects; a segmented worm, a building or an art object could, in principle, be explained as the results of ecological, cultural or neural interactions.

This distinction between natural and artificial is an old one. In the second book of *The Physics*, Aristotle begins differentiating between nature and artifice; natural are those things which have the principle of motion and of 'stationariness' within themselves, whereas products of art have no innate impulse to change.[13]

Furthermore, knowledge of something is, since Aristotle, seen as a grasping 'why' – that is, an understanding of its primary cause. In the case of artificial objects and processes that means understanding their material causes, their origins in a person or 'living creature' and their ends or purposes.[14]

The shock produced by the appearance of components of a cybernetic discourse in the nineteenth century was a result of their challenge to a concept of design widely understood as an end, intention or purpose of a thing originated in a person or 'living creature'. In his teleological argument, or 'argument from design', for the existence of God, the eighteenth-century theologian William Paley extended Thomas Aquinas' reading of Aristotle and argued, through the simile of a watch implying a watchmaker, that since the world seemed designed, there had to be a designer, a purpose or intention which originated outside the world itself. The commotion caused by Darwin's work, which, as we have mentioned, can be seen as cybernetic in retrospect, was the consequence of the blow suggested by the substitution of a designer God by the mechanical, blind processes of iterative reproduction and selection.

AUTOMATION OF THOUGHT

If exorcising the circle from logic had been the pursuit for a whole century of development of formal logic, which culminated in Bertrand Russell and Alfred North Whitehead's *Principia Mathematica*, in 1931 Kurt Gödel finally demonstrated the impossibility of the attempt and showed that anyone trying to do so would be caught in a circular argument.[15] Strangely enough, this impossibility of eradicating circularity from logic was what allowed the automation of logical thought. In an expansion of Gödel's work, mathematician Alan Turing conceived a conceptual device which operated on recursive or circular functions, showing that, as von Neumann pointed out, mathematical logic could be treated from the point of view of automata.[16] Turing machines, as the abstractions behind digital computers are known, are hypothetical devices made of an infinite 'text' or string of symbols and the rules for reading, deleting and writing that text. The significance of this is summarised in media theorist Friedrich Kittler's observation that for the first time, and in contrast to all historical writing (and drawing) tools, texts in the forms of digital codes are able to write and read themselves.[17]

Thus, in the circular recursion of its operations the computer incarnates the same mechanisms that allowed the automation and control of work in the steam engine's governor and the substitution of divine design by the accumulation and selection of accidents in Darwinian evolution. Whereas usually this circularity is subdued to the simulation of processes that are essentially linear, in some specific cases circular agency is made explicit. In genetic algorithms – one of the most common exponents of evolutionary, self-organising or adaptive algorithms – portions of the 'text' that form the memory of the computer are subjected to operations analogous to those of evolution, and accordingly they are re-written (re-produced) or otherwise erased. At a more prosaic level, the writing of this very text in a word processor is the result of a (circular) interaction between myself as a writer and the agency of the spell-checker, which reads, compares, suggests and often automatically modifies the text.

Explicitly or implicitly, the principles of autonomy and agency – and their challenge to concepts of origin, nature and authorship – are at the core of computation. The situation produced by generation through algorithms is one in which the relationship back to an author from a design, its 'causes' in the Aristotelian sense, are complicated by the mediating agency of the computer. If projection implied a point of view (total or fragmented), a mechanism from which one sees and projects, computation means a mechanism that sees; it entails the automation of vision, interpretation and intention that were previously made explicit and canalised by the perspective apparatus.

DENDROID

Dendroid is an experiment I have been developing in collaboration with Swedish artist Arijana Kajfes, which started from our common interest in the work of Gordon Pask and second-order cybernetics in general, and has evolved during the last two years from the production of simple shapes through electrochemical reactions into an elemental analog computer, forming part of a number of installations and exhibitions. In the particular configuration presented here, Dendroid is used for computing geometrical projections such as perspectives, plans or elevations as a sort of computational counterpart to the perspective machines of Dürer or Brunelleschi.

Dendroid is based on work carried out by Gordon Pask during the late 1950s and early 60s on electrochemical computing devices with emerging sensory capabilities. The essential description of his work appeared in his paper with the very descriptive title 'Physical Analogues to the Growth of a Concept', given at a Mechanization of Thought Processes symposium in London in 1958[18] and in *An Approach to Cybernetics*.[19] Chemical computers arise from the possibility of 'growing' active evolutionary networks by electrochemical processes. These trainable machines can improve on their own initial designs by altering their decision functions upon evaluation of past performance, to the degree that Pask's final electrochemical contrivances were capable of defining their own relevant perceptions and actions themselves.

The experiments which Pask carried out in electrochemical assemblages, through the early and mid-1950s, with the intention of constructing an analogue control system, were based on older 'iron-wire' neural models. Similar to those that R.S. Lillie developed in the first quarter of the twentieth century, they originated in the morphological and functional analogies between the growth of dendrites, or branch-like structures, in electrolytic processes and in neurons.

With the increasing information-processing capability of the digital computer in the mid-1960s, the radically different technology of the chemical computer fell into disregard. Pask's devices are fascinating for a number of reasons. First, they belong to a tradition of cybernetics which employs machines as rhetorical arguments, with early examples such as Norbert Wiener's self-steered 'moth-bug' robot or Ross Ashby's 'homeostat' from 1940. Second, in the openness of its operations the chemical computer combines morphological, material and informational processes in mutually affecting, circular causal relations. Last, the chemical computer addresses the epistemological limitations of computation as symbol-manipulation and proposes a strategy for transcending them by allowing free connections and mappings between the symbolic and the material world.

In his analysis of Piero de la Francesca's 'Altro Modo' or 'Other Method' perspective, Robin Evans defends these types of technological 'dead ends'. What

13.1 >Information>
structure>information.

Information in the form
of electric impulses
controls the formation of
metal threads in a
metallic salt solution,
which in return modify
the way that information
flows through them: the
longer the thread between
two points (a cathode and
any of the anodes), the
smaller the electric
resistance and the
reduction of the signal
between them.

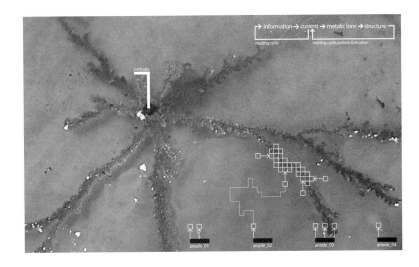

13.2 >Projective
transformations in the
dendritic array.

A 4X4 matrix – identical
to those used in computer
graphics for the
computation of
perspectives,
axonometrics, plans or
elevations has been
mapped into the array of
anodes and cathodes of
the Dendroid system.
Physical events become
computational events, as
information is
transformed by the analog
morphology and structure
of the dendrites.

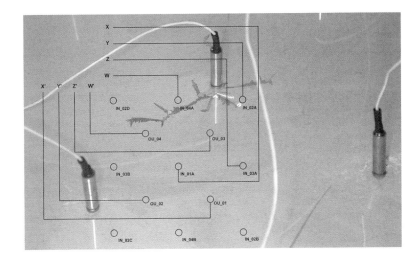

13.3 >Dendroid: 3D
transformation matrix.

The diagrams represent
matrix values equivalent
to those used in the
transformations performed
by the electrolytic cell:
on the left of each
diagram is represented
the input vector (x, y,
z, w); on the bottom, the
output or transformed
vector (x',y',z',w').
The sizes of the circles
indicate the values in
the transformation
matrix, or the analog
values of the resistances
between electrodes. The
set of possible growth
patterns of Dendroid
covers all possible 3D
projections perspective
and planar some of which
are seldom used in
architecture.

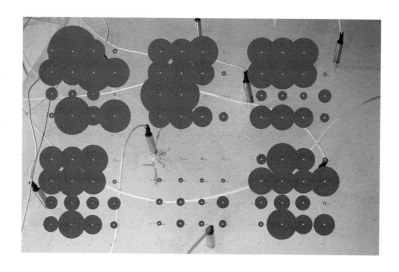

13.4 >Transformations
of a cube through the
electrochemical hardware.

The drawing shows the
geometric data of a cube,
sent and received back
after going through
the electrochemical
device. The lines that
join the vertices of
the cubes, and their
transformations, can be
understood as the journey
of the geometry through
the dendritic computer.

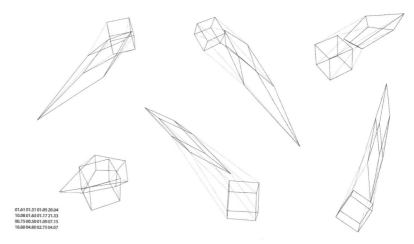

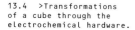

01.61 01.51 01.05 20.04
10.08 01.63 01.17 21.33
00.75 00.50 01.00 07.15
10.88 04.80 02.75 04.07

13.5 >Retinal wiring.

Dendroid connected to light sensor array, an assembly developed together with artist Arijana Kajfes at the Smart Studio, Interactive Institute. In this case the dendritic device works as a recorder of the information received from the light sensors. The changes of light in the space surrounding the machine affect the very slow build-up and growth of the dendritic structures, in a form analogous with the growth and wiring of neurons involved in the processing of vision in the eye and the brain.

Sigfried Giedion dispatched as 'transitory phenomena', safely erasable from the annals of progressive history, Evans vindicates, arguing that '[they] may be of interest because they define where things were given up, suspended, neglected, or left incomplete. They may also reveal a good deal about what was pursued by contrast with what was not.'[20] In the cybernetic tradition of machines as articulations of concepts, and through reference to the similar use of embodied rhetoric in the artefacts and explanations of Renaissance perspective methods, Dendroid addresses the complicated relations between the architectural drawing and computation.

The device consists of an electrochemical bath, a microcontroller circuit and software running on a standard computer. In this electrochemical hardware, the system does the typical transformations involved in projective geometry and characteristic of CAD programs – such as rotation, scaling, and all the different types of parallel and perspective projections. In Dendroid, geometric data in the form of three-dimensional vectors (X, Y, Z) is translated into electric signals which pass through the dendrites in the electrolytic bath, are then read, and are subsequently translated again into geometric information. Signal transformations are equated to geometrical transformations.

The device can work in two forms: it can either be trained, so if initially fed with a set of geometric transformations, such as those corresponding to architectural drawings it can be indoctrinated to produce the standard, average architectural projective transformation; alternatively it can be left to grow arbitrarily, without any learning – in which case, after a period of formation and growth, the device can be used to perform geometrical transformations. This turns the setup in to a serendipitous machine, suggesting different 3-D transformations according to the growth patterns of the dendritic machine.

In a more general sense, Dendroid can be used as an analogue of a number of other circular causal processes, in particular those implying positive feedback and growth. Magorah Maruyama explained in 1963 the morphogenetic properties of what he called 'deviation-amplifying mutual causal process', which encourage the growth of differences and the development of structure through an increase in heterogeneity – in opposition to negative feedback, which inhibits growth and smoothes out disparities. Besides identifying those processes which yield increasing quantities of feedback to the system, Maruyama studied their relationships to the morphological growth of cities, settlements, economies and evolutionary processes in general.[21] After all, Pask had already established the generative analogy between material, thermodynamic and informational processes involved in the growth of metallic threads and those involved in the growth of a concept.

1   >Marshall McLuhan, 'The Gadget Lover, Narcissus as Narcosis' in *Understanding Media, The Extensions of Man*, London: Routledge, 1964, pp. 46–52.
2   >Adrian Forty, 'Language and Drawing' in *Words and Buildings*, London: Thames & Hudson, 2000, p. 30.
3   >Robert Tavernor, *On Alberti and the Art of Building*, New Haven: Yale University Press, 1999, p. 43.
4   >Marshall McLuhan, 'Media Hot and Cold' in McLuhan, *op. cit.*, p. 27.
5   >Walter Benjamin, *The Work of Art in the Age of Mechanical Reproduction*, section XI. <http://bid.berkeley.edu/bidclass/readings/benjamin.html> accessed 24 October 2005.
6   >John von Neumann, *Theory of Self-Reproducing Automata* (edited and completed by Arthur W. Burks), Urbana, Illinois: University of Illinois Press, 1966, p. 9.
7   >Friedrich Kittler, 'There is No Software' in John Johnston (ed.), *Literature Media Information Systems*, Amsterdam: G+B Arts International, 1997, p. 150.
8   >Walter Benjamin, *op. cit.*, section XV.
9   >Russell Wallace quoted in Gregory Bateson, 'Conscious Purpose Versus Nature' in *Steps to an Ecology of Mind*, Chicago: University of Chicago Press, 1972, p. 434.
10   >*Ibid.*, p. 434.
11   >Heinz von Foerster, 'A Note by the Editors' in *Cybernetics, Circular Causal and Feedback Mechanisms in Biological and Social Systems, Transactions of the Ninth Conference, March 20–21, 1951*, New York: Josiah J. Macy, Jr. Foundation, 1953, p. xiv.
12   >N. Katherine Hayles, *How We Became Posthuman: Virtual Bodies in Cybernetics, Literature and Informatics*, Chicago: University of Chicago Press, 1999.
13   >Aristotle, *Physics, Book II, Part 1*, translated by R. P. Hardie and R. K. Gaye, <http://classics.mit.edu/Aristotle/physics.html> accessed 24 October 2005.
14   >Aristotle, *Physics, Book II, Part 3, op. cit.*
15   >Douglas R. Hofstadter, *Gödel, Escher, Bach: an Eternal Golden Braid*, London: Penguin Books, 1980, pp. 21–8.
16   >John von Neumann, *op. cit.*
17   >Friedrich Kittler, *op. cit.*, p. 147.
18   >Another reference can be found in Peter Cariani, 'To Evolve an Ear: Epistemological Implications of Gordon Pask's Electrochemical Devices', in *Systems Research* 1993; 10 (3), pp. 19–33.
19   >Gordon Pask, *An Approach to Cybernetics*, London: Hutchinson & Co Ltd, 1961, p. 105.
20   >Robin Evans, *The Projective Cast: Architecture and its Three Geometries*, Cambridge, Massachusetts: The MIT Press, 1995, p. 158.
21   >Magorah Maruyama, 'The Second Cybernetics: Deviation-amplifying Mutual Causal Processes' in *American Scientist 51*, June 1963, pp. 164–79.

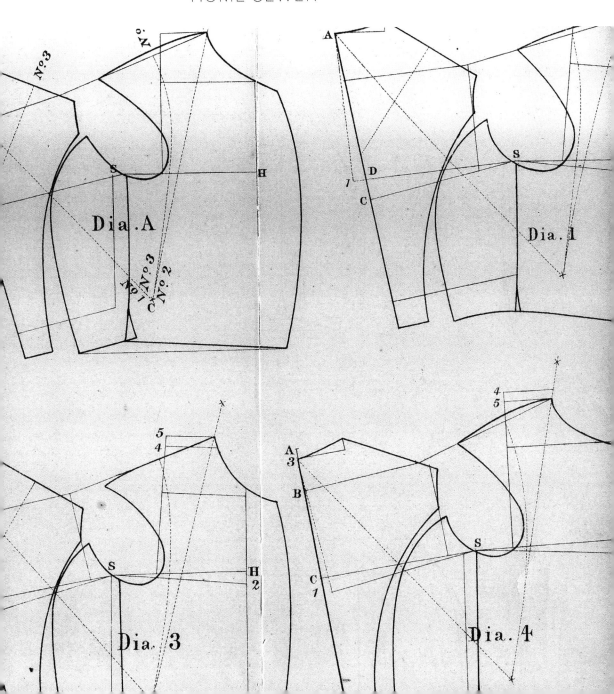

14.1 >The variation of
patterns generated by the
West End Tailoring System
for figures with
abnormalities.

Plate 18: Adaptation of
the system to
admeasurement, *The West
End System: A Scientific
and Practical Method of
Cutting all Kinds of
Garments.*

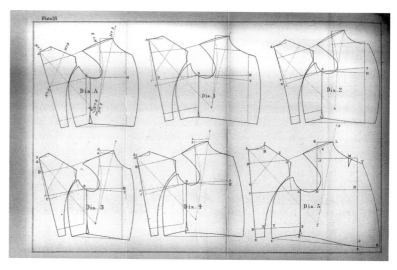

*There, where he had left plain cuttings of silk – there lay the most beautifullest coat and
embroidered satin waistcoat that were ever worn by the Mayor of Gloucester.*[1]

A process or methodology of designing and production is common to any creative
practice – the result of which is an article that is often inhabited, experienced and
used without reference to how it was made.

Once the article has been made and exists as an object it is easy to perceive
the production process purely as a direct transfer from the initial design into a
physical object. This perception would require complete control over the material
world, and in reality the manner in which the initial design is developed into a
physical article is controlled by material and economic limitations as well as
cultural and personal persuasions. Production of a particular article could occur in
variety of ways, and because the production process influences the very existence
and nature of the articles made the choice of a production route is not neutral.

Some creative practices aim to make articles that are not one-off, but that
will be reproduced many times. Within this type of practice the commercial
manufacturer develops the process to ensure cost effectiveness, and the quality
and similarity of the reproduced articles. The article itself loses its status and a
distance is created between the manufacturer and their product.

Bespoke creative processes tend to place emphasis on producing a unique
article, and methods of design and production must allow for modification in order
to incorporate the differences, or develop ways that production can be based on a
set number of variables which parametrically alter the design. These approaches
cater more easily for non-standard situations and produce articles that can relate
to environments which are not man-made, and so cannot so easily be
standardised. A piece of architecture and its relationship with the proposed site is
just such a case, where pragmatic issues due to the site may determine how the
building is designed and how it can be constructed.

Bespoke tailoring produces articles of clothing for specific clients who provide unique sites for these fabric constructions. Relationships between a garment and the body are very intimate, and the shapes and forms of an individual's figure are a unique part of the client's identity which the garment adds to once it is worn. Therefore the production of bespoke garments requires the client's body to be mapped – sometimes in extraordinary ways. By presenting technical texts and first-hand experiences of two techniques of bespoke sewing, a comparison can be made between different methodologies of construction. The two systems examined here – the Gentleman's Tailor sewing for the male figure, and the Home Sewer sewing for herself – act as examples of the manner in which construction processes in all creative practices greatly influence an article's outcome.

TWO PRACTICES

14.2   >Frederick T. Prewett, the originator of the West End Tailoring System.

Front insert: *The West End System.*

In the tailor's shop in Westgate Street the embroidered silk and satin lay cut upon the table – one and twenty button holes – and who would come to sew them, when the window was barred and the door locked?[2]

As with any form of creative process the act of creation is only formalised as a *practice* by methodologies that aim to circumscribe the perameters and the nature of the craft. These provide a structure through which the creative process can be learnt and repeated, and through which specific products can be generated to a predetermined degree of quality. Some methodologies have been set out in books as text and diagrams, suggesting that a successful garment can be achieved by following such a description.

The methodological practices of the Gentleman's Tailor and the practice of a Home Sewer are set up in two instruction books: *The West End Tailoring System* by Edward Giles[3] and *The Complete Book of Tailoring for Women Who Like to Sew* by Adele Margolis.[4] The two practices chosen are not just divided by gender and by the identity of the figures they sew for, but by social and economic factors that also inform the process of construction. The woman creates clothes for herself, often to achieve fashion at a lower price than the High Street, and the Gentleman pays another to make his clothes for him as an exclusive service.

The West End Tailoring System was written as a manual for a methodology of Gentleman's Tailoring which was first proposed in 1890. Chapter One draws our attention to the need to follow every step in order to produce a good result:

> Success can only be obtained or hoped for by strict attention to the various details in a system, amongst which correct measurement is not the least important'[5]

The Complete Book of Tailoring for Women Who Like to Sew takes on a completely different tone as it is directed at a very different type of sewer. It was written much later than the *West End Tailoring System* in the 1960s, when women were encouraged to be as self-sufficient as possible. It is a guide to the Home Sewer to caution and direct her in the appropriateness of her garments. In contrast to the *West End Tailoring System* it does not preach to the third person but aims to befriend and cajole the reader into a particular method of working:

> What a wonderful state of affairs when the pattern and the fabric look as if they were made for one another and both are right for you! To achieve such a happy union you must know something about patterns, something about fabrics and something about what's for you.[6]

To complete the investigation of the two practices I spent some time with Mr. Connock from Connock and Lockie Tailors and drew from my own experience of my mother and my late grandmother making garments for themselves and their families.

The tailors Connock and Lockie had a shop on Sicilian Avenue in London that traded for just over 100 years. Their practice was based on a method that was very similar to the West End Tailoring System. Mr. Connock showed me their instruction book, kept in the shop for everyone's reference. The system is set out as an established series of procedures, adherence to which is clearly paramount in gaining the status of a professional tailor, and which produces results that conform to an expected quality.

In Connock and Lockie there were cutting tables, each with its own equipment. Each had a Tailor's 'Ham', a roll of pattern paper, tailor's chalk and pins in a tray. Tools were named to identify their specific role as a third object to regulate the interaction of the hands and the fabric, giving the uncertain foldings and formings of a direct sewing process a precise action. Their identification enables a clear description of the sequential process required to complete a garment. Emphasis is placed on perfecting particular skills in order to gain an increasing control over the manipulated surface.

The cutting tables at Connock and Lockie were at the back of the shop, not hidden away but visible from the shop window. They were proud that they were still traditional tailors and that everything was made in-house.

Sewing – taught to me by my mother, as she was by hers – has always seemed to me a very intuitive action, where a manipulation of the fabric reacts to previous manipulations. It is an iterative process, which creates a garment. The Home Sewer's method of sewing is never a standard procedure. Every time it is not only a one-off garment but also a one-off series of actions.

In instruction books images of the Home Sewer somehow attempt to elevate her into a position of a professional, with her own room, tools in a work box, hooks and shelves to house the equipment needed.

The McCall's sewing manual, *Sewing in Colour*, suggests:

A pleasant place to work and the correct tools are a 'must' for sewing enjoyment. Try to establish a sewing centre in your home.[7]

The Home Sewer's equipment is not, as suggested by instruction books, permanently laid out on display like the Gentleman's Tailors'. Although my mother and grandmother were frequent sewers they never had a designated space for sewing equipment. This was not because there was no spare room for a sewing space. The sewing machine may generate, mend and alter a large percentage of the fabric surfaces that are in the house, but it is just a means to an end. The Home Sewer's relationship with the sewing machine is not one of awe, as depicted by so many advertisements. Her understanding of the sewing machine is not as a tool that conforms to a standard, but as a tool whose limits in production are to be explored. She understands the imperfections of her tool and can adjust for them. Each time a tool is used she re-evaluates its potential, re-teaching herself how to use it.

The Home Sewer brings together the material and tools within the domestic space to create a site for fabrication. When making curtains my mother's sewing machine moves into the room for which the curtains are being made. The floor of the room is commandeered, the fabric is laid out and the furniture pushed back. The 'sharp scissors' are taken from the cutlery drawer in the kitchen, and the 'pin tin' from the top drawer in the sitting room chest.

In the sitting room chest of drawers a lot of sewing equipment is stored alongside the family photos in the second drawer down, but the arrangement relates only occasionally to the sewing books' suggested pieces of equipment. My mother's sewing equipment is set out in a series of boxes, tins and tubs. These containers might suggest a series of categorisations, but even as a box to hold buttons is created its purpose morphs and the categories become indistinct as buckles, two pins and a needle are added.

The system continuously expands and is modified, adding layer upon layer of intended systems that are always subverted. Unlike the Gentleman's Tailor's prescribed set of relationships, my mother's sewing room is a dynamic complex system of parts that are drawn together for a moment to initiate a change. Her workspace is constantly pieced together and then returned to a space for others. She becomes almost nomadic in her travels through the domestic 'world'. This special relationship between the process of creating and exploring the site of the intended article seems important for the Home Sewer in order for her to translate her desires into a completed form. The Home Sewer submerges herself in all references to the desired article in order to bring together the creation.

The Home Sewer's relationship is with the sewn surface, and so she places little emphasis on the methodology used. Her process is not a premeditated manipulation, but one that occurs in order to achieve a particular result. The production of sewn surfaces is not done for status or for the respect of others, which she could obtain as a designer. It is an intense, almost frightening, conversation with herself, focusing into and beyond her creation as a form of liberation.

While my grandmother was alive I asked to borrow from her extensive collection of books on sewing. She told me to keep them as she had never read any of them and certainly wouldn't now. The Home Sewer's actions are never intended to be repeated and her skills are never easily explained as a set of instructions. In contrast, the Tailor's practice has established itself as a more reproducible form of production through its precise documentation and execution.

TWO METHODOLOGIES

14.3 >Observed abnormalities.

Page 18: *The West End System.*

Round Shoulders	by R S.	Hollow Back	by H B.
High Shoulders	,, H. S.	Large Blades	,, L B.
Low Shoulders	,, L S.	Flat Blades	,, F B.
Forward Shoulders	,, F S.	Long Neck	,, L N.
Stooping	,, S.	Short Neck	,, S N.
Extra Erect	,, E E.	Prominent Hips	,, P H.
Full Chest	,, F C.	Flat Seat	,, F S.
Narrow Chest	,, N C.	Corpulent in Front	,, C F.

The stitches of those button-holes were so neat – so neat I wonder how they could be stitched by an old man with spectacles. The stitches of those buttonholes were so small – so small they looked as if they had been made by little mice.[8]

The approaches of the two practices to the materials they work with, both the client's figures and the way in which they control or utilise the nature of the fabric, can be seen to be determined by each sewer's relationship to the end user. The Gentleman's Tailor distances himself from any reference to the client's body, generating a system that requires the minimum information to produce a satisfactorily fitting garment. The Home Sewer goes on an elusive quest to complete her identity. She translates her search into her sewing systems, which cause her to incorporate the materiality of the fabric and the forms of her body into the sewn article in a very direct way.

THE GENTLEMAN'S TAILOR

The first chapter of the *West End Tailoring System* sets up the procedure of fitting a Gentleman. Six measurements are given that 'students' of the system must take during fitting:

1) The shoulder width.
2) The length from the neckline to the waist.
3) The height.
4) The syre (length from the waist to the floor).
5) The breast circumference.
6) The waist circumference.[9]

The dimensions are then used as the starting point for the shape of each fabric piece, which is drawn in chalk onto the flat cloth. These shapes are then cut out to form the garment.

Not only does the Tailor transfer the length dimensions directly onto the pressed fabric and unravel circumferences into it, but he also uses the proportions of these critical dimensions to extrapolate the outlines of each flat piece of fabric. Each new line the Tailor generates from his geometrical construction takes him further and further away from the starting dimensions. The Tailor abstracts these corporeal measurements into a purely mathematical world, eliminating references to the body of the client. The lines forming each fabric piece are given letters, removing them from the anatomical feature they are intended to lie against:

Make from I to J and from L to M one-sixth of the syre measure, square with the line BK. Form the sleeve head by drawing the curve from B through J and to K. Draw the line K G square with the line K C. Arc from G to H the width of the sleeve required at the hand; now halve the angle of the square at C with the right arm of the square intercepting D; and draw the lines H G and H D.[10]

The diagrams presented in the *West End Tailoring System* illustrate the shapes of each piece of fabric with a series of construction lines dotted in against the actual outlines of each. They are considered very simply as geometrical constructions, totally abstracted from the unpredictability of the body, and do not depict the real nature of the fabric. This system of extrapolation from a set of measurements is based on the proportions of a standard figure and allows the Tailor to require only the minimum amount of information about the individual client's figure in order to generate the patterns.

The Gentleman Tailor's system relies on the fabric being perfectly flat and the construction of the outline of each piece aligning perfectly with the grain of the fabric. However, the fabric is never perfectly flat as warp and weft threads move easily in relationship to one another, and so the fabric challenges the Tailor's system of construction. In order for the Tailor to implement his system, he continuously attempts to return the fabric back to a two-dimensional surface by constantly ironing and pressing the fabric under construction.

The Tailor does not keep material in stock and the fabrics used to make a Gentleman's suit are chosen by the client in consultation with the Tailor and his book of swatches. The material for each garment is specially ordered and factory-made as separate runs, which means that there is a huge wastage of material in cutting out a suit and this is reflected in the cost of the bespoke garment.

Swatches of fabric are regimented families of a particular pattern and weight in varying shades of colour. These small samples reduce the Gentleman's Tailor's contact with the actual material, allowing him to operate within his system that idealises the fabric as a two-dimensional flat component.

Once completed, the lounge or dinner jacket could be read as a covering that breaks the view to the body, providing not a suggestion of what is behind the garment but a presentation of what should be. The resulting shape of the suit depends on how the system has translated the critical dimensions taken by the Tailor. The outline of the fabric pieces, once cut and sewn, together cause each piece to hang against the Gentleman's figure forming a curtain-like covering to the client's body. The critical measurements inform how the pieces fall in relationship to one another and how the shape of the seams constructs the outline of the garment. The fabric itself becomes simply a filling-in of a silhouette.

The garment is fastened to the body at points such as the collars and cuffs, and across the shoulders. These points relate to the critical set of dimensions taken during fitting. Collars and cuffs form a very angular relationship to the man's flesh, creating a garment not as a secondary skin but as a well-defined 'other surface' with clear boundaries between flesh and fabric. In between these moments of fitted fabric there is a leap of the system's own generation, a construction of what should be there. This system produces garments that offer a uniformity of appearance for gentlemen.

Such a rigorous and tightly controlled procedure for creating clothing creates a very formal interaction between the Gentleman and his Tailor, where the Tailor must deny any existence of physical interactions in order to respect the client. Edward Giles warns the student of the West End System against clients who 'absurdly draw in their waists and inflate their chests'[11] during fittings, which could cause inaccurate dimensions to be taken. During fitting, the client's masculinity is being confronted and analysed by another man. His identity is being measured up against the standards the Tailor subscribes to. In this transaction the client is consciously looking to another to make something that confirms his identity as part of male society.

Mr. Connock told me that the garments created should not fit the client in the fitting room; if they do, then the garments are not well made. Body heat is the final pressing of the garments and, as observed by the *West End Tailoring System*, the Gentleman's posture changes from its most natural one during the fitting process. This sense of aiming to miss the Gentleman's presented physicality suggests a subtle way of achieving a particular fit that only reveals itself after the suit has been worn for several days. That way, the Tailor is never present for the union when the suit and body fully acknowledge each other.

THE HOME SEWER

My mother's decisions seem to start with the fabric. The process of finding fabric she likes is so unpredictable that if she finds some she will purchase it without necessarily having a garment in mind. In the world of department store fabrics there are few standard lines, and the wide range of available colours and textures are constantly changing. Fabric trades between my mother and grandmother would occur if one party felt that an unused piece of material would be more useful to the other.

The Home Sewer's purchase of fabrics is purely based on a sensual attraction and it is often completely separated from the idea of making a particular garment, whereas the Gentleman is choosing his fabric to create a very specific item of clothing. My mother will buy 'end of rolls' at a cut price, which limit creative possibilities by their size, or she will purchase a length of fabric and put it in the fabric chest until a pattern is found that might work with it. Fabrics are stored as a treasure of surfaces that she can constantly rework in her mind. She can use the material many times over in her head, but when the moment comes for her to make the first cut into the fabric it is a sacrilege and there is huge anxiety that she is doing the fabric justice.

The physical difference between these two fabrication systems is that if a woman is sewing for herself, it is very difficult for her to fit herself. Therefore, the method to create patterns proposed by Adele Margolis is to use a dressmaker's dummy. This is a static model, made in the size and shape of the woman's torso and it allows the Home Sewer to project her own image onto the dummy as a substitute for her own body. She is being asked to place herself in the position of the observer, liberating herself for a moment from her own physicality.

The dummy should be marked along certain lines with a black tape forming a grid of intersections across the torso. These lines can then be read through the tailoring paper, which is used to create a pattern. The grid marks out the dummy like a piece of landscape that the Home Sewer explores, and it guides the location of seams and how pieces of fabric might join together against the torso.

The Home Sewer works in three dimensions, creating a paper surface that is flattened against the dummy by making intuitive cuts and folds as reactions to the form of this terrain. As the dummy does not describe the entirety of the female body, areas such as the skirt or sleeves become falls of fabric that have to be controlled by seams on the torso.

Unfolding and flattening the paper directly converts the three-dimensional shape that the sewer has created, with all its dimensions and intricacies, to a two-dimensional pattern. This method does not reference any geometrical system or ideal standardisation; it is not a science that determines the placement of the seams. It makes the creation of a garment a more visual and tactile conception based on the creation of form. Using the Home Sewer's methodology the design and manufacture of a garment's pattern becomes incorporated into the same action.

By the nature of her system of pattern-creation the Home Sewer makes a more fitted garment where darts and tucks are placed to lose the fullness of the fabric and draw it into the natural curves of the female body. The use of this system creates garments that tightly describe the female figure and become a secondary skin, as implied by Georgina Howell in her description of Azzedine Alaia's designs:

> Just as a women's body is a network of surface tensions, hard here, soft there, so Azzedine Alaia's clothes are a force field of give and resistance.[12]

The Home Sewer is aware of the connections, not the divisions, between herself and the environment she uses and creates. Her appearance is a combination of her own form and a reproduction of her own form, allowing her to disappear into an ambiguous surface of body and fabric.

The finished garment rarely lives up to my mother's expectations and will always go through a series of adjustments. Amendments can range from tightening the darts to re-sitting a sleeve in the shoulder, to remove excess fabric on the underarm. From my own experience the process of such a manoeuvre is incredibly complex and the more times the fabric pieces are taken apart and reassembled the more the fabric is distorted by the inserted tensions. The fabric becomes increasingly punctured and frayed by holes from the sewing machine's needle. This means that re-sewing becomes increasingly messy and complicated, by multiplying the number of loose threads, crumpled fabrics and interfacings. These amendments become a catastrophe of disorder for which the remedy can only be a series of iterations that slowly resolve the complexity. Large sections in women's sewing books are given over to advising remedies so that such undesired distortions do not develop in the worn garment:

> When the shoulder seam is moved forward, the front is shortened while the back is lengthened. When the side seam of the skirt is adjusted, what is taken off the front may be added to the back and visa versa.[13]

Buying new fabric is only the beginning of the interaction that the Home Sewer has with material. Her contact with garments, linen and soft furnishings continues in their need to be cleaned, mended and replaced as part of maintaining a domestic system. My mother has an established cycle of reusing fabrics where they reappear in different guises. She takes clothes apart; an old shirt might become a pattern for another, and old jumpers are sewn into hot water bottle covers. Her fabric chest contains collars that have been removed from dresses in order to update their looks, and cut-off hems from skirts that have been outgrown by my elder sister and re-fitted for me.

Throughout this cycle the one thing that is maintained is the material. Rarely is a piece of fabric thrown away; at worst it is donated to a charity shop or reduced to a cleaning rag. In contrast to the Tailor's, my mother's system is one of frugality where the constant possession of a fabric surface becomes a focal point in recreating or appropriating the material she sews.

THE END PRODUCT

14.4 >Introduction to the ninth edition of the *West End Tailoring System*.

> In conclusion, we have only to remark that with whatever amount of approbation or censure our united though humble effort to instruct the Trade may be rewarded, time alone can tell. The result we are content to abide. At the same time we are fully cognizant of the comparative great intelligence of the members of our profession, and we are thoroughly convinced they will readily appreciate any earnest and sincere endeavour to increase and disseminate a knowledge of our Art. With this conviction on our minds we submit our work, with some degree of pride and confidence, to the judgment of the Trade,
>
> And subscribe ourselves, most respectfully,
>
> THE AUTHORS.

Everything was finished except just one single cherry-coloured button-hole and where that button hole was wanting there was pinned a scrap of paper with these words – in little tiny weeny writing

NO MORE TWIST[14]

The Gentleman's Tailor's sewing practice starts with very few parameters which are used to create a complex system. It has the advantage of being a fully understood and documented process, and because the craft is repeated again and again proficiency with the system produces a sophisticated result in a predictable amount of time. The Tailor's system is carefully described so that it is comprehensible to both the Gentleman and to the Tailor. It is a form of contract between the two.

The Home Sewer's technique is a constant cycle of learning and re-learning different methods of construction, and so the production process is not assured of a successful conclusion. The creation of a garment becomes incomprehensible and indivisible into separate processes. Each construction is an experiment to find the most appropriate way of forming the garment, and this simultaneous act of design and construction can continue indefinitely. The Home Sewer can, however, produce extraordinary results, which create a woman's own sense of identity and challenge the established processes of garment creation using the potential of the material and tools to the full.

The practice of the Home Sewer has survived mass production precisely because every figure is different and her constant tactical reassessing of the fabric and figure appropriates the garment to her own body.

The Tailor's professionalism and separation from the client causes a curious condition whereby the system attempts to create products from materials and for sites that deviate noticeably from the system's imposed ideals. His use of a standard relationship between his critical measurements means that the system itself has to be constantly protected from the variable nature of the material and site, and this causes separations between the figure and the generated garment. The Tailor's idea of a normal figure fills the place of parameters that have not been considered, and so produces a more stable outcome. He is not seeking to take on board every characteristic of the client, and the end garment is a device that enables the Gentleman to be seen to conform with his own contemporaries.

The methodology for the Gentleman's Tailor has established a system that is less questioning of the sewing process used, and so the development of the art of sewing is not so readily explored. The Home Sewer's outcome is unpredictable in the type of result and in its quality, as it is based on multiple sets of parameters which cause the product to change with every small fluctuation. The parameters observed are all seen as positive indicators of individuality, and as such they are pulled together to create an object based on them. The Home Sewer's parameters do not have any standards as a point of reference, so there is less control and this tends to create more diverse garments.

These two systems for dealing with materials and sites, which are not so easily standardised, present ways in which, to varying degrees, individuality can be incorporated into a production system. Similar methodologies can be seen in other creative practices.

A formalised methodology such as the Tailor's slows technological development over time. In the construction industry, where new technologies and materials will be available and new social and cultural issues will arise, development and chances for change in the design processes should not be lost through standardisation of process and product. The efficiency the Tailor offers is essentially one of time – but it is at the expense of materials and site, which must be selected carefully for this design system to operate.

Despite the unpredictability of the Home Sewer's less-prescribed approach, she offers a methodology which suggests that a deeper understanding of materials, site and methods of construction allow for their efficient use. The close collaboration of designers and makers offers the chance to produce appropriate designs that can utilise more demanding restrictions on materials and site, and give an increased sense of identity to the inhabitants.

1   >Beatrix Potter, 'The Tailor of Gloucester' in *The Tales from Beatrix Potter*, London: Frederick Warne, 1984, p. 41.
2   >Beatrix Potter, *op. cit.*, p. 24.
3   >Edward Giles, *The West End Tailoring System; a Scientific and Practical Method of Cutting*, London: F.T. Prewitt, 1890.
4   >Adele P. Margolis, *The Complete Book of Tailoring for Women Who Like to Sew*, London: Mills & Boon, 1964.
5   >Edward Giles, *op. cit.*, p. 16.
6   >Adele P. Margolis, *op. cit.*, p. 31.
7   >Paul Hamlyn, *McCall's Sewing in Colour*, London, New York, Sydney, Toronto: The Hamlyn Publishing Group Ltd, 1969, p. 60.
8   >Beatrix Potter, *op. cit.*, pp. 42–3.
9   >Edward Giles, *op. cit.*, p. 16.
10   >*Ibid.*, p. 28.
11   >*Ibid.*, p. 18.
12   >Georgina Howell cited in *Fabric of Vision: Dress and Drapery in Painting*, The National Gallery (ex. cat.), Curator: Anne Hollender, 19 June – 8 September 2002.
13   >Adele P. Margolis, *op. cit.*, p. 129.
14   >Beatrix Potter, *op. cit.*, p. 41.

15.1   >*20:50* (1987).

20:50 is probably Richard Wilson's best-known work. It was first installed in Matt's Gallery, London, in 1986, where Charles Saatchi saw it and commissioned it for his Boundary Road gallery in 1991.

Katie Lloyd Thomas: You have tended to describe the oil used in *20:50* in terms of its visual effects whereas commentators are very excited about its sensual and symbolic qualities. Why did you choose this material?

Richard Wilson: When I was conjuring an idea for the gallery in 1986 I did not know I would be using oil. I never start with a material. I start with an idea and because I'm always suspect of it I have to work the idea to get it right. Whilst I'm working that idea I'm trying to think of the best sets of materials to use, so they are enlisted after the event really.[1]

Previous to doing the oil I'd made a casting and I liked that idea of filling a mould up with something like a liquid. It only ended up being oil through a series of mental gymnastics. When I decided I'd be flooding the whole room I quite liked the idea that it was oil because it was off the sculptor's vocabulary for materials. It wasn't a well-known material to use. It was a hazardous waste. It was a bit of a naughty thing to be playing with.

I had some oil in the studio and I could never get rid of it and it had this extraordinary reflection, but at the same time when you banged the side of the barrel it didn't move whereas with water there is always a ripple. This stuff seemed to have a viscous quality, it had a thickness to it. Also you could never ever see a surface. With a mirror or with water there's a surface. With the oil it's almost as if you couldn't see where it began.

People come in and the spectacle of seeing that reflection is quite extraordinary. But I was thinking, 'How can you have an interior space which could be doubled in size?' Maybe it has to be done through illusion or mirrors or lights. Only it ended up being this waste oil. I knew it was going to be a strong effect, but what was so beautiful was that it was such a powerful effect done with such economical means. I didn't have to go and buy this stuff – this was stuff that was being stored in garages and I could go and collect it. Sometimes there are certain restrictions in economy that dictate material.

The thing I really play around with is people's preconceptions of our world, particularly the space we live in – interior space. I want people to look at something and then have another look and recognize that what they thought they saw was not actually what they saw. They had to have a second look. And with the oil they think they've seen someone dig the floor away and then they think, 'My God, it's oil,' and suddenly they're overpowered by the fact it's this gooey horrible stuff that ruins beaches and gets on your trousers and is going to ruin them. There's all this paranoia, but they'll go out and they'll say to their friend, 'I've seen the most beautiful thing.' You've then got to reconsider what you thought was an offensive material and if you see that material in a completely new light then you've got to doff the cap to a load of other things that you think you don't like. You've got to readdress them in some way.

15.2

15.3

She Came in Through the Bathroom Window *was also installed at Matt's Gallery in 1989, and had a considerable impact as it actually modified part of the gallery building fabric.*[2]

KLT: How did the window at Matt's Gallery become the material for the next installation there?

RW: I knew I wanted to alter the boundary of the gallery space using the window. The oil in *20:50* had expanded it in a very illusionistic way. I'd doubled the size of the room. What better way than to go back to that same space and shrink it, but in a very physical way. The thing about the oil, it really did feature the window. That's what most people remember. So I thought I'd cut the window out and bring it into the room and box it back so that part of that architectural detail would be flying into the room and compressing you against the wall. I cut the window out and mounted it into a trolley system where I could wheel it round the room until it found a point where I could work with it. I was working with black polythene and string and ribbon and the window and elastic. I boxed top and bottom with a T-section and angle-iron-section steel and softwood boarding, so it was all boxed in. It mimicked the architecture of the gallery too, and it seemed to sit comfortably with the grid system of the window. The sides were puckered like a shower curtain. I looked at certain plastics and I got that very heavy-duty plastic that you'd have on a lorry that slides back when the pallets are unloaded.

15.2 >*She Came in Through the Bathroom Window* (1989).

15.3 >Matt's Gallery.

15.4

What was lovely – one material was very anti outdoor conditions whereas the other really stood up to them, so there was this blurring in that space between whether it was interior or exterior and the two materials were trying to talk about that in some kind of way. It was all terribly fragile. You could break the glass and you were outside and you could put your wrist through the softboard and you were outside or you could slash the plastic with a knife and you were outside. So there was this sense of fragility that existed between interior and exterior.

KLT: And the window itself was hung?
RW: Yes, very discreetly. It just sat there, suspended in the space. People came to it and stared at it for the first time. You don't go into someone else's house and stare at the window, you stare at the view. You say, 'Oh look, a lovely park,' not, 'A lovely window you've got here.'

KLT: It's almost the opposite of the oil. You don't see the oil, you see the reflection. And here you don't see the view but you see the window. That's very nice.
As with many of your pieces, *She Came in Through the Bathroom Window* recycles something existing. Within an architectural context such a practice would usually be driven by economics or concerns with sustainability. What drives your reuse of materials?
RW: If you're going to challenge people's preconceptions about our world, what better way of doing it than taking something that they think they know? If you

15.4 >*She Came in Through the Bathroom Window* (1989).

15.5

15.6

15.5 >*Slice of Reality*
(2000).

15.6 >The original sand
dredger.

15.7 >*Slice of Reality*
(2000).

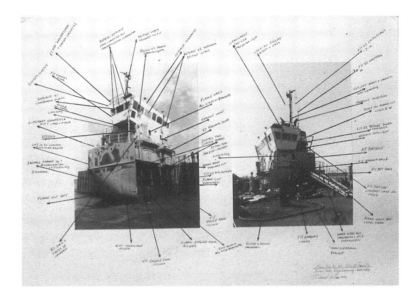

want to challenge someone's preconceptions about an interior space it's no good making some amorphous form that has no reference to what it is you want to talk about. What I do is take a window, cut it out of a building, bring it in and say, 'Look at the way the boundary's changed, look at the way I've compressed the space in the room because I've taken that object, which is not in the vocabulary of sculpture as a material.' I take things from the real world: aeroplanes, ships, rooms, windows, architectural forms, and I play with them rather than inventing them. I've tended to go very much to things that surround me in my world and excite me in terms of the way that they're built or fabricated.

Slice of Reality *was commissioned by the New Millennium Experience Company and the sculpture, a section cut from a disused sand dredger, was moored in the Thames at Greenwich in 2000. Wilson now manages the sculpture and uses it as his office.*

RW: To take a ship – it's like a big set of folded cardboard boxes. It's actually a very interesting form of origami. It's all sheet steel, welded up at 90° or curved, and it's all held together with angle iron or bulb flats, a particular kind of angle iron used in maritime architecture to hold it all rigid. It's fundamentally corrugated-cardboard technology, but on a grandiose scale. You start playing with these things and they become very intriguing aesthetically in how they're put together.

The ship we used for *Slice of Reality* was built like a coal mine – a series of verticals down in the engine room to support the horizontals, above which everything else is then built on. I realized that if I took the main supports out I'd have to put them back somewhere else. It would have been an astronomical amount of money in the fabrication. So I said, 'We'll cut to the very limit of the

15.8

engine room supports,' which gave us a much greater chunk of the ship than I wanted, which should have been five or six feet wide and seventy feet high. I had wanted it much narrower, rather like a slice out of a loaf.

KLT: You've said elsewhere that it's important that you are part of the making process. *She Came in Through the Bathroom Window* was small and lightweight enough to be tested and constructed by you. To what extent are you involved with making large-scale pieces such as *Slice. . .*?
RW: I do delegate on the larger pieces but I certainly work on every idea to develop it to the point where I feel we're ready to start fabricating. Modelmaking and drawing are vital to my practice. I build models and make drawings continuously as a way of getting to understand the idea and know whether the idea is right. Often you get to a point where there's a really crude looking model but I can see in that the potential of the idea. I've noticed that whenever I've called in to my structural engineers, Price and Myers, and put models on the table they're very democratic objects. We all sit and mark them. The models collect everything, even the coffee stains, and I love that. It really is a shared experience.

Although one might have thought one's worked the idea out on paper and in maquettes, what one's really doing is mentally preparing oneself. Things never end up as they're first conceived. When you're cutting ships or spinning façades of buildings it's very difficult to change one's idea halfway through because of the financial implications. You're working with professionals who need to have the scheme drawn up and then adhered to in order to save time and money.

In all of those situations I will be there at every meeting. With the ship it took them five weeks to cut the main ship away and then a month to do all the reinforcing, and I was going up to the shipyard two days a week. I'd be there walking around talking to the team, showing them the drawings, checking on stuff, pointing bits out that needed changing or doing. It's important for me to be making friends with it. Hanging around and just watching things happening and talking and indicating is a way for me to be making as well, if I'm not actually directly hands-on because of the scale of things.

KLT: I'm interested in your decision to cut and finish *Slice of Reality* in a very clean way, unlike Gordon Matta-Clark's cuts which are very rough.
RW: Matta-Clark used to go into timber plastered buildings and cut them with mallets, saws and chainsaws. That's going to tear and shock the material in a very different way to an industrial mechanized way of doing something. The simplest, fastest way of cutting the ship was with oxyacetylene. Oxyacetylene cutting is very neat. If you look at the very edge of the steel on the superstructure high up, you'll see the almost microscopic detail of the cut lines where the flame is burning through. None of that has been ground back or varnished or polished. I have painted the sides and painted up the edge, but that's just been left as it was cut. It was cut by professionals who have spent their lives cutting steel. You would normally cut a neat cut on materials for a ship and I didn't tell them to clean it or buff it. It is just the way it is done.

15.8 >*Slice of Reality*
(2000).

15.9

15.9 >*Slice of Reality*
(2000).

Butterfly, *a crushed aeroplane unfolded in the gallery space by the artist and a team of sculpture students, was Wilson's most recent installation in London and was shown with* Irons in the Fire*, an exhibition of his drawings and models, at the Wapping Project in 2003.*

RW: Talking about things being cleaned and neatened up – there was a very strange experience when I crushed the aeroplane. I bought it as a write-off. I stripped it all down and completely rebuilt it so it was perfect except that it could not fly because it was just a shell. We crushed it over a day so it was completely mashed up as a lump. We hired two guys and a trailer to get the material to the gallery. They went up to this screwed up lump and they started to drag it along the floor. I said, 'Be very careful – you'll scratch it,' and they looked at me as if I was completely mad. I didn't want their hand mark, their marks of damage on my marks of damage. If I choose to smash something up, OK, I've done it my own way. I then don't want someone to come along and smash it up again for me. It's like having a prize car that you've just written off and the AA come along to drag it away for you, and it's a write-off but you say, 'Be careful!' You still have this love for something.

Someone asked me, 'Why did you restore it before you crushed it? Why didn't you just put the wings on and smash it to pieces?' The architecture of Wapping appeared to still be quite raw. It's not dirty but all its history of wear in the fabric of the building is showing because it was disused and fell into disrepair. And I didn't want my derelict thing sitting among that dereliction. I wanted mine to glisten in that rather forlorn darkness, so I wanted something very clean that would catch the light like an insect, so I had to polish it to contrast against all the damaged tiles and brickwork and rusty pipes and everything else. Otherwise my work would just sink in to the environment, into that backdrop and be rather lost.

KLT: All of your works involve fascinating fabrication processes, which are usually unseen. Why did you decide to exhibit the process of unfolding the plane for this particular project?

RW: I wanted to get right back to the basics of a creative act – to take something, screw it up and recover it. I used the analogy of a fiver in your pocket that you forget to take out of your pocket when you wash your trousers. When you find it, there's an extraordinary act which takes place, which isn't about just straightening something out. I've seen my kids do it sometimes. They've unwrapped the tin foil from a sweet. Whilst eating the sweet they've flattened out the screwed-up mess of the foil. There's something quite pleasant about using the soft skin of your fingers to get that ironed out neat and square again. And I thought, that is so sculptural – it isn't just simple unfurling – it is a creative act. You're having to think about how the material is responding to your touch. So I thought, that's what I'm going to do. I'm going to take something and crush it into a lump and pull it back out again, and make public that response to the object.

It was then a case of thinking about what object could be used – in this case an aeroplane. I thought, 'We won't declare it as "art" or anything. We'll have a team of people just putting this thing out creatively and it will be like teams repairing aeroplanes at the Imperial War Museum at Duxford. Here, however, the artists doing it and the team will be making hundreds of aesthetic decisions every moment of the day to try and work out how to get this thing out – something that we're not trained for or know how to do, we'll just lose ourselves in it and while we're doing that we'll just let the public in to watch'.

I didn't want to fall back on my old formal ideas: 'What can the building tell me? I'll make something based around the building'. What the building was telling me was that it was once a hydraulic pumping station. Hydraulics can pull something and it can compress something, and it can do it with extraordinary power. The history of the building is all about pushing and pulling. It pumped water under pressure to the theatres in the West End that operated all the curtains and lifts via lengths of pipeline. The idea of pulling the plane out, and of hydraulics pulling and pushing, was all part and parcel of the piece.

KLT: You've said that oil was chosen as the material for *20:50* because of its aesthetic qualities, and that its symbolic and economic values were more incidental. It seems that in *Butterfly* the history and site of the work becomes more important. To what extent, in *Slice of Reality* in particular, are you interested in the fact that the materials you reuse have a social context?

RW: What has occurred more recently in the work is that it also takes into consideration the notion of context. I worked on a piece *Turbine Hall Swimming Pool* in 2001, located in a disused Methodist Chapel in Southwark Park, and I started to consolidate this idea of the context, looking at why this space was lost to the community. Because the energy had gone out of it, so it fell into disrepair and dereliction. You've got to put the energy back.

The ship was written off and was a discarded object. When I was making the submission to the New Millennium Experience Company I said to them that this was about a slice standing on the Meridian line of Greenwich. It's like the Millennium Dome – it's a skin supported by masts and structures, a big parcel of space. They were all very formal things, but it was also something I didn't explain

15.11   >*Butterfly*
(2003).

to them because I didn't think it would go down too well. It was a doffing of the cap to the river worker and the merchant seaman. These people aren't on the river any more. The industry is completely dead.

My real idea is that *Slice. . .* should rust back into the river: we pile it in, it's this slice of ship, it stands on the GMT line and all that, but it sits there and it rusts away. It weeps itself as a lament. Over a number of years this thing will just corrode and fall away as a reminder of what happened to our empire, our shipping, the whole fact that the growth of London was based around what arrived in ships and went out in ships.

These are examples of the way in which one can take the context of a city, or particularly the discarded elements of a city, and manipulate them. The power of the art is to be able to transform the dereliction into something wonderful for a moment. Suddenly, the social context is interesting. That's a really exciting development for me.

15.12 >Wilson working on
Butterfly (2003).

1   >This is an edited version of a conversation with Katie Lloyd Thomas on 4 May 2005, based on a talk given by Richard Wilson at the Material Matters conference in March/April 2004.
2   >'Richard Wilson's exhibitions at Matt's Gallery . . . are recognised as canonical works within the history of sculpture and installation. Requiring considerable architectural modification to the building, these works reveal the lengths to which the gallery is prepared to go to accommodate artists' ideals and works.' Clare Glossop, 'Infrastructures: Formation and Networks 1975–2000' in Penelope Curtis General (ed.), *Sculpture in 20th Century Britain; Identity, Infrastructures, Aesthetics, Display, Reception*, Leeds: Henry Moore Institute, 2003, p. 237.

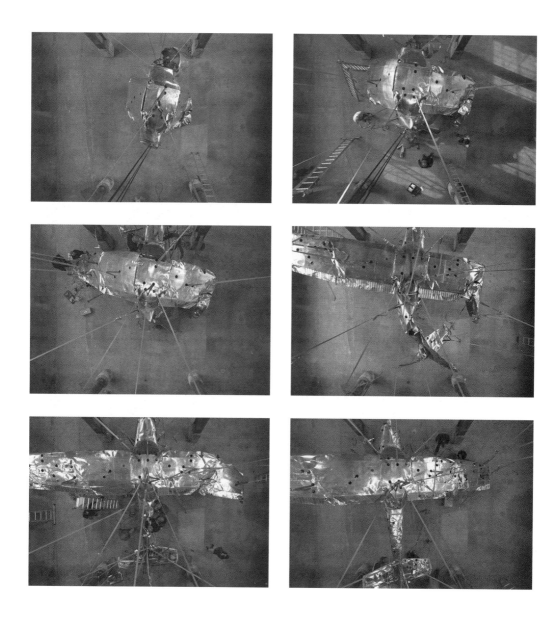

15.13 >Unfolding sequence,
Butterfly (2003).

BETWEEN BIRDS' NESTS AND MANOR HOUSES: EDWARDIAN CAPE TOWN AND THE POLITICAL NATURE OF BUILDING MATERIALS

CHAPTER 16

190

NICHOLAS COETZER >BETWEEN BIRDS' NESTS AND MANOR
HOUSES: EDWARDIAN CAPE TOWN AND THE POLITICAL NATURE
OF BUILDING MATERIALS

I would like to propose that the subheadings presented in this paper offer a way to think about the political nature of building materials in the dominant Western paradigm, namely: 1) their allocation in space, 2) their association with a particular person or groups of people, 3) their position in an historically constructed hierarchy of solidity and temporal permanence, and 4) that their legitimacy is conditioned by their visibility and the visual order of how they are put together.[1] This taxonomy suggests a critique of how materials are often approached in architectural discourse – namely, as structural expression and technological intrigue – and underlines that they are never neutral and are always politicised through the value system of the discourse in which they are embedded. It is, perhaps, precisely because of the material reality of building materials that they appear to be neutral, lack agency and to seemingly escape the inclusionary/ exclusionary practices of power.

I am not suggesting that the modalities I have identified are the only ones or that they occur in every instance. The origins of these ideas are to be found in my doctoral thesis, which looked at the workings of power through space and representation in Cape Town during the late-colonial and pre-apartheid eras in South Africa.[2] Part of this Foucault-inspired[3] unravelling of British architects' and administrators' hegemony over their 'others'[4] included an investigation into the inclusionary/exclusionary legislating and legitimatisation of building materials – especially with regard to social-housing programmes and the domestic architecture of the elite. Consequently most of the observations made in this paper deal with that peculiar period and place, but my contention here is that they have implications for understanding the political nature of building materials in general.

What is apparent is that notions of 'otherness', disease and disorder, as defined through building materials, were fluid, adaptable and often contradictory – for example, thatch was both denigrated as a marker of 'otherness' and valorised as a marker of a bucolic English past. These contradictions emerged as British architects and administrators attempted to resolve the contradictions of colonisation by re-ordering and denaturing 'the native' through increasingly modernist technologies, and by naturalising the coloniser through rewriting settler history and through a phenomenology partly founded on bucolic building materials. It was mainly through British architects representing and reviving the *imagery* of Cape Dutch architecture – arguably a Dutch-developed South African vernacular – that the colonisers began legitimising white domination and British colonisation of the Cape and South Africa.[5] It was also, however, through their immersion in the historical world of Cape Dutch architecture and its rural building materials that they staked their claim on the land. Consider, for example, Herbert Baker's partner Francis Masey's description of the then Prime Minister's Cape Dutch house:

> The straight dominating lines of the eaves and roof ridges of the wine cellar – undisturbed by the aggressive if necessary chimney-stalks – the dark moleskin texture of the reed thatch, the white weather-stained walls, the great oaks giving dignity to the low outbuildings which they overshadow, the green slopes around the farmhouse diapered with trim fruit trees richly bearing golden fruit, the slopes of 'bush' beyond . . . each of these at any time a separate sensation to be enjoyed, but here in combination, with others to

16.1 >Morgenster, Somerset West, Western Cape – bucolic Cape Dutch manor house from the eighteenth century.

16.2 >Top: Meerlust,
Hen-House, Western Cape –
adobe plaster in its
'correct' setting.
Bottom: Wells Square,
District Six, 1917 – adobe
in its 'incorrect' setting
in the city proper.

be added, bewildering the senses and making critical and discriminating writing a not too easy task.[6]

One can smell the moss in the thatch and the lime-washed adobe walls mixing in with spilt wine on damp cellar floors; one can sense the 'coolth' of the shadows in the hot, dry summer air. As Masey himself points out, it was Cape Dutch buildings' overwhelming of the senses, their timeless 'naturalness' in their setting, that blanked out, for example, knowledge of the violence of slavery that was an integral part of these 300-year-old manor houses. The 'embodied experiences', brought on by the material reality of Cape Dutch manor houses, established for the coloniser a spiritual and unproblematic connection to the colonised land. Here, the phenomenology of place makes things entirely romantic (figure 16.1), which is precisely the point: the bucolic, formed from 'natural' materials, bewilders the senses, which in turn depoliticises space and history.

The reason I have included these ideas in this extended introduction is not only to make the point that English rural romanticism was the cause of many of the contradictions in the administration of Cape Town's building materials, but also that material-based phenomenology, unlike the more explicit exclusionary practices disclosed in the sections that follow, is political in its *erasing* of any overt political traces. In other words, this paper is also a cautionary note against a material-based phenomenology that valorizes building materials – particularly 'natural'[7] ones in rural conditions – as these can 'bewilder the senses' and subdue our critical faculties.

THE POLITICAL NATURE OF BUILDING MATERIALS; THEIR ALLOCATION IN SPACE
In a sense, the Cape Dutch manor houses and their phenomenology of place were idealised to the point of delegitimising urbanity itself. At the same time that they were being valorized in the first part of the twentieth century, the heterogeneous and dense old spaces of Cape Town were being problematised. Whilst this is easily recognised as part of the Garden City movement reaction to the 'slums' of the industrial city, it also had as a consideration issues of the appropriate allocation in space of building materials. For example, the Victorian laissez-faire developed houses of District Six came under repeated pressure for demolition and clearance, beginning in 1915 and gaining momentum in 1934 with the Slum Clearance Act, because of their walls being constructed with sun-dried bricks. Part of the remedial work required to avoid expropriation and demolition was to remove, in some cases, the adobe plaster on the building façades and have them 'steel trowelled true and smooth'.[8] The softer marks of otherness had to be removed from the harder surface of the city (figure 16.2). In short, adobe, as a rural material exemplified in Cape Dutch houses, had no place in the city proper. Here, the moss and staining hints at uncontrollable disease and decay – and at the potential undoing of industrial capitalism, as the fabric of the city potentially and literally melts away to primitive mud.

This idea of the correct allocation of a material in space may go some of the way in defining the problematic nature of the segregated black residential spaces of pre-apartheid South Africa, called 'locations'. Before these were restructured through Garden City ideals in the 1920s, locations were, as Gary Minkley characterises them, 'native space' within the city.[9] In the locations that were in

16.3 >Left: Corrugated-iron dwelling at the periphery of the city. Right: 1920s Municipal sponsored corrugated-iron dwelling in Athlone, Cape Town (photographed in 2002).

close proximity to the 'white' space of the city, materials such as adobe and thatch were problematic. The inverse was true for tribal areas. For example, in the Tuberculosis Report of 1914, the rural hut of 'natives' was considered in a largely favourable light, the understanding being that there was a symbiosis between 'natives', the organic materials of their huts, and the natural environment in which they were both located. The primitive 'native hut' and its materials had its right place in the world, and it was not within the space of the European city.

THE POLITICAL NATURE OF BUILDING MATERIALS; THEIR ASSOCIATION WITH PEOPLE

Yet, it was also their association with a particular cultural life, or perceived lack thereof, that drove the legitimacy or illegitimacy of building materials. While not underplaying the importance of spatial issues, even when located in their 'correct' space, materials carried with them the potential of negative associations:

> To put the matter in an extreme way, the native home is essentially a place of refuge from the weather, from wild beasts, from the observation of possible enemies, and for the fulfilment of those perfectly natural functions of cover and shelter that savour rather of the bird's nest than of the highly organized and complicated villa which the European considers as essential for his requirements.[10]

One can hardly be unaware of the negative sentiment carried in this comparison with animal qualities – quite in contrast to Gaston Bachelard's romantic and phenomenological reading of 'nests'.[11] In the rural 'native' areas of pre-apartheid South Africa, the association of 'natural' or organic building materials with animal qualities was a condition of their association with a class or type of people. Furthermore, much of what was valorized in the material make-up of the Cape Dutch manor houses – their rough-textured adobe walls, their thatch roofs – was precisely that which was problematised in the self-made houses of 'natives' in the locations of cities. Whilst the use of thatch and adobe in the Cape Dutch manor house is a romantic conceit – bound within the safe borders of settler history, its rural space and a legitimised cultural life – the potential for their uncontrolled and 'meaningless' use in the same location rendered these materials problematic.

This differential privileging of mud and thatch did not begin and end with the inhabitants of historical Cape Dutch houses and African *kraals*. Although rammed earth as a form of construction was officially excluded from the space of the city through building regulations, a number of holiday homes were nevertheless built

16.4 >Ndabeni, c.1921
– the first racially
segregated residential
area of Cape Town, similar
to British concentration
camps of the South African
War. Note the wattle-and-
corrugated-iron
windbreaks.

with this material in the 1920s in Camps Bay,[12] the area that today contains some of the most expensive residential properties in South Africa. Admittedly, Camps Bay was located somewhat at the periphery of the city which, no doubt, played a large role in the approval of building plans making use of this material. However, the point is clear that wealthy white holidaymakers give mud a different value to that of the self-built wattle-and-daub structures of black job-seekers.

The allowances made to the privileged class also extended to less romantic building materials. Consider the following two examples from the meeting minutes of the Cape Town Public Health and Building Regulations Committee from the early 1920s. The first is contained in a letter written by Cape Town's Medical Officer of Health, Tom Shadick Higgins, to the Town Clerk. The second concerns the case of a reverend and his summerhouse, erected on his property in the suburb of Rondebosch, which – despite being wholly in contravention of the building regulations in its use of sailcloth, thatch, and timber on the property boundary – was condoned:

> In regard to the huts referred to by Mr. Simon, I find that there are six of these recently erected and occupied by natives on Mr. Robert Blake's property near the Muizenberg cemetery. Two of them are wattle and sacking, 6 feet high, with rounded tops, and four of them of paraffin tins and sheet iron, 6 feet high. They have no windows. They are occupied by 13 adults and 3 children. The huts being inhabited by natives, it does not appear that there are the same objections to pulling them down as are felt when they are occupied by people belonging to the ordinary population of the Municipality, and I therefore recommend that steps be taken to demolish them.[13]

And:

> The Sub-Committee found that the structure, consisting of 6″ Jarrah poles, set in cement, with boarded floors and thatched roof, was being erected within a few feet of the boundary of the property. The Rev. Mason had now applied for permission to board in three sides of the structure.[14]

And again:

> That permission be granted to enclose three sides of the structure with poles
> similar to those forming the boundary fence, the inside to be lined with sail
> cloth, the structure to be subject to the usual terms and conditions governing
> temporary structures and that the Rev. Mason be called upon to submit the
> necessary plans.[15]

Once again, the observation can be made that there is a gross disparity
of judgement as to the legitimacy of materials, the one having catastrophic
consequences for its builders. Here again, the matter hinges on the material's
association with the person or people contained therein rather than their location
in space. The fact that the dwellings of the 'natives' were in a rural setting where,
given the colonial administrators' spatial logic, one would expect some leeway
with regard to their use of organic and other materials, illustrates that their
illegitimacy was partly conditioned by the illegitimacy of their inhabitants. That the
Reverend was producing a place to play out a politically desirable cultural and
aesthetic life, and was using very similar materials to those informal settlers at the
periphery of the city for these ends, points to the value of materials lying not
necessarily in their romantic or inherent material qualities but in their association
with particular people or groups of people.

THE POLITICAL NATURE OF BUILDING MATERIALS; TIME AND THE HIERARCHY OF PERMANENCE

Outside of the associative qualities of sack and wood and mud, there was also a
simple hierarchy of building materials that acclaimed solidity and permanence
over the temporary. The editor of the *Architect, Builder & Engineer* spells this out in
an article titled 'Freak Houses':

> Recently there has been some discussion in the Press, both overseas
> and here, of cheaper methods in building houses, and someone has put
> forward the suggestion of adopting a Japanese idea of erecting paper
> houses; to make them more or less weather-proof they would have to be
> oiled. This scheme seems to have a certain amount of popular fancy, and
> the result is there are all sorts of amateurs bringing forward suggestions
> for cheap houses, varying from brick to pisé and in the intermediate stages
> are glass, wood, iron, tin, asbestos, oiled silk, etc., almost varying from
> the present state to the snow hut of the Eskimos. There is no getting away
> from the fact that wherever one may go there are oddly built houses, but
> they do not conform to any idea of stability . . . All credit may be given to
> the owner for doing the best he can on a limited purse, purely from an artistic
> and serviceable view-point, but the fact remains that many of these buildings
> are solely temporary, and may therefore be classed as freak houses.[16]

Even as the city explored alternative construction systems to alleviate the housing
crisis post World War I, materials were still considered in a hierarchy of solidity.
For example, sun-dried bricks were considered superior to wattle and daub.[17]
There was, however, a brief flirtation with the idea of rammed-earth (or *pisé*)

16.5 >Aerial Photograph
of Langa, 1935 –
controlled African space
and failed garden suburb.
Cape Town City Council
with labels by Nicholas
Coetzer.

construction, with two councillors in 1922 voicing their support for this method as
a possible solution to the housing shortage.[18] This motion was not carried. It was
the government's Central Housing Board that essentially quashed any exploration
of these alternatives by refusing to provide municipalities with loans aimed
at alleviating the crisis if mud construction was used.[19] In the logic of loan
repayments and infrastructure investment, houses were required to last for 50 or
60 years without deterioration.

If mud was sometimes slightly ambiguous as a potential building material,
then corrugated iron was the one material whose meaning and value was
immutable, and its transient nature was only one of the reasons for this. The
former president of the Cape Institute of Architects summed up general opinion on
corrugated iron in an article titled 'The Corrugated Curse' by saying, 'Cursed be
the makers and users of galvanised corrugated iron. Ugly, temperature conducting,
temper provoking, inefficient metallic monstrosity – avaunt.'[20] The dominance of
the Arts and Crafts movement at the time would help explain why Cecil Rhodes'
summer cottage in Muizenberg was 'restored' after his death by using thatch to
replace the building's original corrugated-iron roof. Yet, a deeper reading could
be suggested. Unlike other parts of English-influenced South Africa and other
colonies such as Australia, the 'Mother City's' architects did not include
corrugated iron as part of the city's valid modes of colonisation precisely because
the city's stewards had pretensions to an organic, mythical past where settlers
were part of the pre-colonial vernacular landscape. The Cape Dutch revival and
preservation proponents presented the old homesteads as being a vernacular,
having literally grown from the earth, and were horrified to find that 'boorish'
farmers had begun to replace the thatch roofs with corrugated iron. This English
fantasy of their pre-historical or permanent possession of the land was sundered

Figure 16.6 >Top:
Dwelling in Pinelands
Garden City, Cape Town.
Bottom: The 'barracks' at
Langa for single, male,
migrant labourers, c.1934
– the space is produced as
a controlled white space.

by the intrusion of this anachronistic, industrial material. Here, material permanence is not simply literal but also connected to the natural or 'that which has always been'.

THE POLITICAL NATURE OF BUILDING MATERIALS; THEIR VISIBILITY AND THEIR VISUAL ORDER

Yet even as the most reviled of materials, corrugated iron found its way into the domestic space of Cape Town. In another case of a contravening summerhouse being brought before the City's committees, the owner resolved to 'avoid the unsightly appearance of the corrugated iron roof [by covering] the same with spars so as to give the structure a rustic appearance.'[21] In essence then, the importance of sight and the visual in the qualification or disqualification of a building material should not be underestimated. In a move somewhat out of kilter with the Arts and Crafts sensibilities of the time, it seemed that as long as an inferior building material was 'out of sight' and thus 'out of mind', it would be tolerated. This attitude allowed corrugated iron (as a wall material) to be authorised in certain areas of Cape Town as the housing crisis unfolded, albeit only for temporary houses. Yet, the idea of the visual played a role here too; the corrugated-iron zones were located outside of the generally white and middle-class areas and away from the main transportation routes, allowing their problematic nature to be tolerated (figure 16.3).

The idea of the visual also played out in the combination of materials and an associated sense of order. An example of this is given in a quote from the *Municipal Journal of South Africa* in an article focusing on locations and the housing crisis:

> The Housing Problem has received so much prominence lately in the press that the time seems opportune to draw attention to the conditions under which our Natives live in our Municipal Locations, with a view to their betterment. With a few exceptions, the average hovel, hut or wattle and daub structure provided as a residence, more particularly in most of the inland locations, is an absolute disgrace and unworthy of civilization – old bags, paraffin tins, scraps of galvanised iron often playing an important part in the completion of the structure . . . A very large proportion of these structures would not be considered fit to house a thoroughbred horse or cow; yet human beings are allowed to exist under such conditions.[22]

There is a sense that it was something in the haphazard jumble of materials that the houses of the location contained that helped lead to the establishment of municipal housing programmes for black people in South Africa, beginning in the 1920s. There is an aesthetic sensibility that suggests that building materials should be put together in an ordered manner, and this should necessarily be purposefully done. But it goes beyond that. The quotation carries a sense of disease that goes with the disorder, the rust, the sense of decay; things have fallen apart before they have even been made whole. This suggests a similarity to the condition Homi Bhabha recognises in the rag-tag clothing of the 'mimic man',[23] namely, that the coloniser sees his own tenuous nature and his own undoing in the 'improper' use of materials and their incorrect combination made manifest by 'the native'. In this discourse on 'native housing', 'natives' displayed none of the sense of design and order that were so valued by the middle-class British officials who were involved in deciding their housing fate. As two Cape Town city council members stated in 1922, 'They are their own architects and their own builders, and their ideas of house planning and house construction are not such as are likely to receive approval of our officials.'[24]

The anxiety produced by the 'mimic man' was temporarily alleviated by the residentially segregated Garden City locations of Cape Town, which became highly ordered and controlled, and which were places where conditions of otherness were not allowed to emerge. Ndabeni had initially been conceived as a suburb of freestanding cottages as an extension of the Victorian 'civilising' mission,[25] but was built more on the lines of the British concentration camps of the South African War thanks to emergency corrugated-iron Nissen 'tents' being used when the plague struck the Cape in 1901 (figure 16.4).[26] In 1927, the 'model native township' of Langa replaced the 'eyesore' that Ndabeni was considered to be, and was hidden in a forest on the outskirts of Cape Town (figure 16.5).[27] Although Langa was also a greatly compromised version of its original proposal as a garden suburb, it nevertheless eradicated the ambiguities of meaning and contradictions that building materials had hitherto allowed. All the buildings at Langa were constructed of brick and most with roof tiles (at least in the first few phases of Langa's construction) at a great monetary cost to the city council and its budget. The residents were not allowed to add to or change any of the dwellings, making them visually ordered and, in this context, part of the white space of the city, temporarily on loan to the 'natives'. In contrast to this, the white garden suburb of Pinelands had also begun its long history of development, the use of thatch being an early developmental requirement in an attempt to secure the picturesque sensibilities of the Arts and Crafts movement (figure 16.6).

CONCLUSION

Building materials and their cultural meaning should not be discounted in the workings of power through the built environment. In the examples given in this text, the same materials were either considered legitimate through their association with a privileged group, or were the very means by which a particular group was stigmatised and delegitimised. Furthermore, the location of materials in a hierarchised space and their relation to each other as a composition also carried various positive and negative associations, moderated through the aesthetics of the visual and of the sense of sight in general. Within the logic of British imperialism, materials and their associated meanings certainly played their part in the legitimising of colonisation and racial residential segregation long before apartheid tightened this spatial practice through the Group Areas Act of 1950.

The conditions identified in this paper continue to play themselves out in Cape Town and the post-apartheid context, which suggests that the values and attitudes leading to the exclusion/inclusion of building materials, and their role as markers of 'otherness', have not shifted. Nor have the battles of wealth and poverty, and class and race, around which these attitudes coalesce, been resolved. Building materials, then, are not neutral and inert – simply practical and technological applications in the service of shelter or aesthetics – but are part of a discourse that makes them exemplars of Foucault's dispersed or hegemonic power. The lines architects draw, conjuring up the patterns of our material reality, are always part of a battle of inclusion or exclusion, of legitimacy or illegitimacy. Whether from an historical or a legislative sensibility, these lines literally inscribe or underline what is proper and improper and what is a proper and improper way to be in the world. Architecture, in its most material form, engages with the production of the colonial and post-colonial city as a white space.

1   >What has not emerged from this study is how the other senses can be involved in the structuring of the political nature of building materials. Another underdeveloped component here is how their manufacturing process conditions their associated value.

2   >Nicholas Coetzer, 'The Production of the City as a White Space: Representing and Restructuring Identity and Architecture, Cape Town, 1892–1936', unpublished Ph.D. thesis, University of London, 2004.

3   >The thesis' concern with 'representing' links to Foucault's 'archaeology of knowledge' is summarised in Michel Foucault, 'The Order of Discourse' in Robert Young (ed.), Untying the Text, Boston: Routledge and Kegan, 1981; whilst the concern with 'restructuring' links to Foucault's interest in the spatial instruments of domination, as suggested in Paul Rabinow (ed.), The Foucault Reader, New York: Pantheon Books, 1984.

4   >This term in this context will be familiar to those versed in post-colonial theory. The British constructed a hierarchy of skin-tone 'otherness' – ranging from Afrikaner to Greek, Portuguese, Jewish and other 'dark' Europeans; followed by the predominantly Muslim 'Malays', the Creole 'Coloureds', and Indians; whilst 'natives' were categorised as Christian or 'married Natives', as opposed to the migrant worker, or 'raw kafir'.

5   >Nicholas Coetzer, op.cit., see Chapter 3: 'Possessing the Land / Possessing the History'.

6   >Francis Masey, 'The Beginnings of our Nation, VI. Schoongezicht: The Residence of the Hon. J. X. Merriman, M.L.A.' in The State, vol. 1, no. 6, June 1909.

7   >As if unformed by human hands.

8   >Cape Archives, 3/CT–1/5/13/1/1: Slum Clearance Special Committee, 1935.02.11.

9   >Gary Minkley, ' "Corpses Behind Screens:" Native Space in the City', in H. Judin and I. Vladislavic, (eds.), Blank – Architecture, Apartheid and After, Rotterdam: NAi Publishers, 1998.

10   >'Native Housing. Physical and Social Conditions' in Architect, Builder & Engineer, vol. 6, no. 10, May 1923.

11   >Gaston Bachelard, The Poetics of Space, Boston: Beacon Press Group, 1994, p. 93.

12   >Cape Archives, 3/CT 1/4/7/1/1/12: Public Health and Building Regulations Committee, 1921.02.16.

13   >Cape Archives, 3/CT-4/1/5/1248 (N75/5): 1923.10.31: letter from Shadick Higgins to Town Clerk.

14   >Cape Archives, 3/CT-1/4/7/1/1/14: PH&BRC, 1921.10.12.

15   >Cape Archives, 3/CT-1/4/7/1/1/14: PH&BRC, 1921.10.25.

16   >Architect, Builder and Engineer, vol. 7, no. 11, June 1924.

17   >Cape Archives, 3/CT-1/4/7/1/1/12: PH&BRC, 1921.03.01.

18   >Cape Archives, 3/CT-1/4/7/1/1/15: PH&BRC, 1922.05.10: report of Councillors Henshilwood and Somerville.

19   >Cape Archives, 3/CT-1/4/9/1/1/2: Housing and Estates Committee Minutes, 1920.12.07, From the Secretary Central Housing Board, 10 November 1920.

20   >Architect, Builder and Engineer, vol. 13, no. 10, May 1930.

21   >Cape Archives, 3/CT-1/4/7/1/1/14: PH&BRC, 1921.10.25.

22   >C.M.V.C. 'Municipal Locations', in Municipal Journal of South Africa, vol. 1, no. 4, November 1919.

23   >Robert Young, White Mythologies: Writing History and the West, London: Routledge, 1990, p. 147.

24   >Cape Archives, 3/CT-1/4/7/1/1/15: PH&BRC, 1922.05.10.

25   >J. Comaroff and J. Comaroff, Of Revelation & Revolution: The Dialectics of Modernity on a South African Frontier, London: University of Chicago Press, 1997, 'Mansions of the Lord' pp. 287–301.

26   >V. Bickford-Smith, E. Van Heyningen, N. Worden (eds.), Cape Town, The Making of a City, Cape Town: David Philip, 1998.

27   >Cape Archives, 3/CT-1/4/10/1/1/1: Native Affairs Committee, 1924.08.27: meeting with Prime Minister Hertzog.

CLARE MELHUISH >CONCRETE AS THE CONDUIT OF EXPERIENCE
AT THE BRUNSWICK, LONDON

The public and critical reception of the Brunswick Centre is closely bound up with the materials of its construction. This distinctive mixed-use development, built in Bloomsbury during the 1960s and finished in 1973, was hailed as a pioneering example of a low-rise, high-density approach to urban renewal. But it is the 'concrete-ness' of this grand architectural intervention which seems to have impinged upon the public consciousness more than almost anything else about it, inspiring some less than complimentary epithets – 'concrete monstrosity', 'concrete jungle', 'Alcatraz', and so on – but also, from other quarters, unabashed admiration. The critic Theo Crosby wrote that it was, quite simply, 'the defiance of new concrete set in one of the most consistent brick environments in London [which] makes the project interesting as an urban adventure and worthy of analysis',[1] and it was this appraisal, among others, that eventually led to the listing of the building by English Heritage in 2000, in order to ensure its protection and preservation for posterity as an architectural production of remarkable vision, accomplishment and significance to the nation's heritage.

Much has been made of the ideology of concrete construction in the history of architectural Modernism, but the truth behind the Brunswick story was that concrete was never part of the original conception. The architect, Patrick Hodgkinson, has clearly stated that if he was ideologically wedded to anything it was the use of brick. He took his inspiration from architects such as Louis Kahn in the United States, and Alvar Aalto in Finland, and not the much-vaunted Central European modernists whose influence dominated teaching at the Architectural Association when Hodgkinson was a student there in the early 1950s. The idea of the Brunswick as a grand ideological statement in concrete form-making and construction is, therefore, fundamentally flawed, yet it has been of considerable influence in the evaluation of the building's significance in architectural history.

The aim of this paper, then, is to challenge the conventional readings of the Brunswick offered on the one hand by sometimes adulatory architectural discourse and on the other by often dismissive popular opinion. By adopting an anthropological approach to the study of the building, I am striving towards some insights into the interactions between people and the material qualities of the built environment, which have been effectively relegated to the sidelines of discussion both by the prevailing 'ideology' of materials, as presented in the architectural critical tradition, and by strident popular stereotypes.

Hodgkinson described his own scheme for this important site as a 'town room'.[2] By contrast, the Brunswick has been presented as the formal expression of an obsessively rationalising, functionalist philosophy of social organisation and city planning – manifested in the factory-produced building materials of the industrial world, and imposed on a traditional neighbourhood without regard either for the inherent spatial and material qualities of the existing environment, or for the local community. I endeavour to look beyond that neatly closed architectural *idée fixe*, to use ethnographic methods to hear the many contrasting voices which make up the multi-layered narrative of architectural intervention, and to develop a phenomenological understanding of the Brunswick complex in a more holistic way as a cultural production of its time. To this end, I have set out to uncover crucial aspects of the design, life and reported experience of the building which bring to the fore issues of materiality, sensory perception, and embodiment or 'being-in-the-world' at the individual and collective level.

THE BRUNSWICK: A BRIEF SURVEY

The Brunswick scheme was initiated by the developer Alec Coleman[3] on the site of decayed and war-damaged Georgian terraced houses in Bloomsbury (including the birthplace of Ruskin), which were designated for clearance. In 1963, the London County Council (LCC) granted outline planning permission for the low-rise high-density scheme submitted by Hodgkinson and Leslie Martin, in whose office he was working. Hodgkinson had been employed by Martin, the retired chief architect of the LCC and designer of the acclaimed high-rise Alton Estate in Roehampton, on the basis of a low-rise housing scheme which he had designed as a student for a site in Brixton, and which was subsequently adapted by Hodgkinson and Martin for a site in west Kentish Town for St Pancras Borough Council.[4] When the Brunswick scheme received planning permission, Hodgkinson was appointed as sole architect for the main residential and retail part of the site and opened his own office in London where he worked closely with McAlpine's, the contractors for the project. However, the progress of construction was disrupted by financial problems, as a result of which McAlpine's took over as developer-contractor of the site. On Hodgkinson's initiative, the housing element of the scheme was sold off to the newly-created London Borough of Camden Council as a flagship project for the new council. Camden drastically reduced the specification of the design, and both Coleman and Hodgkinson were eventually dismissed by McAlpine's. The scheme completed in 1973 was a truncated and reduced version of the original, in terms of extent and specification. It comprised some 600 flats with an open-ended, open-air shopping precinct at ground level. This is what we see today, although the refurbishment programme started in February 2005 will result in the closure of the north end of the precinct with a new single-storey building block containing a supermarket.[5]

The long, raised shopping precinct is enclosed along its east and west edges with monolithic concrete A-frame blocks containing studio, one-bedroom and two-bedroom flats on seven floors. The complex has a monumental porticoed entrance onto Brunswick Square to the east, under which a cinema is located, but the better-used, if more modest, entrance is on the west from Marchmont Street, a shopping thoroughfare which has experienced a marked decline since the construction of the Brunswick. The most distinctive feature of the development, apart from its sheer scale and its unabashed use of exposed concrete, is the cascading glass terraces on both sides of each block: the famous 'wintergardens' to the flats, which glint in the light on a bright day and give a view of the sky from within.

The development was originally designed to create an upmarket shopping environment with a grand, civic presence. The now open precinct was to have contained a covered market hall, and public gardens were planned for the terraces looking over it at second-floor level. However, the market hall was never built, leaving a rather empty windblown piazza, and the terraces were eventually closed to the public for security reasons, the grand external staircase leading up to them removed. The office units located at terrace level are mostly occupied, but not quite as the 'professional chambers' envisaged by the architect. A large percentage of the flats, which were originally intended for mixed-income occupancy, have been designated as sheltered accommodation for the elderly and fragile. While some have been sold under the right-to-buy scheme and then sold on to more affluent, professional incomers, a significant number of flats remain in the occupancy of long-term council tenants, many of whom were among the first to move in.

At the time of writing, refurbishment of the Brunswick is underway, focused primarily on the shopping centre but also including the comprehensive repair and painting of the external façades of the whole complex. For years, however, the Brunswick had been clearly in urgent need of maintenance and repair. The concrete façades were stained and damaged in many places, revealing the underlying red load-bearing brickwork used to build the walls to the flats; a surprising 'inconsistency' in a building where the impressive internal A-frame structure of the housing blocks makes such a strong statement about the integrity of concrete construction. The general atmosphere of neglect and decay was alleviated only by the efforts made by individual inhabitants to brighten their balconies with fresh paint and plants.[6] At ground level, most of the retail units behind the colonnades of bush-hammered concrete columns now stand empty and gutted as work progresses on the refurbishment of the precinct, intended by the owners, Allied London, to transform the Brunswick into a desirable shopping destination.

CONCRETE V BRICK

The Brunswick has had a very mixed press over the years, but the perception of the building as a concrete edifice is a consistent point of reference, along with an awareness of its scale. Indeed the two attributes seem to be intrinsically linked. As English Heritage pointed out in 1993, 'the multi-functional "megastructure" is monolithic in its architectural form, the concrete of which it is built reinforcing the expansive scale of the structure.'[7] As a concrete building it was admired, but also condemned by both professional commentators and the public. On the one hand, concrete symbolised the idea of modern life – immensely strong and stable, allowing for the construction of large-scale structures, and capable of mass production – and architects in Britain had been experimenting with the material since the end of the nineteenth century. On the other hand, it was perceived as aesthetically unappealing, lending itself to scalelessness, and, progressively, problematic in terms of maintenance. Reyner Banham defined the Brunswick as a 'megastructure' essentially on the grounds of its scale and grandiose appearance (above all, 'it looks like a megastructure'[8]), criticising the terraces which go on 'scalelessly for ever'.[9] But the vast scale of the Brunswick complex (compared to its surroundings), combining many different functions, and the sheer extent of the use of concrete as a structural and a cladding material, was regarded as ground-breaking in the context of 1960s planning philosophy and architectural ideology, and highly significant for the future of urban living.

Crosby's enthusiastic assessment emphasises a visual, aesthetic appreciation of architecture, in which materials are invested with semiotic or iconographic significance as 'signs' of a particular ideological position. This line of architectural discourse has led to the Brunswick frequently being identified as a legacy of Corbusianism, and being placed within the historically important 'Brutalist' tradition of British architecture. However, Hodgkinson was never part of the concrete-building tradition and was frankly antagonistic to the work of Le Corbusier, whose Fort l'Empereur project for Algiers was identified by Banham as the origin of the megastructure idea, and indeed to the European Modernist tradition in general. Hodgkinson described the Unité d'Habitation in Marseilles, which he visited at the end of his first year at the AA, as an 'impenetrable slab unacceptable for towns and society ... stranded, alien to its surroundings, severing the continuity of space or time.'[10] By contrast, and against the general tendency of the AA at that time, he looked to the writings of Lewis Mumford, particularly his concept of the 'superblock',[11] and to the architecture of Louis Kahn, maintaining that Kahn's first buildings made him committed to using brickwork at an early stage of his training as an architect. After a spell in Aalto's office, he joined Martin's practice in Cambridge in 1955, where he worked on a scheme for a group of brick libraries which he now says, 'would have been hailed as very Kahn'[12] – except that there was little interest in Kahn generally at that time. He also worked on the scheme for Harvey Court, completed in 1961 in Cambridge. This was a brick courtyard structure – a series of buildings on an elevated plinth which allowed for underground servicing and car parking, and the initial inspiration for his first Brunswick scheme.

The 'Brutalists' called for an 'anti-design', a-formal approach, in which the use of 'raw' and 'exposed' materials, denuded of finishes and claddings, was fundamental. In part, this was a reaction against the Welfare State ideology of an older generation of architects – also known as the 'William Morris Revival', or 'People's Detailing' (celebrated in the architecture of the Festival of Britain 1951) – which was derided by the new guard as anodyne and soft. Alison and Peter Smithson were central to the movement, and developed what has been called an 'anthropological aesthetic'. They embraced the techniques of industrialised mass-production as the authentic expression of a modern-day vernacular, in particular the use of concrete. The use of concrete in the design of the Brunswick has thus been used to give it a central role in the evolution of Brutalism in British architectural history. But in reality, Hodgkinson, who had rejected Peter Smithson as a tutor in his last year at the AA along with the whole cult of Corbusianism, consciously distanced himself from Brutalism, and has stated, 'I thought it was a fetish'.[13] The fact that the Brunswick was originally designed as a brick building has been effectively concealed or ignored by a narrative of architectural history intent on a Brutalist classification or, alternatively, conveniently circumvented by the concept of 'brick Brutalism' proposed by Banham in 1966 and used to designate much of the Cambridge School work – including Harvey Court, regardless of Hodgkinson's own antagonism to the idea.[14]

CONCRETE AS LIVED EXPERIENCE

Albert, a sheltered tenant who has lived in the Brunswick for ten years since his accident, says he 'thought it was like a prison.' More specifically, he focuses on its 'big ugly blinking walls.' He says, 'they should knock down the flats and put glass in and turn it into a monkey house.' But his neighbour Doris, who has been there for fifteen years and previously lived locally in Taviton Street and Drury Lane, comments more mildly that 'you get used to living in a concrete building.' And June, who watched the building go up, thinks 'it's wonderful what they've done.'[15]

The concrete construction of the Brunswick repeatedly comes up as a topic of conversation about the building, suggesting that its materiality is very much to the fore in people's own perception of their experience of living in the building and

the way in which they communicate that experience. There is an intense awareness of the material fabric of the complex, mainly deriving from the many problems which are associated with it – in particular water penetration, damp, heat through solar gain, and cold through heat loss. Hence the experience of living in the Brunswick is, at a banal and everyday level, closely related to a range of physical sensations, particularly those of discomfort. Ironically, then, the people who frequent the building in varying degrees of intensity, may have a greater sensitivity and awareness of its materiality and are more articulate about it than those living in a more traditionally constructed building.

It was only when changes in the building regulations meant that the structure would have to be built in concrete that the materiality of the Brunswick was radically rethought. At that time, Hodgkinson recalls, the architects in the office thought concrete would, indeed, be more appropriate because the building was 'so monumental – it was bound to look and feel more important,'[16] reflecting the prevailing ideology surrounding concrete. He himself was eventually persuaded that the use of concrete was the right thing, partly because of his conviction that if it was built in brick the contractor would use an eclectic mixture of poor-quality bricks, compromising the materiality of the building in a possibly disastrous way. Indeed, Camden's budget would run only to the cheapest type of fair-faced concrete, without any kind of finish. It was not pre-cast, except for the housing slabs, but fabricated on site using 'an enormous crowd of navvies'; an extremely labour-intensive process which Hodgkinson, brought up with the progressive ideas of Buckminster Fuller, found bizarrely archaic.

The materiality of the Brunswick is central to the critical discourse surrounding the building, yet it represents a complicated story which subverts the simplicity of that reading: the Brunswick as a statement of modernist conviction, where the use of concrete represents a fundamental tenet of that faith. Not only was there no commitment to concrete at the outset, but the way in which it was finally fabricated was profoundly un-modern and, furthermore, the apparent integrity of the resulting concrete construction is not what it seems to be, for behind the concrete cladding a considerable part of the building consists of load-bearing block and brickwork, used in the construction of the flats. Finally, Hodgkinson never intended the cladding itself to be left untreated, but envisaged that it would be rendered and painted in the manner and hue of London's Regency heritage. The finish, along with many others, was dropped by Camden Council to cut costs; although, indeed, David Levitt (who worked on the original project with Hodgkinson) and others had argued from the outset that the idea was flawed, due to the necessity and cost of regular maintenance.[17] They proposed brick or tile cladding instead.

ARCHITECTURE AND DRESS; MASCULINE V FEMININE

There is, then, an extensive discourse of materials and materiality which is central to any understanding of the architectural expression of the Brunswick, and of the Brunswick as lived experience. From this perspective, the building may be considered rather as a body, an architectural corporeum, than simply as a vessel or container. Hodgkinson's own strong interest in a notion of 'appropriate dress' in architecture serves to bring this conception of the building into focus. It was this notion, framed by what he acknowledges to be a rather conservative outlook –

'brown shoes for the country, black shoes for the town' – which helped to persuade him that concrete was the appropriate material for urban architecture, whereas brick was perhaps more suitable for rural buildings after all.[18]

The earliest conception of the development as a glamorous, upmarket shopping arcade was largely dependent on a high specification in terms of materials, including the use of gold mosaic for the columns of the shopping arcade and high-quality paving. All of this was stripped away to the most basic and raw standard of material treatment. Hence, it can be argued that the building that stands today is one which has effectively been unceremoniously disrobed of its envisaged wardrobe, its flesh and bones denuded and exposed in a manner never intended. The strongest impact of this exposure is perhaps that of the sheer hardness of the concrete and glass surfaces, exaggerated by the angular outlines of the structural geometry, and the absence of the verdant landscaping on terrace and balcony levels which led the initial design to be described as the 'hanging gardens of Babylon' in one of the more enthusiastic reviews which hailed its unveiling.[19]

At the time of the Brunswick's construction, concrete was not considered, in the words of Levitt,[20] a 'naff' material, but rather one associated with notions of progress, technological development and the future resolution of many social problems – particularly the lack of adequate housing provision. Many architects were very excited by the structural, material and decorative possibilities of concrete. But at the same time it had its antagonists, including Hodgkinson, and was never really taken on board as an 'upmarket' material capable of connoting the values of luxury and comfort associated with elevated social status. By and large, it was used as the material of institutions, commercial offices, and large-scale housing blocks, reflecting the fact that its outstanding qualities of hardness, strength and (as was hoped) durability, rather than comfort and sensuous appeal, are indissolubly tangled with notions of masculinity and public life, as opposed to femininity and private, domestic life, in a decisively gendered dialectic rooted in the nineteenth century.

Penny Sparke, who traces the origins of this dialectic in her analysis of gender and taste,[21] cites Thorstein Veblen's summing up of the difference between the sexes. He invokes a belief in biological difference that underpinned the association of women with the private and men with the public realms of social life. Men were judged to be better equipped than women to deal with the ruthless, amoral world of work; while women were allocated the responsibility of creating and maintaining a tranquil, comfortable home environment, insulated from the pressures of public life, offering their husbands physical and emotional sustenance.[22] Hence, women became charged with the role of 'home-maker' as part of a 'cult of domesticity' which emphasised the role of taste, comfort, and 'soft' feminine qualities in the organisation and experience of the private realm.

According to Sparke, one of the major implications of Modernist design ideology was the denuding and erosion of the female realm, and female power within it, through its assertion of a utilitarian, anti-bourgeois ethic. One of the most obvious attributes of modernism was its embrace of hard, 'hygienic', strong, unyielding materials – notably concrete, steel and glass. From this perspective, Modernist architecture can be interpreted as a specifically masculinist, anti-feminine movement which sought to eliminate feminine qualities and power even within the formerly sacrosanct female realm of the home. From this point of view, the Brunswick itself may be regarded as open to critique as a spatially aggressive, indeed aggrandising, statement of male values expressed through an inherently 'masculine' language of materials, notably concrete and glass. Beatriz Colomina's analysis of 'domestic voyeurism' in the architecture of Loos and Le Corbusier, as an architecture which subtly undermines the status of women as subjects, adds a further dimension to such a discussion, and one which again raises the subject of dress, or clothing.[23] She argues that the houses designed by both Loos and Le Corbusier persistently frame their occupants in such a way that '[a]rchitecture ... is a viewing mechanism that produces the subject' – and there are aspects of the Brunswick which might be interpreted in the same manner. However, Loos also placed a strong emphasis on the 'covering' of architecture as primary, compared to the structure as secondary, writing on the relationship between fashion and the house exterior in terms which evoke Simmel's view of clothing: in Colomina's words, as 'a mask which protects the intimacy of the metropolitan being.' Interestingly, Loos' view also evokes Semper's discussion of the primary importance of the wall, as representational surface, over that of structure in architecture[24] – which was fundamentally antagonistic to the Modernist conviction of the integrity of structural expression, and which bears a strong similarity to Hodgkinson's own sensibility.

A CONDITION OF UNDRESS

There seems to be an awareness among residents at the Brunswick of a condition of undress and uncomfortable exposure underlying the material identity of the complex that equally generates problems in their own experience of relating to, and interacting with the building. The prevalence among respondents of complaints and comments about dirt, disrepair and neglect, strongly linked to the discourses of security and domestic complaint previously mentioned, is encompassed within this. Damp seeps, very visibly, through the walls of the flats; the structure and surfaces are blemished by holes, stains, and, occasionally deliberate disfigurements; and, in certain places, bits of rusty reinforcement metal have started to emerge through the surfaces. Water accumulates on the terraces like 'swimming pools'. A strong sense of the building's decaying, permeable, exposed and vulnerable body clearly pervades occupants' everyday experience of living at the Brunswick: it is an uncomfortable proximity and intimacy that is not just visually offensive, but assaults all the senses. The building has a funny strong, dusty smell when you come in, comments one respondent, and she didn't use her hot-air heating system for two years because she was convinced the air coming out of it was bad. Indeed, a warden claims it is killing sheltered clients with chronic airway disease. Sound travels by unexpected routes through the structure, throwing you into unwelcome proximity with strangers and their activities: for instance, shouting and fighting with no evidence of its source; and, more bizarrely, for one respondent, the sound of bells jingling around the feet of a belly dancer in the Indian restaurant in the precinct below.

MAINTENANCE AND TECHNOLOGY

Issues of maintenance and technology are closely connected to the physical and synaesthetic experience of the building as material fabric. Its heating and

plumbing systems are widely considered to be idiosyncratic and, increasingly, inadequate. According to the former estate manager, the Brunswick always had a bad reputation for repairs and maintenance, largely because of aspects of the design – such as the expansion joints, which have caused problems due to water penetration ever since the building was first opened, the open-ended design of the blocks (allowing easy entry both to undesirable weather and intruders), and the glazing to the 'greenhouses'. She states that after thirty years the whole complex is due for rewiring, replumbing, and a new heating system. Some of the lighting to the access galleries no longer functions, and cannot be replaced because asbestos in the ceilings means nobody will do the work. But Mr. P. suggests that the design and technology of the Brunswick is simply beyond Camden Council's capacity to maintain and manage successfully. He reveals an extensive knowledge and experience of the technical systems – air pump and fan, hot-water pressure and the ballcock operation, balcony drainage, airbricks to prevent condensation, etc. – which effectively activate the flats as dwellings. Mr P. believes that both the Brunswick and its Georgian neighbours are simply too complicated for the council to manage. The wardens add that the fact that the services are located in the basement of the complex causes huge problems of access because of the division of ownership of the building, and creates the need for constant negotiation between council and freeholder.

While such observations and complaints may be considered as part of a more general 'discourse of domestic complaint' running through the history of British housing, they also serve to reinforce a reading of the building as an inadequately clothed and vulnerable body, in which the technological systems vital to the smooth running of the building represent a form of artificial intervention. Due to lack of expertise and routine maintenance to these systems, it becomes impossible for the building to function properly and thrive.

PROPOSITION

Such a reading of the building's materiality, prompted by people's reported experience through the whole spectrum of sensory perceptions, reinforces an idea of the Brunswick as a living, if vulnerable, organism which its inhabitants relate to at an intense personal level, rather than an abstract, imposed intellectual idea. In the words of Merleau-Ponty, 'sense experience' becomes 'that vital communication with the world which makes it present', forging a bond between 'the perceived object and the perceiving subject', termed 'intentional tissue.'[25] Thomas Czordas points out that 'the notion of "experience" virtually dropped out of theorising about culture' during the 1980s because of the great emphasis on structuralist analysis, and he proposes that it be reinstated.[26] But he also stresses that the process of perception, the 'deployment of senses and sensibility, and not only their content, is emphatically cultural' – that is, the way that individuals use their senses and their particular responses to phenomena is highly determined by their specific cultural context and conditions, and not simply the result of universal human attributes.

Czordas' position indicates the way forward for a new wave of research into modern architecture, one which looks beyond the prevailing discourse of aesthetic ideology on the one hand, or of Modernism as alienation, abstraction, and cultural fragmentation on the other. We need to explore the multiple meanings embodied in any significant building, understood as a multi-faceted cultural production, in which the material surfaces represent the primary experiential interface between individuals, the larger collective identity, and its architectural expression.

1   > Theo Crosby, 'Brunswick Centre, Bloomsbury, London' in *The Architectural Review*, Vol. CLII, No. 908, 1972, p. 211.

2   > Patrick Hodgkinson, 'Foundling Conception' in *The Architectural Review, op. cit.*, p. 218.

3   > Alec Coleman was also responsible for building the Tricorn Centre in Portsmouth, now demolished.

4   > The predecessor of the London Borough of Camden.

5   > In February 2005, work finally started on the implementation of a long-debated refurbishment programme initiated by freeholders Allied London, the aim of which was to upgrade the Brunswick shopping centre to make it commercially more attractive, both to shoppers and to retailers.

6   > Strictly speaking this is forbidden by council regulations, along with the visible positioning of washing lines and laundry.

7   > London Advisory Committee, English Heritage (1993): response to planning application to make alterations to the building.

8   > Reyner Banham, *Megastructure: Urban futures of the Recent Past*, London: Thames & Hudson, 1976, p. 185.

9   > *Ibid.*, p. 187.

10   > Patrick Hodgkinson, 'A Handful of Homes: British Post-War Housing' in *A3 Times*, No. 9, 1987, pp. 19–20.

11   > Lewis Mumford, *The Culture of Cities*, London: Secker & Warburg, 1938/1940. See particularly section VIII, 'Biotechnic Civilisation' and image section 28 on Urban Rehabilitation. Also: Lewis Mumford, *The Highway and the City*, London: Secker & Warburg, 1964, Chapter 1.

12   > Patrick Hodgkinson in conversation with the author, November 2004.

13   > *Ibid.*

14   > Banham claimed that the planning concept at Harvey Court is related to the Smithsons' interest in ancient sites. It has, he said, 'the air of a sacred enclosure'. See Reyner Banham, *The New Brutalism: Ethic or Aesthetic?* London: Architectural Press, 1966.

15   > All respondents quoted in this paper were interviewed during fieldwork undertaken at the Brunswick by the author in 2000–2001.

16   > Patrick Hodgkinson in interview with the author, July 2001.

17   > David Levitt in interview with the author, December 2000.

18   > Patrick Hodgkinson in interview with the author, July 2001.

19   > Ena Kendall, 'Babylon comes to Bloomsbury', *Observer magazine*, 2 December 1973, p. 33.

20   > David Levitt worked on the original project in Hodgkinson's office, and it is his practice, Levitt Bernstein, who are today responsible for the refurbishment scheme in collaboration with Hodgkinson.

21   > Penny Sparke, *As Long As It's Pink: The Sexual Politics of Taste*, London: HarperCollins, 1995.

22   > See Joyce Henri Robinson, 'Hi Honey, I'm Home: Weary (Neurasthenic) Businessmen and the Formulation of a Serenely Modern Aesthetic' in Christopher Reed (ed.), *Not At Home: the Suppression of the Domestic in Modern Art and Architecture*, London: Thames & Hudson, 1996, pp 98–112. Also discussed in Clare Melhuish, *Modern House 2*, London: Phaidon, 2000, pp. 20–1.

23   > Beatriz Colomina, 'The Split Wall: Domestic Voyeurism', in Beatriz Colomina (ed.), *Sexuality and Space*, New York: Princeton Architectural Press, 1992, pp. 73–128.

24   > Kenneth Frampton, *Studies in Tectonic Culture: The Poetics of Construction in 19th and 20th Century Architecture*, Cambridge, Massachusetts: The MIT Press, 1995.

25   > Maurice Merleau-Ponty, *The Phenomenology of Perception*, London: Routledge, 1989.

26   > Thomas Czordas, 'Embodiment and Cultural Phenomenology', in Gail Weiss and Honi Haber (eds.), *Perspectives on Embodient: The Intersection of Nature and Culture.*

I can't quite say when it happened, but one day I woke to find that my things – or rather the things – I felt then that I could no longer call them mine – had taken over. Piles and piles of them now occupy the space I once considered my own . . . I find my way barred by the myriad objects that have vomited themselves over every last corner . . . If once they helped me, if they told me – when I forgot – who I was . . . now they have become a terrifying incarnation of all that sustained me for so long.[1]

Jason Oddy, 'After All'

18.1 >Introduction:
A multitude of
maintenance activities
are deemed necessary to
preserve the much
publicised 'neutral'
backdrop of the American
Air Museum, Duxford.
American Air Museum:
excerpt from cleaning
schedule.

Check/clean barrier matting
Wipe Public Seating
Empty Rubbish Bins + entrance bin
Litterpick Area
Clean/Check Interior Signs
Clean Prefab Windows / Floor entrance
Check/Clean Mess Room
Check/Sweep outside AAM Entrance
Return Stones in front of Glass Structu
Sweep/Clean AAM foyer & Balcony
Check Liveside Barrier for Litter
Remove graffiti/hand prints from exhibits
Vacuum Carpet Area
Check Disabled Loo Alarm in AAM
V Mop floor
Tidy Bomber Jacket /explainer areas
Check Red Safety Line & Chain in plac

Cleaning schedule Area 'C' two weeks commencing,
Daily cleaning week one: Return stones in front of glass structure

Architecture's habitual representation in public is as the complete and distinct object – an individual creation, captured in an ephemeral instant and effaced of all traces of activities that produce and maintain it as such.[2] This paper explores the dialogue between two stories of making that challenge this representation. One follows the creation of a 'paper room' by architects 5th Studio; another unravels the daily activities involved in maintaining the American Air Museum building at the Imperial War Museum, Duxford.

The selection of these stories is a personal one. At 5th Studio from January until May 2003, I was involved in designing and constructing the paper room – an exhibition/corporate-event space constructed from and showcasing paper/fibre-based products. Whilst I ploughed my way through a plethora of legislation required to establish this paper room as a public place, at the American Air Museum my partner, in his job as museum assistant, waded through a multitude of maintenance activities all deemed necessary to preserve the public representation of a building repeatedly presented in architectural journals as a 'neutral backdrop'.[3]

BACKGROUND

18.2 >Background: The enclosure of the paper room uses materials normally associated with waste for its construction.
Paper room: perspective drawing, 5th Studio.

Events/miscellaneous: Ensure runners are free from obstructions.

The Paper Room

In January 2003, as part of a strategy for the Paper Trail Project in Hemel Hempstead, 5th Studio was appointed to design a paper room within an existing paper mill. The Paper Trail Project embraces an area of over five hectares and includes creating a new visitor attraction and innovation centre for the region, based around a working paper mill. The strategic plan was approached through the mill's connection to the topography of the landscape in which it sits – notably the presence of water, which infiltrates the entire papermaking process. Across the site the experience of water shifts in relation to its use and location. By simultaneously acting as chemical/transportation/power resource for use in the papermaking process and as a distinctive body of landscape that extends beyond the mill itself, the existing presence of water challenges perceived separations between natural and industrial landscapes. Highlighting this latent overlap between process and topography, with its clear implications for layout and distribution of spaces, forms the basis of 5th Studio's strategic plan across the entire site. Rather than contain exhibitions depicting the processes of papermaking, it proposes the creation of a number of landscapes or garden spaces that embody them.

While the brief for the paper room was simply for a space in which to launch the strategic plan, its construction forms the first incarnation of an ongoing test bed and working exhibition of paper products. Its enclosure is made between a series of new insertions and an existing warehouse within the paper-mill building. An entrance ramp and screen, displaying microscopic sections of paper fibres, climb up one side of an existing brick wall. At the top of the ramp, an opening within the wall forms the entrance to a 100m^2 room. The parameters of the room are created by paper bales, paper honeycomb, cardboard sheets, fibreboard panels and the brick wall itself.

As a public building used for exhibitions, conferences, seminars and public events, the paper room's use of paper and fibre-based materials explores the potential of these products to structure and enclose space.[4] In this way the paper room is a fragment that expresses the ideas and qualities of the larger strategy.

The American Air Museum

Designed by Lord Norman Foster and opened by HM The Queen in 1997, the American Air Museum is located at Duxford near Cambridge. Commissioned by the Imperial War Museum to display its collection of American military aircraft, the building forms part of a complex that welcomes over 400,000 public visitors each year and was awarded the Stirling Architecture Prize in 1998.[5] The form of the building is based on an arched geometric shape – a torus, or ring doughnut. Made up of pre-cast concrete panels, a single-span vault forms the major enclosure to the building, which is completed by a glazed façade, 90 metres long and 18.5 metres high, to the south east. Aircraft of every shape and form hang from the concrete structure. Whilst the building has been designed to offer a neutral backdrop to the aircraft, its dimensions and entrance sequence are directly influenced by the largest aircraft that it houses: the vast B52 bomber. Its 16 m-high tail fin and the 61m wingspan were the key influence on the building's height and width. Moreover, visitors enter the museum, via a partially submerged entrance to the north east, to find themselves midway in the volume of the building, facing the nose of the B52.[6]

The American Air Museum has been heralded as an embodiment of the methods and techniques used in the production of aircraft. An article in *Building*, written just before its completion, describes how 'in the construction of the aeroplanes themselves there are no frills . . . you can see how everything is put together. The same is true here [of the air museum].'[7] Indeed, as an article in *The Architects' Journal* proclaims, the size of each pre-cast module is a function of the optimum size for buildability whilst maximising the amount of repetition – there are only five panel types for the whole roof.[8] Yet complex geometry and cutting-edge structural engineering are but a few of the hidden processes behind the production of this building. Its apparent neutrality is reproduced on a daily basis by a multitude of practices and processes with both dramatic and subtle effects.

MAINTENANCE ACTIVITIES

In recycling cardboard and packaging, the paper room uses materials normally associated with waste for its construction. This establishes a materiality which is very different to that of the American Air Museum, whose materials have been manufactured and refined for the sole purpose of its construction. However, formal arguments surrounding 'high-tech' or 'low-tech' architecture are not the basis of this paper. Rather, it is an investigation into the very processes and practices that constitute creative production. This investigation stems from earlier research which explored the practical work of artist Mierle Laderman Ukeles through the theoretical lenses of Gilles Deleuze, Felix Guattari, Rosi Briadotti and Moira Gatens.[9]

For Ukeles the role of the artist is not privileged and detached; art must play an activist role in empowering people to act as agents of change. This agenda stems from a feminist concern with challenging the privileged and gendered notion of pure creation and the myth of the independent artist. Ukeles' 1969 *Manifesto for Maintenance Art* proposes the dismantling of the notion of art as fixed and complete, through the literal transformation of everyday activities into 'art'. In her manifesto she proclaims, 'Avant-garde art, which claims utter development, is infected by strains of maintenance ideas, maintenance activities and maintenance materials.'[10]

In *I Make Maintenance Art One Hour Everyday*, a project that took place in 1976, maintenance staff at the Chemical Bank in Water Street in downtown Witney were asked by Ukeles to designate one hour of their daily work as 'art'. Ukeles then took Polaroid photographs of the workers every day over five weeks while asking them whether they were doing 'work' or 'art'. In the performance *Wash* in 1973, Ukeles fastidiously scrubbed the pavement of the public space outside the AIR Gallery in New York City. This performance pushed the hidden and static conceptions of 'woman' and 'woman's work' together in a public space to examine the processes of subjectivation and the power differentials at work within both conceptions.

Ukeles' projects use actions and performance to express how differential power structures produce, and are produced by, apparently mundane and banal activities. By presenting private and hidden routine maintenance activities as art through performance and acts of gratitude, her work engenders shifts in the status and meaning of 'work' and 'art'. For the critic Helen Molesworth, her work is an 'attempt to rearticulate the terms of public and private in ways that might fashion new possibilities for both spheres and the labour they entail.'[11] Her performances explore how practical actions within specific contexts help to actualise certain conceptions. Furthermore, they highlight the fragility of oppositions such as public/private, clean/dirty, acceptable/abject activity, which, as Moira Gatens describes, 'attempt to capture bodies in stable forms,'[12] so challenging the social construction of aesthetic and cultural values that coagulate them into binary oppositions.[13]

In Ukeles' projects the socio-spatial and temporal assemblage of a human body and its circumstances imply specific conditions regarding the status of maintenance activities in society. This notion of places as assemblages of discursive and non-discursive practices forms the basis of the following exploration of the paper room and the cleaning schedule of the American Air Museum. While Ukeles' work explores the role that habitually hidden dimensions, including legislation and maintenance activities, play in the production of 'ideologically appropriate subjects,' this paper explores the role they play in the perception and implementation of architecture.[14]

Whether creating a new environment or restoring an existing one to its 'original' state, both the paper room and the American Air Museum require constant attention and ongoing tending. Within traditional assumptions of architectural production both are seen as very different activities: one involves the creation of a new space and one is simply the restoration of an existing one. This assumption forms the starting point of the five sections of this paper that position fragments of the construction of the paper room alongside selected maintenance activities. However, as the sections progress they start to uncover similarities and overlaps in the processes and practices that go into creating the paper room and those that maintain the public representation of the air museum. Ultimately, the readings of the construction processes involved in making the paper room and the cleaning activities in the American Air Museum form paired comparisons in order to ask: When does restoration at the level of the daily maintenance activity become re-creation? Further, by investigating the implications of such activities for rethinking places, it explores what is at stake for architecture and perceptions of place if maintenance is thought as a creative act comparable to others within the building process.

1. TRESPASS: INTERVENTION V RESTORATION

18.3 >Trespass: In the Museum, clutter is dangerous: 'Foreign Object Debris.' Maintenance activities remove all trace of this 'out of place' matter. American Air Museum: maintenance staff drawing.

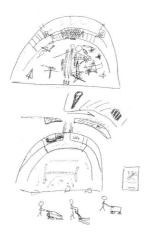

Beware of FOD (Foreign Object Debris): if you create or see any please ensure you pick it up.[15]

The paper room forms one element of a strategy involving the regeneration of a paper mill in Hemel Hempstead. Taking the existing mill's interrelation with its topography as a precedent, the wider strategy develops a series of spaces that negotiate between perceptions of natural and man-made topographies. In this context, the paper room is a prototype: a landscape that embodies papermaking processes – becoming a means through which they are encountered and understood.[16] Part of a peripheral warehouse is stripped out and swept, and a new assembly of fragments inserted. Each embody different manifestations of paper: a vertical paper-bale structure, a corrugated cardboard plane, a honeycomb panel, cardboard tubes and a glowing glazed screen of enlarged paper fibres.

Like the war machines it exhibits, numerous elements of the American Air Museum are at the forefront of technical innovation.[17] In contrast, countless low-tech activities – including polishing, mopping, scrubbing, wiping, dusting and vacuuming – maintain the building every day. The daily maintenance staff consists of a maximum of five people, whose adherence to a six-page cleaning schedule, a fortnightly roster and a 22-page handbook combines with over 60 different implements/machines and 15 types of cleaning fluid to form the basis of an endless maintenance strategy that serves to reinstate this so called 'neutral' backdrop. At the entrance, around a series of commemorative glass structures, whether gleefully kicked or stumbled upon, grey stones migrate across a tarmac path. Every morning, the path is swept. Each stone must be located, collected and returned to its designated place. In the shop, cardboard 'holes' become embedded in the sliding-door track. To prevent malfunction, these packaging inserts must be carefully extricated and disposed of by vacuuming. These are but a few of the incessant minutiae whose presence consistently threatens to disrupt the workings of the museum.

In and around the paper room what was a clutter of outmoded machine parts becomes re-established as part of a new landscape that resonates with the paper hills and cardboard escarpments that already reside there. Here the practice of clutter constitutes another aspect of ordering time and place.[18] Rather than a series of obstructions, the situation of the room becomes a framework through which it is perceived. In the museum, the stones and cardboard inserts are clutter: dangerous 'foreign objects' whose 'material presence confronts an alternative use of the spaces that they occupy'.[19] Maintenance activities remove all trace of this 'out of place'[20] matter, ensuring it does not pile up and impede the smooth flow of people, or hinder the much publicised comprehension of the building as 'simple, right' and 'stripped down to elemental basics.'[21] Its actions are rudimentary and functional, mere restoration, a removal of accretions and a reversion to an original state.

2. COAGULATE: MATERIALISATION OF LEGITIMATE EFFECTS

18.4 >Coagulate:
To make the paper room 'public', fire legislation designates the cardboard plane the authority of a 'proper' ceiling.
Paper room: cardboard ceiling.

Cleaning in general, bullet point one: Do not overstretch or use unbalanced equipment.

Cleaning exhibits, bullet point two: Exhibits over two metres must only be accessed using a cherry picker or a platform tower.[22]

The designation of the paper room as 'public' makes it subject to specific regulations. Below the cardboard layer a manic sprinkler system, in addition to the existing one above, sets up a new horizontal plane. This interpretation of the fire legislation affords the cardboard plane the authority of a 'proper' ceiling, and pronounces the enclosure of the approved and accepted standard to be a 'room'. Gaps in the bale structure prove more difficult for the location of required fire signage. Yet regulations prevail. Openings become exits, whose presence designates the pile of 24 paper bales a 'wall'.

In the museum a 'dust horizon' collects two metres above the floor. The museum assistant's handbook states that maintenance staff must be specially trained to put up a tower and to use a cherry picker. Yet, few are selected for training and cherry pickers must be specially hired. Meanwhile the dust gathers . . . its presence instates a miasmatic manifestation of the restricted cleaning level.

The way in which spaces are perceived is premised on a set of assumptions: conventions and rules that have material bearing on the way lives are lived.[23] These conventions do not merely describe or represent, they intervene in the world, functioning to organise its 'social character.' They instigate a 'framework of intelligibility' which maintains explicit propositions about bodies and places, deciding what types of utterances may be 'legitimately' extracted from them. Categories such as 'public /private, active/passive' may be read as 'clusters of specific affects [*sic.*] and powers, organized around an exclusive binary form through various complex assemblages,' social, environmental, cultural, linguistic as well as legal.[24] Complex interpersonal and spatial rules govern and position public minutiae, and the legitimisation of certain actions and activities allocates designations and makes present certain material effects. The status of the paper room and the museum as 'public' entails their operation within particular sets of rules that transcribe a framework for their use and perception.

3. DISPLACE: SHIFTING MATTER

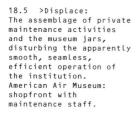

18.5 >Displace:
The assemblage of private maintenance activities and the museum jars, disturbing the apparently smooth, seamless, efficient operation of the institution. American Air Museum: shopfront with maintenance staff.

'you missed a bit'
'you can clean my windows any time'
'bet it's like the Forth Bridge'[25]

Part of the enclosure to the paper room is made by baled waste paper. Discarded aspects of everyday life create a new 'public' enclosure. Memories of office work, birthdays and breakfast are piled on top of each other. Here, both domestic and commercial commodities: the memo, the birthday card, the sugar packet shift in status and meaning. Displaced from their everyday location and wrested from their passage towards recycling they become objects of construction, contemplation and curiosity.

In the museum, while cleaning activities are transcribed by public legislation they are simultaneously hidden and strictly timetabled – involving a specific uniform, stance and in-visibility. Restricted to a private and even abject realm, their occasional presence during opening hours regularly prompts personal responses or elicits complete repudiation. Marked by personalisation or by dismissal, the assemblage of these private maintenance activities and the public space of the museum jars. It momentarily disturbs the apparently smooth, seamless, efficient operation of the institution.

Through shifting the location of objects and activities associated with habitually disregarded or hidden actions to an exposed and public space, spectators are forced to conceptually and tacitly engage with them and their surroundings in a different way. In the paper room the transformation of domestic objects associated with the rituals of breakfast and work into 'architecture' subverts aesthetic and cultural values which separate mundane and artistic creation – 'work' and 'art' – into binary opposites. Their shift in location reveals the practices and places which define them, and their new location within everyday spaces and processes, as domestic/urban, public/private.

The presence of maintenance activities in the museum exposes the public institution to the pressures of what it conventionally prohibits or makes invisible. Here, static conceptions of public and private are pushed together in a space, allowing an examination of the processes of subjectification and the power differentials at work within both conceptions. Their presence unveils the socio-spatial and temporal assemblage which supports the utterances of public/private, clean/dirty, acceptable/abject activity, and shows how each 'new' and pristine building – each 'original' 'work of art' – is, in fact, infected and influenced by 'mundane' 'maintenance activities.'[26]

4. DISINFECT: EDITING MATTER

Weekly cleaning: A.A.M before 10 am:
Wipe public seating
Check/polish entrance doors
Sweep/clean foyer and balcony[27]

18.6 >Disinfect:
Before the paper room
could be officially
opened to the public,
'contaminated' paper
bales were removed.
Paper room: wall
constructed from paper
bales.

Before the paper room could be officially opened to the public, 'contaminated' bales of soft porn texts and hospital records were removed and replaced with bales of 'acceptable' everyday debris. In the museum, before opening hours, areas of maximum visual impact are carefully selected to undergo scrupulous levels of rinsing, polishing and buffing to attain a presentable public face. The removal of fingerprint contaminations on the glass entrance balcony takes priority over the ramp balustrade. While identical and seamless in terms of architectural details, the prioritisation of cleaning certain areas over others establishes counter thresholds, imperceptible in construction but indicated by tidemarks left on the fabric of the building. Defamiliarisation is a 'momentary bracketing of conditioned modes of perception.'[28]

The use of common materials in unusual ways challenges existing economies of architecture. Likewise, the exposure of mundane activities necessary to maintain an image of neutrality challenges the production of this image itself. Here, maintenance becomes complicit in the desire to represent architecture as independent and timeless – yet its very existence, its relentless repetition, destroys this apparent neutrality it seeks to preserve. In each action an editing process is at work, produced by and productive of specific spatial experiences and representations, in which this paper is also complicit.

5. STAIN: TRANSLATING MATTER

18.7 >Stain:
The cleaning routine
of the museum exerts
specific material and
political translations:
what can be cleaned by
whom, when and how.
American Air Museum:
entrance ramp.

Sweeper: removal of matter: lumps, wrappers, loose debris: entrance: daily

V mop: collection of matter: mud, dust, fine sediment: ground floor: daily

Scrubber Dryer: addition of sheen: ecoclean, antifoam, scrub head: ground floor once a fortnight on Mondays.[29]

In the paper room cardboard honeycomb is released from its everyday use, becoming an optical delight: simultaneously concealing and revealing, illuminated by backlit paper sheets. Here, the insertion undergoes a transformation – yet what transformations do these insertions exert on the original building? What materialises out of the traces that are uncovered, and what role do residual remnants have? Offset by the new space around it, the wall between emerges. What was once a mere line of separation becomes significant. Through a glass screen of enlarged paper fibres, residual dust and cobwebs become translated into a further layer of texture.

In the museum the cleaning routine exerts specific material and political translations. An 'exhibit' becomes translated into 'stand' and 'case', having priority to be cleaned before a certain time, or is designated a 'priority structure' to be cleaned by conservators only. Likewise, the fabric of the building becomes translated into 'edges and ledges', each with its own cleaning machine and associated practice.[30] A floor mopped over and over, an expansion grille lifted and dusted beneath; the repeated removal of all traces of inhabitation forces a specific and intimate occupation at the level of the detail. Here, large-scale order and perception becomes connected to minute and local practices.

In both the paper room and the museum, subtle interventions act as translations. Parallel objects and activities set up an exploration of other possibilities. 'Bearing traces of its former self the object [the building] emerges like a stain, neither wholly present nor fully absent, marks not just of what has been but also, perhaps of what is to come.'[31]

CLEANING UP

18.8 >Cleaning up:
The insertions that
create the paper room
and the maintenance
activities of the
air museum act as
translations: playing
a key role in the way
the 'host' or existing
building is perceived.
Paper room: interior
view.

In the paper room a new assembly of fragments carve out and trace a different set of paths and stories. In contrast, the maintenance routines of the American Air Museum appear quotidian, banal and repetitive – simply cleaning up – innocent, expedient and straightforward. This perception of artistic versus mundane creation is premised on a series of assumptions that maintain, and are maintained by, everyday activities and places – what should be done and where.

For validation and credibility, architecture traditionally depends on a level of public reception and recognition.[32] To be recognised as 'public' both the paper room and the cleaning regime of the American Air Museum must adhere to specific regulations organised through various social, political, environmental, cultural, linguistic and legal assemblages. In the paper room, paper bales and cardboard must be afforded conventional parameters of ceiling and wall, while in the museum the very presence of matter produced by regulations serves to record, reinforce and re-produce them.

Shifts in assemblages of objects and activities which coagulate certain conceptions can make present habitually disregarded places. In its location between two stories of making, this paper is an action that shifts the way both are perceived. In the paper room everyday private objects are manipulated through accumulation and displacement into an industrial landscape. My interpretation explores how this 'unconventional' use of materials reveals and stretches the framework of the legislation that effects and produces the room's situation as public and safe. At the same time, in its exploration of the museum's maintenance activities this paper reveals the hidden activities and regulations absent in both daily and architectural representations of the American Air Museum. This 'contamination' of the American Air Museum by maintenance challenges its public presentation as a 'neutral,' static and pristine backdrop, revealing the plethora of human activities this reception depends upon for its production. In both readings there is a subversion of the familiar that reveals and challenges the fictions of public and private.

As Kevin Hetherington describes in his paper 'Secondhandedness: Consumption, Disposal, and Absent Presence': 'Social relations are performed not only around what is there but also sometimes around the *presence* of what is not.'[33] In my readings of the paper room and the museum maintenance activities, private acts and objects assemble to create public representations. Rather than define a rigid boundary between public and private, these objects and activities propose their contiguity – making any such clear-cut divisions impossible.

The idea of restoration is based on the premise of simply returning to an original state. In contrast, this paper explores how maintenance activities, whether subtracting or adding matter, take part in a constant making of building. In this way maintenance activities might be seen as ongoing acts of translation: creative actions of making, comparable to others associated with building.[34] This subtle level of re-making, where interventions act as translations, has a resonance with the fragments that together constitute the paper room. Ultimately these interventions not only shift the way materials are used but also affect the way their new locations are perceived. Here, in place of the complete and distinct object architecture is instead made as a series of interferences or contaminations. These have an empathy with the existing fabric of the host building, editing it and uncovering latent situations, whilst creating new settings between it and its adjacencies.

The activities of cleaning take an editing role in the reception of the American Air Museum, reinforcing or establishing a 'politics of use' and translating it into a series of surfaces for the collection of matter. Likewise, the insertions that form the paper room are translations that not only gain strength from the presence of the original building, but also add something new to its perception.

In *Architecture from the Outside*, Elizabeth Grosz describes how architectural assumptions work on the premise of the 'building as a fixed entity or given stable object' entailing an acceptance in its neutral role as the 'containment or protection of [specific] subjects' rather than their production.[35] The translational potential of architecture is a notion that challenges this idea of architecture as neutral. Here, a building is no longer merely a container but becomes instead a living part of its own circumstances.[36] Further, the assumption of architecture as a 'fixed entity or given stable object' is challenged by the notion of maintenance itself. The long tending that goes into a building constitutes a constant remaking of it through a plethora of maintenance activities: all the different activities specific to materials – polishing, sanding, wiping, dusting, vacuuming – some subtracting material and others adding; all the tiny rituals and practices that constitute the daily mechanisms of place.

Through the lens of habitually hidden legislative and maintenance activities, then, architecture becomes recast as a series of processes and practices: an assemblage of physical, psychological and temporal dynamics – 'situations' continually in-the-making, as opposed to pure creation.[37] Here, the human being cannot be separated from its relations to the world.[38] It is not a distinct and separate entity, but is an ongoing process in, to, and of the world. Ultimately, this process of continual remaking of places is a site for resistance. By rethinking place as a fluid assemblage of practices, it challenges imposed representations of identities and places which attempt to position and preserve architecture as an independent and neutral object. While exploring how subjectivities become manifest through an assemblage of everyday activities, stories, events and performed places, this reviewing simultaneously releases the possibility of rethinking and moving *beyond* the fictions that structure traditional, and stratified, assumptions of architecture, place, and identity.

ACKNOWLEDGEMENTS
I am particularly grateful to Katie Lloyd Thomas for advice and direction on this paper. Likewise, I am grateful to the Imperial War Museum, Duxford, for allowing me to take and reproduce photographs of the American Air Museum and to Museum Assistant, Nick Cheek, for explaining the museum's cleaning schedule to me. I would also like to thank 5th Studio, Cambridge, for providing me with the stimulating opportunity to be involved in designing and constructing the paper room.

1   >Jason Oddy, 'After All', in 'Paris: Georges Perec', *AA files* 45/46, London, Winter 2001, p. 87.
2   >For a discussion of the representation of architecture as objects in relation to the work of 5th Studio, see Tom Holbrook, 'The Commonplace' – an essay forming part of the catalogue published on the occasion of *Presences*, an exhibition at The Architecture Foundation from 29 March–13 May 2001.
3   >One description of the American Air Museum reads, 'Simple in form, the building provides a neutral backdrop for the Imperial War Museum's collection of US aircraft': Isabel Allen, 'Duxford's Plane and Simple Museum' in *The Architects' Journal*, London, 14/21 August 1997, p. 10.
4   >5th Studio, *Paper Trail Masterplan*, and practice brochure.
5   >Cambridge Network directory: Imperial War Museum Duxford, <http://www.cambridgenetwork.co.uk/pooled/profiles/BF_COMP/view.asp?Q=BF_COMP_6667> (accessed 25 September 2004).
6   >See Barrie Evans, 'Concrete in Flight' in *The Architects' Journal*, London, 6 November 1997, pp. 51–4; David Andrews, Gabriele Del Mese, Kevin Franklin and Chris Wise, 'The American Air Museum, Duxford' in *The Arup Journal* 3/1997, pp. 10–15; Gus Alexander 'Chocks Away' in *Building*, 1 August 1997, pp. 16–19; and David Wood, 'Cost Study: American Air Museum, Duxford' in *Building*, vol. 262, no. 8011 (41), 17 October 1997, pp. 54–9.
7   >Gus Alexander, 'Chocks Away', *op. cit.*, p. 19.

8   >See Barrie Evans 'Concrete in Flight,' *op. cit.*, pp. 51–4.
9   >See Helen Stratford, 'Collective Assemblages, Embodiment and Enunciations' in Judith Rugg and Daniel Hinchcliffe (eds.), *Recoveries and Reclamations: Advances in Art and Urban Futures Volume 2*, Bristol: Intellect Books, 2002, pp. 107–17.
10   >Mierle Laderman Ukeles, 'Maintenance Art Manifesto' (1969), in Kristine Stiles and Peter Selz (eds.), *Theories and Documents of Contemporary Art*, Berkeley, London: University of California Press, 1996, p. 623.
11   >Helen Molesworth, 'House Work and Art Work', in *October 92* Spring 2000, p. 96.
12   >Moira Gatens, 'Through a Spinozist Lens: Ethology, Difference, Power', in Paul Patton (ed.), *Deleuze: A Critical Reader*, Oxford: Blackwell, p. 182.
13   >See Helen Stratford, *op. cit.*, pp. 107–17.
14   >Helen Molesworth, *op. cit.*, p. 77.
15   >Duxford Imperial War Museum, Cleaning Schedule and Museum Assistant's Handbook.
16   >5th Studio, *Paper Trail Masterplan*.
17   >See Barrie Evans *op. cit.*; David Andrews, Gabriele Del Mese, Kevin Franklin and Chris Wise, *op. cit.*; Gus Alexander *op. cit.*; and David Wood, *op. cit.*
18   >For a discussion of how the way in which the practices related to clutter constitute another aspect of the ordering of time and space in the home, see Saulo B. Cwerner and Alan Metcalfe, 'Storage and Clutter, Discourses and Practices of Order in the Domestic World' in *The Journal of Design History*, No. 3, 2003, pp. 229–39.
19   >Saulo B. Cwerner and Alan Metcalfe, *op. cit.*, p. 235.
20   >See Mary Douglas, *Purity and Danger: an Analysis of the Concepts of Pollution and Taboo*, London: Ark, 1984.
21   >Jonathan Glancy, 'Flying Fantasy: Erotic Spaces: American Air Museum' in *Blueprint*, London, May 1997, p. 44.
22   >Duxford Imperial War Museum, Museum Assistant's Handbook.
23   >For a greater discussion of this idea of spatial perception, see Eleanor Kaufman 'Living Virtually in a Cluttered House' in *Angelaki*, vol. 7 no. 3, 2002, p. 161.
24   >Moira Gatens, *op. cit.*, p. 178.
25   >Examples of typical comments made by visitors to museum assistants whilst cleaning.
26   >This argument draws upon Ukeles' work. For a discussion of Ukeles' work in relation to the public institution of the museum see Helen Molesworth etc.
27   >Duxford Imperial War Museum, Cleaning Schedule.
28   >Eleanor Kaufman, *op. cit.*, p. 163.
29   >Duxford Imperial War Museum, Cleaning Schedule.
30   >*Ibid.*
31   >Simon Groom, essay forming part of the catalogue published to accompany the exhibition *Parallel Objects* by Jane Dixon at Kettle's Yard, Cambridge, 30 September–5 November 2000, p. 17.
32   >While architecture can and does thrive in the 'private' realm of domestic interiors and private houses, a constant drive is its publication and recognition in the public realm through architectural journals, exhibitions and the like. This argument draws upon Helen Molesworth's discussion of Ukeles' work as a feminist critique of 'art's traditional reliance on a public sphere for its legitimacy and value': Helen Molesworth, *op. cit.*, p. 82.
33   >Kevin Hetherington, 'Secondhandedness: Consumption, Disposal, and Absent Presence' in *Environment and Planning D: Society and Space*, volume 22, 2004, p. 159.
34   >For a discussion of the role of restoration and translation in paintings, poetry and buildings, see Fred Scott, 'Notes on New and Old Work', an essay forming part of the catalogue published on the occasion of *Presences*, an exhibition at The Architecture Foundation from 29 March to 13 May 2001.
35   >Elizabeth Grosz, *Architecture from the Outside: Essays on Virtual and Real Spaces*, Cambridge, Massachusetts: The MIT Press, 2001, pp. 6, 59.
36   >For a discussion of the possibilities for architecture to become a living part of its environment see Ragana Sigurðardóttir, Preface to Anna Hallin, Kristin Ómarsdóttir and Ósk Vilhjálmsdóttir, *in and out the window*, Reykjavik: Salka, 2003.
37   >Gilles Deleuze describes how 'we don't desire an object … rather, we find ourselves in situations.' Gilles Deleuze, 'L'Abécédaire de Gilles Deleuze' (1996), conversation with Claire

Parnet, directed by Pierre Boutang, translated by Charles J. Stivale, Wayne State University, Roman Languages and Literatures. Online: <http://www.langlab.wayne.edu/Romance/ FreD_G/ABC2.html> (accessed 15 February 2004).
38   >Gilles Deleuze, *Spinoza: Practical Philosophy*, (trans.) Robert Hurley, San Francisco: City Light Books, 1988, pp. 122–30.

19.1 >Women's networks on women's dresses.

19.2 >Beginnings.

'PUTTING TOGETHER AND SHARING'

In Mandingue, one of the six main languages spoken in Senegal, 'Kambeng Kafoo' means 'putting together and sharing', 'using collectively'. My paper deals with the circulation of matter, knowledge and desire through this process of 'putting together and sharing' within a group of women who have organised themselves in a cooperative in order to save money, buy land and construct their own houses in a self-initiated community called 'Cité des Femmes', located in Keur Massar, a suburb of Dakar. A 'cité'[1] in Senegal is a collective housing estate including some few hundred dwellings built 'en dur', out of long-lasting materials, and provided with modern servicing; it is a small 'city' in itself, holding a certain identity and autonomy, a symbol of urban emancipation. Kambeng Kafoo is the name of the group who initiated the project, which includes women from Casamance who work as 'bissap'[2] sellers in Dakar.

This paper, which focuses on the beginnings of the Cité des Femmes project, is written from a materialist position, which tries to bring together questions of matter and politics and to acknowledge that the *material* of a *building* refers not only to its physical components but includes also many kinds of *matters* and processes of negotiation within different economic, sexual, social and political contexts. It also positions itself within a long tradition in feminist theory and practice which tries to restore the links between matter and *mater* and to reframe the issues of materiality, emergence and generation within a gendered approach to place-making.

I learned about the Cité des Femmes project from Madjiguène Cisée, one of its initiators, who has also been a spokesperson for the 'sans-papiers' movement in Paris. In 1996, a number of illegal immigrants, most of them Africans, decided to organise a public protest and claim their rights to live and work in France by temporarily occupying spaces in Paris, including warehouses, theatres and churches. After a few months of protest most of them received immigration cards, except for their political leaders who were directly or indirectly forced to return to their home countries. This was the case for Madjiguène, who chose to go back to Senegal and work with women. She created a women's network, Refdaf (Réseau des femmes pour un développement durable en Afrique) – a federation of women's organisations throughout the whole country, which helps women to realise their own projects. Kambeng Kafoo and the other groups who participate in the Cité des Femmes project include women (mostly single – unmarried, widows or spouses renounced by polygamous husbands – or women whose husbands are retired or unemployed) who are taking care of their children and have decided to save money together in order to buy land and build their own houses. Most of them are currently renting rooms in collective flats or living in the street, working in the informal economy. Most women in Senegal are active within the informal sector, which is of vital importance to the country. They have, for example, the monopoly in vegetable and fruit trading. Yet even if the household economy is mostly covered by women, traditionally they don't have any right to own their own homes – as in most Muslim societies, this right is always transmitted through masculine lineage. The Cité des Femmes aims to break with this tradition and demonstrate women's capacity to organise themselves to fund, build and manage a home according to their own needs.

19.3 >Naming.

19.4 >Construction workshop.

19.5 >Collective kitchen and construction workshop.

The women participating in the project each plan to save 1000 Francs CFA[3] (equivalent to £1) per day in order to be able to buy a 150m^2 or a 300m^2 plot of land in two years' time, and to have their own houses built after four more years.[4] Seeking creative solutions within such a long-term project, Madjiguène contacted me and artist Alejandra Riera to work with them on the project. In October 2003, we decided to go to Dakar for a first visit and to start with an initial consultation and a process of documentation.

From the very beginning we were interested in the material and collective aspects of the project, in how an architectural project could be realised through a principle of 'putting together and sharing' and how this principle would affect the design process. We were concerned with the materiality of this process, but also with how our own position is politically defined through it; with what we, as European women, 'put together and share' with the women of the Cité des Femmes. What kind of reciprocities, mutual agreements and two-way exchanges do we put in place in our collaborative design project?

AFRICAN MATTERS

From a European point of view, Africa has always been perceived as a source of primary resources – material, energy and labour – to support the economy of the northern hemisphere. The routes that connect Africa to Europe have been the same for hundreds of years, but now they are taken by immigrants instead of slaves. The products exchanged have also remained the same: Senegal's main exports are still fish, peanuts, petrol, phosphates and cotton, just as in colonial times. Like most African countries, Senegal's current contribution to the global economy is mainly material.

THE STREET: A MODEL OF SHARED SPACE

Generally, women do not participate in this large-scale economy but only in a local, informal economy. This economy takes place in the street, in direct connection with the domestic realm. We began to look at the streets of Dakar, not only to identify issues of poverty but also to learn about another kind of urban space. Rem Koolhaas has warned us, ironically, that African cities are the model of our future cities, which, by arriving at such a level of complexity, will have to adopt the ultimate solution of self-organisation.[5] So, rather than looking for source material, we went there to learn what our modern Western tradition has failed to teach us: modes of managing space without hierarchy, female strategies of place-making for living in more and more chaotic and unsustainable urban contexts.

The street taught us about a certain understanding of the notion of 'sharing' which is emphasised in the project as a principle of self-organisation, and about what a 'shared space' means as opposed to the Western idea of 'public space'. A 'shared space' is a model of space that welcomes the informality of everyday life, the contiguity between the intimate, the domestic and the public. Its sense of community is reinforced by the imperative of giving and sharing with others, which is one of the traditional principles of Senegal.

The street in the African city is the matrix of urban life. It allows a mix, without hierarchy, between the opposed categories that usually organise the modern city. Here 'living' and 'production', 'activity' and 'leisure', 'rural' and

19.6 >School and health centre.

19.7 >Community garden.

'urban', 'poverty' and 'prosperity' coexist without contradiction. A quarter of Dakar's population is transient, which means more than 500,000 people coming every morning into Dakar from villages and suburbs. Some of them hang around in the city hunting small job opportunities, others are just paying visits to their relatives, knowing that, according to the traditional rules of hospitality, their hosts have to share their food with them. This has become a social trick that enables the poor to survive. As Fatou told us, she has always to plan three times more rice than she needs for her family, knowing that there will always be unexpected guests showing up for lunch.

SAND, DIRT AND DUST

The shared space is formed through collective and individual appropriation of public space and a continual negotiation of its rules. The management of the street is not publicly run but self-organised, autonomous and resistant to order imposed from above. The street has no 'function' but 'use'. This multiple, fluctuating use is most of the time a misuse, a 'détournement' of the original functions of the modern infrastructure that was constructed during the colonial period, including roads, traffic signs, pedestrian routes, street furniture, urban greenery, etc. Here, the street contradicts modern planning principles: it allows more 'matter' than 'form', more 'use' than 'function', but not without consequences. On the streets of Dakar clean, controlled and disciplined public spaces are replaced by freely shared space which hardly benefits from public services, and the remains of its over-occupation – piles of rubbish, dust and sand – are multiplied in time. If modern occidental civilisation positions domesticity in opposition to dirt,[6] in the African streets, domesticity is installed in the dirt. This is due of course to poverty, overpopulation and lack of infrastructure and maintenance services, but also to a certain cultural tolerance to *dirt* – understood as a shared and collectively produced matter. Dirt is the 'matter' which undermines the traditional authority of 'form' within the city. If, in the Occident (as Katherine Shonfield has reminded us) 'dirt is matter out of place',[7] in the African city, dirt is *matter making place*.

THE 'BÉS BU NEKK' ECONOMY
In addition, we looked at the Dakar street because it is the working (and living) place for most of the women in Kambeng Kafoo. The street is the space they experience and manage every day. Women work in the informal sector because it is the only one they can afford: a flexible, self-controlled, day-to-day way of producing goods. Most of them participate in the production of goods and services which are related to everyday life – working as bissap, fish and peanut sellers, and as fabric dyers, launderers and millers. Some of them use the street as a working space because they can't afford to rent a proper space for their activity. They wash and sell on the street whilst also doing their own domestic work: for instance, cooking and looking after children. As such, they extend their domestic economy into an everyday informal economy that brings them some small benefits, just enough to have food every day for their family. It is an economy of daily survival which is exclusively based on the solidarity networks that women have created for resistance in the absence of financial or social support from the state. 'Bés bu nekk', as they say in Wolof, denoting the temporality of this economy.

The whole economy of the Cité des Femmes project is directly dependent on this 'bés bu nekk' system. The women produce just enough to live from one day to another and that is why they have created a cooperative, Kambeng Kafoo, which periodically recycles the savings by the members of the group. By running a communal saving scheme – a 'tontine'[8] – they produce a small benefit which can be used in turn by each member to increase her individual contribution to the collective saving. This circular horizontal dynamic which feeds the economy of the project also spins its construction process.

A PLACE CONCEIVED BY WOMEN FOR THEMSELVES
How critical is a dwelling place made by women for women, imagined by them and funded by the economy of their everyday lives? How far does it go beyond a male-dominated symbolic system in which women are confined within fixed and permanent walls? If the spaces that women provide for men are always associated with *wombs*, than what about the spaces that women provide for themselves? How fixed and permanent will a Cité des Femmes be, and to what extent must it be conceived and built as the other 'cités': 'en dur'?

We were concerned with the idea of conceiving a project in the feminine, together with the fact of conceiving a project in an African context, which would emphasise the importance of everyday life and solidarity networks – issuing from a specific culture in which objects and gestures have a different symbolic value to the one we are used to. We tried to imagine a spatial embodiment of the women's desires, and decided to organise a consultation that would take place as a picnic discussion and model-making session on the site of the future Cité. We asked women to bring objects from home and to use them to construct the model. Once again, it was a way of enacting 'putting together and sharing': putting together personal objects and ideas related to them and sharing the resultant meanings.

At the picnic, the Cité was modelled as a place for assembling relationships between persons, objects and thoughts. This place was formed by personal objects placed in relation to one another, objects which brought personal ties and formed collective meanings, and enabled a material and symbolic understanding of the space-time relationship through a performed negotiation between the

19.8   >Mosque.

19.9   >Market.

individuals and the group. The improvisation brought unpredictability and surprise as unexpected dimensions of the Cité emerged.

The model-making turned, unexpectedly, into a ritual performance and we discovered the 'magic' aspect of the participatory approach and realised that our current compulsory and highly prescriptive practices of participation have evacuated the poetics of improvisation and playing – and that we have forgotten to think of architecture as a magical act. The model-making interpreted architecture as a women's ritual and shared activity – just like cooking, dancing, chatting and playing. Everyday familiar objects became metonyms of uses, programmes and spaces. They operated simultaneously in the realm of representation and that of reality, participating in mapping imagination and acting ritualistically within everyday life.[9]

AN OBJECT-ORIENTED DEMOCRACY

The circular structure of the tontine, which financially supports the project, also became the way of conceiving the architectural model of the Cité. Just as in a tontine, where goods and money are put together on the table 'turn by turn', women planted the objects brought from home one by one in the sand. They brought symbolic objects (such as clocks, jugs or prayer mats), but also insignificant things, improvised on site, such as wrapping paper, pieces of wood and grass, because life gathers all these things without hierarchy. The Cité was created through both the symbolism and the direct physicality of these things: their size, their materiality, their position and their use. The women's bodies themselves became the metonyms of the Cité's possible reality; through their presence, they constructed a continuity between the imagined world and its use. Simultaneously imaginary and real, the Cité has emerged through performative gestures and words – not as an abstract model, but as a live model which enacted its 'body politic'. This way of doing also rephrased the issue of representation within a design process.

In his exhibition *Making Things Public, Atmospheres of Democracy*, Bruno Latour proposed a way of thinking about the principles of democracy which starts with what constitutes our material world and what should be the 'matter of concern' within any kind of governing system; he emphasised the role of objects and things that are tied to humans and their actions and that constitute the 'materiality' of politics. He proposed the idea of an 'object-oriented democracy' which understands the different processes of 'representation':

> What we call an 'object oriented democracy' tries to redress this bias in much of political philosophy, that is, to bring together two different meanings of the word *representation* that have been kept separate in theory although they have remained always mixed in practice. The first one, so well known in schools of law and political science, designates the ways to gather the legitimate people around some issue. In this case, a representation is said to be faithful if the right procedures have been followed. The second one, well known in science and technology, presents or rather represents what is the object of concern to the eyes and ears of those who have been assembled around it. In this case a representation is said to be good if the matters at hand have been accurately portrayed . . . The first question draws a sort of

19.10   >Football field.

place, sometimes a circle, which might be called an assembly, a gathering, a meeting, a council; the second question brings *into* this newly created locus a topic, a concern, an issue, a *topos*. But the two have been taken together: *Who* is to be concerned? *What* is to be considered?[10]

The model-making performance helped us to define both an assembly and a topic for discussion. '*Who* is to be concerned with the Cité?' Who are the actors, the makers, the users? And also, '*What* is to be considered for the Cité?' What are the needs, the desires, and the uses?

A 'PALAVER' WITH OBJECTS
This kind of discourse, collectively constructed through performative gestures and the manipulation of objects, became an enactment of 'an object-oriented democracy' within the Cité. It became a 'palaver' with objects. The 'palaver' is a performative form of collective decision-making which is still operating in most West African communities. The 'palaver' involves a large number of members, including women, and is a traditional form of governance: a public discussion which seeks collectively negotiated solutions to problems concerning the community or individuals belonging to it, in such a way that consensus is not imposed from the beginning but is found during the discussion through dialogue and participation.

As in a palaver, the model-making became a highly interactive and negotiated process, in which the participants placed themselves as *social persona*. The Cité emerged through an intersection of verbal, kinesic, and material elements in the setting. The model was not so much representational as generative of ideas and desires. Statements were reproduced both verbally and spatially – through gestures and the manipulation of objects – generating a form of *material thinking*. The objects brought as many representations of the project as there were women participating.

The complicity between us and them was also a complicity of interpretation and logics. We have adopted a logic which accepts contradiction, like Freud's 'logic of dreams', or like the logic of magical thinking. We accepted that impossible things can happen if, as in many African folk tales, we suspend our disbelief. In the process of generating the Cité, women wished for things that they could build but also for things that they will probably never be able to build, such as a school, a maternity clinic, or a hospital.

By analysing the model, we also discovered other details. For example, all the proposed spaces were collective places: the women chose to start with the 'collective' and 'the common'. They imagined the Cité by thinking about others: how to give space to others (children, men), with football grounds, schools, or hospitals. They also began from the 'necessary' – with those functions that concerned the transformation of matter, such as the construction workshop or the collective kitchen.

THE MATTER OF THE BEGINNING

The model was built on sand. What was not taken into account in the beginning was the importance of the surface of sand. The model created a world that was not heavy, stable and solid, but light and liquid. Rather than a Cité 'en dur' it suggested a liquid community, continually moving and changing shape while keeping the same materiality.

Sand is the basis of all Western African cities. It is also the 'dirt' and the 'dust' of the streets; the space women use for their everyday activities. Present everywhere in Dakar, sand has also become the most usual material for construction. The bricks of the Cité are most likely to be made from this sand. The Cité is literally made out of the ground, which is both its support and its matter. It is the element of continuity between the current location of women's activities and their future context – between the current modelling process and the future construction process, which will take place in the same place and use the same material. The Cité is thus already there, embedded in the ground of sand. It is *matter* rather than form.

In her article 'Stabat Mater', Francesca Hughes marks the difference between 'matter' and 'materiality' and notices the difficulty (modern) architecture has in representing matter rather than form, a difficulty inherited through a metaphysical tradition which starts with Aristotle and continues with Descartes and modernity. This is, Hughes suggests, because matter doesn't deal with precision, similarity and repetition, but with emergence and difference:

> If matter is, in Aristotelian terms, potential form, it might become form and it might not, materiality presents matter irreversibly poised to become form: in the wings, no turning back, at our disposal. The doubt or threat that promised form might be lost and matter return is removed. Materiality is matter domesticated, successfully colonised by formal criteria. If matter is birds in the bush, materiality is birds firmly in the hand. We well know which is worth more.[11]

Sand is still 'birds in the bush' here, potential 'cité', not yet materialised and colonised by any form, not yet domesticated by any prerequisite function other than the desires of those participating in the model-making. Belonging to another knowledge tradition, which is not philosophical but oral and performative, the performance-model of the Cité des Femmes suggests the possibility of an

19.11 >Maternity clinic.

architecture which represents, or rather re-presents, *matter* in the sense suggested by Latour. If the 'palaver' has transformed objects into 'things', sand is not only 'matter' but also a 'matter of concern'.

Hughes builds her article around questions of generation and maternity, playing once again on the connection between the figures of 'matter' and 'mater' or 'mother' that other women theorists and practitioners – such as Elisabeth Grosz, Katherine Shonfield or Jennifer Bloomer – have also brought into architecture. Together with them, she parallels the political exclusion of feminine knowledge in theory with the exclusion of matter in architecture, and tries to restore their contemporary legacy.

MATTERS AND MOTHERS

In the same way, the women imagined the Cité as a theatre in which matter acts like a 'mother'. Its 'belly' of sand receives and nurtures objects in a loose order. No 'form' is suggested for the Cité – only temporary marks on sand, which disappear soon after the event when what was a Cité becomes, again, just matter.

The maternal role of sand recalls for us the figure of 'chora', which Plato, in the *Timaeus*, designates as the place of generation, and to which he assigns three aspects: the recipient and receiver ('dekhomai', 'dekhomenon') of the world, always changing and changeable, and a 'third kind' which participates in both the sensible and the intelligible.[12] For Plato, chora is the place of the conception and the construction of the world. This figure has nourished the imaginary of many feminists and contemporary architectural theorists,[13] and provides an alternative to the Aristotelian–Cartesian tradition as a reference for work with space.

Just like the Cité, which is drawn with objects rather than with precise shapes or functions, the chora in Plato's text is a place expressed through metaphors and metonyms rather than concepts which belong in the realm of the maternal: chora is described like a 'nurse', a 'matrix' or a 'mould'.[14] If chora is still a kind – a 'third kind'– it is not a form. It is that which 'gives shape to all forms without having herself any form'.[15] It is space understood as a receiver – welcoming, tolerant, hospitable – not as stretched-out void-space or as gap

19.12 >Kambeng Kafoo's 'shaking'.

or distance to be conquered. With chora, the question of space is not that of measurement, possession and formal mastery, but that of generation.

Plato's chora also functions like a sieve, or other 'instruments' which work by being moved or shaken and which, in return, transmit movement to seeds so that they can be sifted. Thus, chora's work is one of spacing-out, of giving space in the amorphous mass of the material which is to be filtered. The order established through shaking privileges relations and associations rather than identities. This shaking of chora allows a separation from before the separation, from 'before everything was organised'; separation where 'the thought of the demiurge is absent': a separation 'without either reason or measure' ('alogos kai ametros', in Plato's words).

The question asked by the women's performative model which involved associations of movements, bodies and objects was 'how to give birth to a project': a question which interprets the model 'without either reason or measure', as a Platonic 'third kind' which participates in both the sensible and the intelligible representation of the Cité.

'BIRTH GIVING'

In order to mark the place of the maternity building in the Cité, one woman took a piece of fabric and folded it under her dress. She played at being pregnant and giving birth at the exact place where she would like the maternity clinic to be built. Someone lent her a child, who she fed at her breast to make the game more realistic.

We understood this playing not only as a performance but also as a performative act (as in Judith Butler's feminist interpretation); as a discursive enactment which brings into being that which it names, while keeping the possibility of its reproduction and resignification.[16] Women's playing-out of *giving birth* interpreted the Cité as a 'Cité of Mothers' but also as a *mothering space*, as a chora – suggesting an understanding of the whole process of planning and designing as 'birth giving'. The scene of 'birth giving' marks the moment of passing from containment to delivery in the process of 'conception' of the Cité. It is not a metaphoric representation, but a material and embodied performance of thinking and doing through emergence, differentiation and self-organisation.

The group of women play *chora*, reminding us that the beginning of the Cité des Femmes, as in an African folk tale, is also a re-enactment of the beginning of the world. They bring into play the reproductive force of all mothers, suggesting that life matters are those which make place.

Together with other women from the northern hemisphere, who have developed a materialist approach to architecture and theory, Kambeng Kafoo and the women of the Cité des Femmes taught us that the material of thinking and building in architecture should not be separated from the material of living, and that, before 'form', a place is made through the shaking and filtering of life 'matters' and the materiality which results from everyday economies, politics and social life; that this way of making involves a position of a 'third kind', which is 'without either reason or measure' and which reiterates performatively the hospitality and generosity of mothers.

1   >Cité is a French word that comes from the Latin 'civitas', just as the English word 'city' does.

2   >Bissap is a plant from the hibiscus family, which is widely used in the West African diet for its high nutritional properties and vitamin C. Rural women cultivate bissap on the fields around Dakar to be sold within women's networks in the capital. Kambeng Kafoo is part of these networks, which include sellers of bissap and its products: fresh bissap drinks, bissap dishes, etc.

3   >The Franc CFA is a currency used by some francophone countries in West Africa. This common currency is meant to encourage exchange between them and the former colonial power.

4   >If the average annual income in Senegal is around US$490 (source: World Bank statistics in 2001), the average income per day is around US$1.20 (approximately 1000FCFA), which is exactly what a woman might need to save in order to acquire her piece of land in two years. But at present most of them are able to save only 100FCFA per day; this means that they will need 20 years to obtain a piece of land, and 40 more to build a house.

5   >See the film *Lagos/Koolhaas*, written and directed by Bregtje van der Haak, produced by Sylvia Baan for Pieter van Huystee Film.

6   >In her seminal book *Purity and Danger*, Mary Douglas reminds us that 'dust' and 'dirt' are matters negatively associated with women. See *Purity and Danger, An Analysis of the Concepts of Pollution and Taboo*, London: Routledge, 1966. Also in the article 'Dust' of his Dictionary, Georges Bataille gives the image of a domestic woman fighting against dust, confirming once again this association in occidental culture that makes 'dust' the metonymy of woman. See also Allan Stoekl (ed.), *Visions of Excess: Selected Writings*, 1927–1939, translated by Allan Stoekl, Carl R. Lovitt and Donald M. Leslie, Jr., Minneapolis: University of Minnesota Press, 1985.

7   >This is the title of Katherine Shonfield's architectural installation which transformed a Victorian lavatory outside a Baroque church in Spitalfields, London, in 1991. Her installation – which included texts, architectural plans, urban maps and cleaning products – questioned the role of architecture in the 'war against dirt as matter out of place'. She announced also the 'era of de-regulation through feathering', by covering the interior walls and ceiling of the unused lavatory with a layer of white, delicate 'dust' of feathers, and sought 'to undermine the way the architecture delineated and defined the literal production of dirt'. See Katherine Shonfield, *Walls Have Feelings*, London: Routledge, 2000, pp. 48–51.

8   >At a first glance, the 'tontine' is a very simple and affordable form of collection of money and goods. It is based on proximity, confidence and close connections between persons sharing a common interest. The contribution of each member, in money or goods, is defined for a period agreed collectively (usually weekly or monthly). Classified between the forms of informal and alternative funding, the management of the tontine doesn't require training and involves no rules other than a mutual agreement. This form of saving plays an important role in the African economy, allowing many women to put together capital for housing construction, family ceremony or business.

9   >The consultation and model-making took place at Keur Massar on 17th October 2003. The women participating included: Madjiguène Cissée, Ndèye Yacine Diagne, Fatou Sow, Balanto, Diarétou Diallo, Diara Diagne, Amy Bass, Aïda Diallo, Fatou Dramé, Aida Guèye, Ouley Ba, Moayang Gaye, Aïta Ndoye, Awa Mbaye, Mainouna Diop, Delfine Mousso, Dia Zeynaboussi, Aissatou Gaye, Sokhna Diagne, Khoury Diop, Nafi Sour, Ndiaye Khumba, Aïda Touré, Fatou Gaye, Oumy Senne, Adama Dhiakhel, Oulimata Ndiaye , Cadou Ndiaye, Ammi Bass, Mariama Diallo, Diaretou Diallo, Kine Dallo, Mabayang Toure, Ouréye Assim, Salla Niang, Awa Diallo Diaw Gweye, Doussou Touré, Moussou Koto Diary, Diabou Bala, Bana Djitté, Moussoukeba Darry, Betine Fabiada, Seyni Gassama, Siré Souna, Fatou Sania, Khady Cissé, Souma Diané, Khady Braya, Sadama Biaye, Tremineté, Alry Biaye, Maty Touré, Téné Diandy, Tounaka Faty, Awa Djitté, Benetou Mandiam, Amy Diouf and members of the groups Kambeng Kafoo, Afème, Jappoo, Santa-Yalla, Afi Gorée, Sobeya, Bokk-Wërsëk and Fatima Alto Beish.

10   >Bruno Latour, 'From Realpolitik to Dingpolitik or How to Make Things Public' in Bruno Latour and Peter Weibel (eds.), *Making Things Public, Atmospheres of Democracy*, Cambridge, Massachusetts: The MIT Press, 2005, p. 16.

11   >Francesca Hughes, '*Stabat Mater* – On standing in for matter' in Doina Petrescu (ed.), *Altering Practices: Feminist politics and poetics of space*, London: Routledge, 2006.

12   >'. . . and a third Kind is ever-existing Place, which admits not of destruction, and provides room ('edron') for all things that have birth, itself being apprehensible by a kind of bastard reasoning by the aid of non-sensation, barely an object of belief', Plato, *Timaeus*, 52b W.

(Heinemann edition), translated by G. Bury, Boston, Massachusetts: Harvard University Press, 1975.

13   > The concept of 'chora' entered architectural debate, especially in the 1990s, following the theoretical 'excavation' of Plato's text by Jacques Derrida. What has followed was the influential project 'Choral Works' by Jacques Derrida and Peter Eisenman, which has become an important reference for deconstruction in architecture and has generated wide discussions and publications. Other contributions came out at about the same time from the feminist side, referencing the work of Luce Irigaray and Julia Kristeva on chora and its feminine figurations: i.e. Elisabeth Grosz's article 'Women, Chora, Dwelling' in *ANY* No. 4, 1994; Claire Robinson, 'Chora, She Folds' in *Folding in Architecture*, Architectural Design Profile, 1994; my own text on 'Chora or the Impossibility of "Thinking" about Space', included in my Ph.D. dissertation, 1995; and many others.

14   > 'For it is laid down by nature as moulding-stuff (*ekmagéion*) for everything.' Plato, *Timaeus*, 50c, *op. cit.*

15   > 'It is right that the substance which is to be fitted to receive frequently over its whole extent the copies of all things intelligible and eternal should itself, of its own nature, be void of all the forms [*amorphon*: 'formless', 'informe']'. Plato, *Timaeus* etc.

16   > Judith Butler's notion of 'performativity' developed in *Gender Trouble* and further in her subsequent work, is a key concept for theorising new non-essentialist approaches to gender in feminist theory. For Butler, gender is not an inherent attribute of the subject but it is constructed through 'performative reiteration': that is, as the subject's constant attempt to embody hegemonic norms. See, notably, her *Gender Trouble; Feminism and the Subversion of Identity*, New York, London: Routledge, 1990.

MATERIAL RESPONSIBILITY AND THE WORK OF RURAL STUDIO

ANDREW FREEAR >MATERIAL RESPONSIBILITY AND THE WORK
OF RURAL STUDIO

*Rural Studio was founded by Samuel Mockbee (known as Sambo) in 1992 to expose
architecture students at Auburn University 'to their social responsibility as
architectural citizens, along with the principles of design and construction.'[1] The
studio is based in Newbern, a rural community in Hale County, the poorest county
in Alabama, where second-year students can spend a semester working together to
construct a house, and fifth-year students stay a whole year designing and building
community projects. Rural Studio's projects are well known internationally for their
invention, poetry and resourcefulness – particularly in relation to the use of
materials. Here, Andrew Freear, who took over the running of Rural Studio after
Mockbee's death in 2001, talks about the educational and material implications of
working hands-on in the specific economic and social circumstances of the deep
South.[2]*

Andrew Freear: Having the opportunity to build is an amazing 'carrot'. At
architecture school you and I were probably never given $10 to build a bookshelf –
let alone $25,000 to build a house or $50,000 to build a fire station. Students take
the opportunity and the responsibility very seriously. In the studio, if you or I talk
to a student about a paper project it's as if we're begging them to think about it
and make a design move. But when a donation of materials arrives at the Rural
Studio it changes the design and I don't even have to tell them to do it. They learn
iteration without the professor having to beg them to be iterative, which is a
magical thing. Suddenly there is something at stake, a 'real' relationship with a
family or a community of people who will be hurt if the building leaks. This tends
to temper outrageous statements and proposals. Students begin to realise the
implications of the drawn line. Is it a two-by-four or a piece of steel? How heavy
will it be? Can they get it to site? Will they nail it or weld it?

    I'm certainly not suggesting that everyone should have a Rural Studio, but
it's interesting that it has evolved in a generation where the computer has become
such a dominant tool. I visit many schools and there are often complaints from the
Luddites about how no one uses the workshop any more. If the Rural Studio is
waving its hand saying, 'What about how this material smells or feels or weighs?'
that's terrific. Some of the publicity makes Mockbee out to be a guy who wanted to
save the world. I lived with him for four years, and nothing could be further from
the truth. It's a successful programme because its very clear goal is teaching
architecture students. Of course there are some nice spin-offs and benefits to
the community. The students are very lucky to be so immersed in a small rural
community which is such a contrast to their previous existence, either as city
dwellers or suburban dwellers. The studio focuses on making architecture,
communicating as well as is possible with the clients and making an architecture
that has aspiration and that does not patronise clients.

THE SUPERSHED AND PODS: STUDENT ACCOMMODATION, 1997–2000
AF: One of my first projects at the Rural Studio was the cardboard house, probably
the most interesting of the pods under the Supershed. As housing for Rural Studio
students it is a perfect example of the possibilities the pods offer us to really
experiment on ourselves. I feel we have a responsibility to try this stuff because
few others have the opportunity afforded by our isolation. So at the same time as
educating students, being sustainable, being responsible, I am very aware that if

20.1

20.1 >The rear view of
the cardboard house.

20.2 >The cardboard
pod appears from under
the supershed.

20.2

we don't do cardboard houses or carpet houses and be provocative and push the envelope, there are very few folks out there with this opportunity.

Aside from experimentation with cardboard, the challenge of the cardboard house for young students was very simply: how to make straight precise things like wood beams and metal and glass attach to big fluffy objects. Did we all learn very much from the technology of building with cardboard? I don't think so. Could we have learned more? Certainly, but we have very limited scientific resources. We learn by doing and inhabiting then watching, and our students are not so interested in research in the classical sense. So in the end we used the cardboard as building blocks and stacked them on top of each other. We wanted people to see that the building was made from cardboard. It is still sitting there today and it looks fantastic. Nothing has happened to the cardboard. The house has a big roof, and it is well drained, raised slightly off the ground and has a gravel surround. It illustrates the basic principals of building in this location. Students look at which buildings have survived: all the old wooden buildings around here that have been here for 150 years have all got big roofs that protect the walls and they're all off the ground.

NEWBERN LITTLE LEAGUE BASEBALL FIELD, 2003
Katie Lloyd Thomas: The cardboard technology you developed then appears much later in a quieter way, used in the outfield wall for Newbern Little League Baseball Field.
AF: The Baseball Field is a very grown-up project. We were offered such a poor piece of land and there was so much work in the ground – it was all about drainage. With cardboard bales used for the outfield wall, our intention and understanding was that the metal braces on the cardboard would eventually snap. So we piled dirt over the top of the bales and seeded it with grass. Our hope, which is being confirmed, was that as the bales disintegrated the dirt and the grass would hold it all together. It's lovely, if a little kid runs into it she's not going to hurt herself. And the cardboard bales were going to go in the ground anyway as landfill. The bizarre thing is that we got the cardboard bales for free for the house, but when you start ringing up a manufacturer and saying we need another 500 of these things they start asking you for money. Supply equals demand! What they were trying to do was to make back the money that they were previously paying to put them in a landfill.

KLT: At what point in the design process did you select the material to use for the audience enclosure?
AF: There were many conversations about which nets to use, and then suddenly in a jury someone said, 'What about catfish nets?' A 'lightbulb went on in the room', a magic moment. Until that point, it had been, 'Well, we don't know if we're going to be using chain-link or some kind of mesh.' The guy who runs the team is a catfish farmer and he knows how to mend the net. It's free and the farmers have lots of it spare that is used for patching the big nets. Then you research it and of course it's great against UV light, it doesn't rot and we discovered that its qualities are virtually the same as the materials used in Major League Baseball stadiums. For us it was total serendipity.

20.3

20.3 >The catfish net slinky winds its way around the field.

20.4 >Evidence of how the catfish net has been fixed – note the cardboard bales.

20.4

MASON'S BEND COMMUNITY CENTER, 2000

AF: I think our best use of materials is when the discovery of an appropriate material 'just happens', instead of deciding right at the beginning of a project to use a particular material. They are just occurrences that come at a particular moment in a project and you don't really know how they happen or where they come from. I suspect the use of windshields at Mason's Bend Community Center came from a conversation that was happening at the time in architecture schools, where everyone wanted to do 'fish-skins' in their buildings. Anyway, the students found that the side windows of the Chevrolet Caprice had pre-drilled holes in them; they picked them up from a wreckers' yard in Chicago, built a mock-up and the rest is history.

20.5, 20.6, 20.7

Mason's Bend Community Center is one of my favourite buildings by Rural Studio. But nobody maintains or cares for it; everybody looks at it and asks why, and I have to send my folks down there every so often and get them to clean it up. We have made mistakes where projects have no clear community ownership or tenuous programming, perhaps. But we learn from our actions. More recently we have tried very hard to look for communities that are willing to go and find the money themselves, and when they become our client they take more ownership.

A lot of our early projects were projects we were doing for ourselves. We graduated to public projects, and when you do a public project with public money you've got to be grown up. We can't build such things out of toilet rolls and plastic or tin cans. First of all, it is patronising. The detailing has to be designed more sustainably, and with a greater understanding of local perceptions. We have a project down in Thomaston, the farmers' market, which rusts. The artful architects think rust is cute but the local folks equate rust with decay. As a result of this, in our second project in Thomaston we have been brutally aware that we have to make sensitive choices of materials that shouldn't need maintaining. The projects also have to respond to the fact that the clients have no money and no time to 'share the sweat' because they are out earning a crust. The average income in Hale County is something like $15,000 a year. You don't expect people like that to volunteer – if they are going to work, they are going to go somewhere and earn some money.

MUSIC MAN'S HOUSE, 2003

AF: I want to use means and methods that are not patronising to either the students or to my clients. Just because you collect tin cans doesn't mean I should make you live in a tin-can house. Whenever you see publicity about us they always show Music Man's House and Lucy's House. Music Man's House is a reflection of 30 students building a house for one man, who was there every day and completely bought into the process. The metal hogwire with the infill is appropriate, in my view, because Music Man has appropriated it with his own signs and it has actually become a place that he has taken over. It has become an armature for him. So I have always worried about it being patronising, but it is *so*

20.5 >Chevrolet Caprice windows with pre-existing holes.

20.6 >Students removing windows.

20.7 >Mock up.

20.8 >Forrest Fulton installing the windshield.

20.8

20.9

20.9 >Masons Bend
Community Chapel.

20.10 >Windshield
Detail.

20.10

Music Man. He enjoyed the process so much that you just have to buy into it. But do I struggle with that? Yes. I don't know if my students do, but I want them to look at it and think about it.

LUCY'S HOUSE, 2002

I came on board the project to build Lucy's House as an observer, when Sambo died. On the face of it carpet tiles are pretty nasty things, but we went through the whole process of how to use the tiles and we talked to the manufacturer. Interface are a large corporation, but we decided they were actually pretty good folks with a decent sustainable ambition. They wanted to close the cycle and to stop taking any minerals out of the ground. So in their new process they rent their tiles to people, and when they're worn out Interface take them back and put them back into the process. They come out as new tiles again. I think that's honourable; that's why we've worked with them. The tiles we were able to use in the house, which were more than seven years old and therefore no longer 'off-gassed', were seconds and samples and had just been sitting in storage, so they were very clean.

So, the question to the manufacturer was: how can you build a house out of carpet? I asked him, 'How would you use these tiles if you wanted to keep water out and stop fires?', and he said that he would lay them horizontally. 'What about stacking them?' I asked. 'Perfect,' he said. So we went back to Rural Studio and started stacking them and spraying them down with water, compressing them, slightly slanting them to see it made any difference. We made all of these mock-ups. We sprayed the wall with water, and the water penetrated a little but with good ventilation it had dried out after a few hours. So what you build is virtually a monolithic wall, like stone. You put a huge great roof over it, you lift it off of the ground, and it's still there, it's in better shape than the overhanging plywood eaves! The wall is fantastic – just bleached and there's no vermin. It allowed us to give them a house. It's a big family in more ways than one, and they used to live in two rooms. The kid, AJ, used to be a disaster at school; now he has his own bedroom, some privacy and he's doing great at school.

ANTIOCH BAPTIST CHURCH, 2002

AF: At Antioch Church we recycled the complete building. Nobody else would have taken the time to do it; they would have just demolished the existing church. The congregation helped us demolish the thing, and what's nice is that they know that all the wood in the new church is from the old church. One of the student's mothers planed all of the reused boards to take the paint and finish off. She spent weeks pushing pieces of wood through a planer that now wrap the inside of the church.

All of the infill webbing on the trusses had been the structure of the original church. Originally we wanted the bottom chords to be wood, but we didn't have long enough pieces. When we actually drew the truss, there was so much metal in the chords that we thought, 'Why don't we just make them out of metal?' So now you have a lovely datum that runs all the way around the room.

Some of the church is original wood, and some is donated. The concrete blocks that form the whole north wall and foundation wall, they were blocks from one of the dormitories at Auburn University. They get the kids to go and buy concrete blocks to make furniture with in their dorms, and at the end of every year

20.11   >Music Man.

20.12   >Main family carpet room with Lucy's bedroom to the right.

20.13   >The students hand-stacked and cut 72,000 carpet tiles.

20.14   >AJ, standing to the left, has his own room and privacy.

20.14

20.13

20.12

20.15, 20.16, 20.17

the caretaker just throws it all out on the street. So we sent the students back to Auburn, and they stacked them up on the truck and brought them out here.

The congregation put new pews in and hung pictures all over the walls. Some areas are full of plants, and they've got light fixtures on the ceiling fans now. They have taken it over as theirs and they love it. They know that it is their building recycled into the new one. It gives them the baptismal font and the restroom they wanted, so it's a perfect facility for them. There's one big window that looks right out over the cemetery. For that small congregation, that's very important. That's their connection to their family. None of these folks can talk about the way the architecture looks, but they always talk about how calm the space is. The calmness to the place is very Baptist in its way. There's no decoration or ostentatiousness to it.

PERRY LAKES PARK FACILITIES, 2003

KLT: It has been suggested that Rural Studio is able to work in this way in part because there are no building regulations and no building inspectors in Hale County, and you don't have to produce and submit drawings for approval.

AF: That's true. There's the 'Southern Building Code' which covers the region, but our local government is not wealthy enough to pay a building inspector. When the students built the tower for the toilet rooms at Perry Lakes Park, the structure was all anodised aluminium, so there was a lot of welding involved that we couldn't do, and the students did 50 shop drawings for it of the highest quality. The welder had never had drawings like that before; he couldn't believe it. But I told the students, 'You've got to do this well because the guy is doing it for free, and he has to do it fast and he has to do it right: be professional and you'll get a professional result'. And they did it.

The current projects have become large and complicated, and the only way any team can get their heads around the problems and the project is to draw – but because there is no professional building inspector to check these drawings, we do it ourselves. Of course, the situation is both frightening and wonderful! But we don't take it lightly at all. We are very lucky to have a group of engineers from all over the world who are interested in working with us. As professionals they have to start somewhere: so they start with the building codes.

20.15 >The original Antioch Baptist Church.

20.16 >A student's mother planing boards form the original church.

20.17 >The throwaway blocks from the student dorms.

20.18 >'Inventory' of materials (piles of material donated or recycled).

20.18

20.19

20.20

20.19 >The datum running around the room, and the view to the cemetery.

20.20 >View of the blank south-facing wall of the church.

Sure, the argument is made that it's easy for us – and on the one hand it is, but on the other hand we have to make moral judgements. It's actually a burden for me and for the students to understand, 'We probably should have a handrail here but we're not going to.' We have an opportunity to challenge the codes, to make more rigorous, better buildings and give greater value for money for the most folks possible. My students are the first ones to want to know where they are relative to the codes and I think that's good. The way we work down here is a kind of social agreement – like when I agree to drive on the right-hand side of the road, because if I don't you and I will crash into each other. Fortunately, it's not a litigious society at present. At the moment everyone buys into the process: the politicians, the clients, the students and the teachers. But times will change and that will mean the end of the Rural Studio.

1   >Samuel Mockbee cited in William J. Carpenter, *Learning by Building: Design and Construction in Architectural Education*, New York: Van Nostrand Reinhold, 1997, p. 63.
2   >This is an edited version of a conversation with Katie Lloyd Thomas on 1 July 2005, based on a talk given by Andrew Freear at the Material Matters conference in March/April 2004.

20.21   >View from the tower toilet.

20.22   >Mound toilets and tower.

20.22

The renewed or recycled has had much play in recent years as a result of interest in, or perhaps anxiety about, the state of nature. Our built culture in general, and material practices in particular, have come under close scrutiny in a new environmental critique. This critique has been made possible by innovations in the natural and material sciences – most notably in the development of ecology, the study of the world's ecosystems. This environmental critique, however, is as much dependent on language as it is on science – or rather, dependent on its ability to cause language to mutate in its favour. Like any other narrative, it seeks to persuade by successfully implanting new terms and repositioning familiar ones: terms like the overextended, and hence almost meaningless, 'sustainability'; and others, more specific, like 'environmental impact', 'global warming' and 'recycling'.

Within the built environment, environmental design seeks to model the production and operation of buildings as closely as possible on the paradigm of the ecosystem. Ecosystems are closed, with life inside them built on a network of interdependencies: of organism and habitat, and organism and organism. Energy is consumed, waste is produced and, instead of being thrown away, it is kept within the system. The detritus of a completed process becomes the raw material of a new process, a pattern most apparent in nature in something like the food chain. Here, the used is not only re-used but re-formed, so that it is no longer recognisable as itself, becoming something new: the worm, eaten by the bird, becomes the bird; the cow, eaten by the boy, becomes the boy.

It is a waste-not/want-not circular model of consumption found in what's left of 'nature' – as opposed to our second-order linear model of consumption, in which energy and resources are sucked in and wastes are thrown away. This linear pattern of consumption exists nowhere in nature, and, before the Industrial Revolution, was not found to any extent in human culture either. The desire for it may have been there, but the sheer time and effort of the handmade gave pause for thought. It was much easier to re-use than to throw out and start again. Within environmental design, a building or group of buildings can be analysed in terms of how far short it falls of this ecosystem model, by measuring what is going in to sustain the building – fuel, food, goods – and what is coming out as waste products – CO_2, sewage, rubbish. The lower the amounts entering and leaving the building, the closer its metabolism is to the virtuous circle of the ecosystem – and the closer it is, the 'better' it is.

Apart from the desire to be unlike nature, to assert culture as a higher – and incorruptible – order, what is the cause of our resistance to such virtue? Perhaps it is environmentalism's insistence that we keep our eyes on the limitations of matter – including our own – rather than imagine that our transcendences – most recently, the digital – are independent of them. The fact that we are corruptible and recyclable, from man to maggot, makes most of us kick against the reality of the material. But like it or not, the appearance of new matter on the planet, whether born or made, is in fact a re-appearance, a recycling of pre-existing matter – like the generations that come before and after us: new, and yet not new. During these life cycles, none of this matter is created or destroyed, so that although in constant metamorphosis from one state to another, one form to another, substance has an essential sameness – a fact noted by, among many others, Gottfried Leibniz:

21.1 >Parthenon, Athens.

21.2 >Altes Museum,
Berlin, K.F. Schinkel.

Each portion of matter may be conceived as a garden full of plants, and as a pond full of fish. But every branch of each plant, every member of each animal, and every drop of their liquid parts is in itself likewise a similar garden or pond.[1]

In nature, then, the 'new' is found in a transfer of matter from one form to another, all based on the same carbon. In material culture, the model is the same: the 'new' is found in the transfer of raw materials into manipulated materials – bauxite into aluminium, sand into glass – and manipulated materials into one form or another of new artefact – books, jets, buildings. In both nature and culture, we perceive the change in matter through the change in its form. Until the nineteenth century, change in form in material culture was almost as gradual as the change in form in nature: an incremental evolution from style to style. As a result, there was often no dramatic difference between the new and the renewed, as the transformation of new building materials into new buildings resulted so often in the renewal of old forms: for example, from the Parthenon (figure 21.1) to the Altes Museum (figure 21.2).

At the beginning of the twentieth century, however, attitudes to the new and the renewed changed, largely because the formation of the new changed. The effort of the handmade – and therefore the incentive to re-use – vanished in the slipstream of the assembly line. Until this acceleration, a new that was essentially a renewal was unproblematic. It tied into Western tradition at its deepest level; into myths of rebirth, of the earth and of the individual. As such, something decayed brought back into vigorous use was to be prized as a symbol of the universality of this possibility rather than spurned as 'not new'. With the totalising effects of industrialisation, however, the model of rebirth was supplanted, though unwittingly, by the model of resurrection.

Resurrection is a step beyond rebirth; history ends. There is no repetition of either disintegration or return, as there is in the passing of the seasons or the recycling of objects. With resurrection, repetition is replaced by a dream of once-and-for-all reconstitution: the body miraculously transcending its corruption and remaining permanently new. When talking about the cultural artefact rather than a (natural) body, once-and-for-all re-constitution becomes once-and-for-all constitution: the new thing transcending decay and remaining permanently new. This may be nonsense, but it is powerful nonsense, drawing on our anguish over the decay and loss of the specific – the individual – and negating any solace to be had in the continuity of the general – the generation, the species.

The permanently new was precisely what the founding fathers of the Modern Movement aspired to. In a tract such as Le Corbusier's Towards a New Architecture, the intention at first appears to be to urge us to escape a past which is irrelevant to the establishment of 'a new order' based on change rather than tradition:

Construction has found new means.
Architecture finds itself confronted with new laws.
Industry has created new tools ...[2]

But this change is driving towards a new 'standard', as the Parthenon was a standard for its epoch and beyond:

> Let us display, then, the Parthenon and the motor-car so that it may be clear that it is a question of two products of selection in different fields, one of which has reached its climax and the other is evolving.[3]
>
> ... [T]he Parthenon appears to us as a living work, full of grand harmonies ... [I]ts correspondence is ... with those huge impressive machines ... which may be considered the most perfect results of our present-day activities, the only products of our civilisation which have really 'got there'.[4]

'Getting there' means becoming typical of the epoch in question; a type, a standard, or in effect, a classic. At that point, evolution ceases – although it is not clear precisely when that point occurs:

> When once a standard is established, competition comes at once and violently into play. It is a fight; in order to win you must do better than your rival in every minute point ... Thus we get the study of minute points pushed to its limits. Progress.[5]

Unlike the traditional standard, the new Modernist standard is distinguished by the entirely new conditions that have brought it forth: conditions of continual change. The new 'classics' – the Barcelona Pavilion, the Villa Savoye – could not therefore, ideologically, be allowed to show their age. Ageing implies an ever-increasing distance from the ever-appearing new, and the new typified the new epoch (or the epoch of 'the new'?), in which we are still trapped. As being typical of the epoch was the prime requisite of the standard, and as architects like Le Corbusier aspired to creating the architectural standard for his epoch, their work had, of necessity, to continue to appear 'hot off the line'. Thus, the decay of the materials of the Villa Savoye was as unacceptable as the decline of the ideas that produced it. What was wished for was the once-and-for-all constitution described above: the new thing that transcends decay and remains permanently new.

This is very well described in David Leatherbarrow and Moshen Mostafavi's book *On Weathering*, in which they identify an anxiety about the weathering of Modernist buildings.[6] A movement driven by conscious rupture with a failed and decayed ancien régime could not itself be perceived as subject to the same decay when what was wanted was an end to linear time, an end to the passage of objects from new into old – a metaphysical state of permanent erection, rather than resurrection.

Not all Modernists were this wishful. Some realised, long before Mao Tse-tung's wife, that the only way to engage in the paradoxical activity of maintaining the new was to instigate a state of 'permanent revolution' – permanent impermanence. Filippo Marinetti, the 'caffeine of Europe', poet and leader of the Italian Futurists, declared that each generation must destroy the cities of their parents and begin again, in order to preserve humankind from history. The Russian Futurists were just as adamant, 'I write nihil on anything that has been done before,' said Mayakovsky.[7] The old was to be bulldozed away for the new, and the new in art was to reflect the new in the rest of material culture: a violent, repudiative, man-made new – the 'second nature' celebrated by Karl Marx, forged by us to provide for us where the 'first nature' does not. There is no once-and-for-all new here, and certainly no renewal. This is Marinetti at full tilt in his manifesto for Italian Futurism, published in *Le Figaro* in 1909:

> Set fire to the shelves of libraries! . . . Flood the cellars of museums! . . . We would deliver Italy from its canker of professors, archaeologists . . . and antiquaries. Italy has for too long been the great market for the second-hand dealers.[8]

And so the practice of renewing the built fabric was to be replaced by the Modern Movement's tabula rasa.

The cult of continuity (new-as-renewed) was not entirely supplanted by the cult of originality (new-as-novelty), however. It merely went underground, waiting to return. Environmentalism has brought it back, to counter the collapse of the new into novelty. Today, so-called 'late capitalism' has reduced the Modernist project for ceaseless revolution to rampant consumerism: novel objects in novel forms in ever-increasing numbers, flowing from arrival into obsolescence with increasing speed, to promote increased consumption and profit. As the distance between sites of production and sites of consumption continues to increase, so too does the consumer's inability to see the human and environmental price of this production. It is easy to believe in a completely unproblematic 'second nature', more bountiful than the first, if one knows nothing of the material processes that drive it.

Not everyone has remained ignorant, however. The ever-accelerating flow of matter – off the production line and onto the tip, briefly by way of the consumer – has led many to reflect not only upon the social costs of consumerism but also the environmental costs, which transform an industry's financial gains into a nation's financial losses – from pollution to ill health, climate change and overexploited resources. In other words, the power to transform matter at will, with ease, in the service of a profitable novelty carries material consequences. While primary energy and building materials are produced in such problematic ways, the making of objects is burdened with environmental as well as social consequences. A 'second nature' consumerism driven by novelty has proved unsustainable by the 'first nature'. Worldwide, there is too much extraction, too much through-put, and too much waste for slow natural processes to either provide raw materials or absorb wastes quickly enough. The built environment is heavily implicated in this overexploitation:

> 50% of material resources taken from nature are building-related. Over 50% of national waste production comes from the building sector. 40% of the energy consumption in Europe is building-related.[9]

Add to this the 40–50 per cent of greenhouse gases contributed by the built environment, and the cult of the new cannot be ignored by architects for much longer. Buildings move much more slowly through the production/consumption cycle than most other objects, but they take a great deal of energy and material

21.3 >Norton House,
Venice Beach, Los
Angeles, Frank Gehry.

21.4 >Paramount Laundry,
Culver City, Los Angeles,
Eric Owen Moss.

to make. There is also energy embodied in the materials themselves. This is the amount of fossil fuel it takes to extract, process and transport them. Embodied energy, and the environmental damage of one kind or another that it represents, are irrecoverable and irreparable. The deed is done. So the specification of materials is of far more than aesthetic importance:

> Wood has the least embodied energy at 639 kilowatt hours per ton. Brick is next (4 x the amount for wood), followed by concrete (5 x), plastic (6 x), glass (14 x), steel (24 x), and aluminium (125 x).[10]

So the aim is now to reduce the environmental impact of the act of building – first by reducing the consumption of energy, which requires a re-framing of the perception of the new.

Neither architects nor their clients are in the habit of asking whether a proposed building is necessary in the first place. For both groups, the new building – new in form and substance – is the sine qua non of architecture. Environmentalists, in the interests of reducing the enormous environmental impact of the building industry, are asking us to get back into the loop of a circular model of consumption, and, where feasible, to consider recycling buildings before building the new. The existing building represents energy already spent and pollution already caused. The longer its life, the less new energy needs to be spent and the less new pollution caused. Certain environmentalists within architecture declare that all new building must cease. This is patently absurd. It is the case that an existing building may very well take more energy and cause more pollution to restore and run than a well-built new building – in which circumstances, the new is entirely justified environmentally.

The birth and death of a building are now as important as its life. The profligate waste of building materials during construction represents a waste of energy and needs to be avoided. And the ease with which a building can be deconstructed is now as important as its efficient construction. As much as possible of the building's materials needs to be recycled, as in an ecosystem where the waste of a spent process becomes the raw material of a new process. With global warming increasing for the foreseeable future, an economy of means may become a matter of survival as well as aesthetics – but it is aesthetics, specifically the aesthetic preference for the new, that often stands in the way of this. The environmental cost of making building materials like brick, glass and concrete suggests that we should ensure that their lives last as long as possible, through reuse or recycling. The cultural resistance to this, however, is not easy to overcome. Persuading designers and their clients of the desirability of the 'not new' can perhaps only be done by other designers, seducing with their solutions rather than hectoring about moral imperatives. Frank Gehry's playful Norton House in Venice Beach, Los Angeles (figure 21.3) is an example of recycling as bricolage, as is Eric Owen Moss's more hard-edged Paramount Laundry in Culver City, Los Angeles (figure 21.4). That the new-as-novelty ever needs to be justified antagonises many within architecture. In the schools, old Modernist ideas of originality, and of a 'paper' architecture of novelty, carry no environmental price. And in the profession, the call to consider the environmental as well as the aesthetic and financial impacts of materials specification seems an

21.5 >Restoration of
Sans Souci Palace,
Potsdam.

21.6 >Carre d'Art,
Nimes, Norman Foster.

intolerable extra burden on practitioners already overburdened with limits and
strictures.

Is there any way of reconciling the nature-based paradigm of the new-as-renewed – new substance in recycled forms (figure 21.5), recycled substance in new forms – with the culture-based paradigm of the new-as-novelty – new substance in new forms (figure 21.6)? Is there any point at which a seemingly puritanical environmentalism and a plush consumerism intersect? Is there any way in which environmentalism can avoid being seen as nothing but a return – to the stasis and conservatism of pre-modern culture? The answer is yes, and in more than one way. Unless one is a particularly psychotic Futurist, both the new and the renewed are culturally and emotionally meaningful to us. Why else would the Russian Communists have restored the czarist palaces? As Emanuel Levinas says, 'that the New and the Renewed are peaks of human life, that one can define humanity by the desire for the new and by the capacity for renewal – is perhaps a basic truth, but a truth.'[11]

Most of us have a deep attachment to renewal-as-continuity – the indefinite continuation of cultural memory through the indefinite continuation of its material embodiments – and a deep need for the new-as-different. Here is Levinas again:

> The Desire for the new in us is a desire for the other; it distinguishes our being from existing, which is self-sufficient, and which … perseveres in existing … In the natural throbbing of the being of beings, the human would thus be the rupture of this ontological rhythm.[12]

Culture, then, severs us from the unthinking being of our 'natural' state. To force change is to step outside the ceaselessly renewing order of life. And yet the continuity of the renewed at the same time reassures us and steadies us against the vertigo of novelty – so that we swing between the poles of resurrection and rupture, the desire to avoid loss and the desire to be free of that which we fear to lose.

Does environmentalism, therefore, sit at one end – trying to reintroduce old ways of doing and being, old-fashioned 'natural' materials and old buildings, in an attempt at the renewal of the biosphere – while the new sits at the other? Does environmentalism's measurement of the environmental cost of materials mean that architecture must keep within the limits of environmental functionalism? Or does environmentalism – and environmental architecture – in fact straddle both the renewed and the new? Environmentalism, after all, isn't exclusively about return; it is also about rupture. There are more technical and formal innovations in environmentally designed architecture than there are in sentimental recidivism.

Modernism is getting old: around 2,500 years old, if marked from the ancient Greeks; around 300 years old, if one thinks it emerged in a materially recognisable form with the Industrial Revolution. One of the mainstays of its project – to overcome and replace nature – is dangerously obsolete, causing us more problems than it solves. There are many reasons for viewing environmentalism not as a repudiation of Modernism's undeniable liberations but as a new form of Modernism: as Modernism's rupture with its own past, a Modernism turning away from trying to overcome nature, and, in Ulrich Beck's terms, towards overcoming itself – its own heavy-handedness, its own sadism towards people and the biosphere.[13] That this also involves 'overcoming nature' – overcoming global warming and a polluted environment – seems to contradict what has just been said, but the old Modernism overcoming nature and the new Modernism imitating nature to overcome nature-in-revolt-at-over-exploitation are two very different, if awkwardly expressed, descriptions.

The redefinition of Modernism's project in environmental terms is thus paradoxical – at once a break with a past that is about the privileging of the new, and, at the same time, the renewal of an old paradigm: that of nature as a model for material culture. Not, as in the past, a formal model (though that, too, is happening in architecture which explores complexity theory), but an operational model. At first sight, this may look like two ways of saying the same thing – a rupture with Modernism equals a resurrection of pre-Modernism. But such is not the case. It is simply not possible to go back. The new aim of overcoming Modernism may contain within it a return to nature – but to the materially sophisticated workings of nature, not to a 'state of' nature. This return is only possible through new environmental sciences capable of understanding our dependence on ecosystems and measuring our damage of them; on new environmental technologies, like photovoltaics and wind power, which enable us to extract what we need from nature without destroying what we need; on new environmental methodologies that enable us to design buildings – new or renewed – whose materiality does less damage to the natural matter from which it springs, and yet isn't all wattle and daub.

In the cauldron of materials manufacture, the overcoming of Modernism has yet to arrive, but in the not-too-distant future we will grow building materials, not forge them. They may well be animate as well as inanimate, engineered from living matter, or at the very least endowed with the same properties as living matter. This is Jeremy Rifkin in his book *The Biotech Century*:

> Scientists in the chemical industry are talking about replacing petroleum, which for years has been the primary raw material for the production of plastics, with renewable resources produced by microorganisms and plants. A British firm, ICI, has developed strains of bacteria capable of producing plastics with a range of properties, including variant degrees of elasticity. The plastic is 100% biodegradable and can be used in much the same way as petrochemical-based plastic resins. In 1993, Dr Chris Sommerville, the director of plant biology at the Carnegie Institute of Washington, inserted a plastic-making gene into a mustard plant. The gene transforms the plant into a plastics factory.[14]

Has environmentalism, then, succeeded in causing language to mutate in its favour? Has it successfully implanted new terms – and repositioned familiar ones? Has it provoked a cultural shift? Not entirely, and certainly not yet in architecture. The new is still privileged over the renewed, innovation over conservation. However sensitive to what is already there, however shaped in response to exogenous pressures, the newness of the material object, the newness of the gesture in an existing context, is unquestioningly privileged over the simple renewal of existing fabric; or, even more radically, the act of walking away and leaving self-organising, bottom-up/patch-up initiatives to fill the place of The

Architect. This is emphatically not to say, however, that the architect-as-prime-mover, heroic or otherwise, should be repudiated. On the contrary, aesthetic seduction is an extremely potent weapon in the armoury of any ideology trying to establish itself. The point is not that architects as conventionally conceived of are now unwanted, but that they may sometimes be unnecessary, that before any energy-intensive intervention is made the unasked question needs to be asked: does this new building need to be built?

The idea of the new and the renewed held in tension within an environmentalist critique of materials, with neither privileged over the other, remains remote – and such a future may anyway become irrelevant. It is the fast-approaching revolution in materials manufacture that will cause language to mutate in environmentalism's favour, by means of a rupture with both industrial and craft manufacture: a rupture that is a return – since, in one sense, growing materials, like growing vegetables, could hardly be more 'natural'.

1   >Gottfried Leibniz, *Monadologie*, cited in Gilles Deleuze and Felix Guattari, *A Thousand Plateaus*, London: Athlone Press, 1993, p. 19.
2   >Le Corbusier, *Towards a New Architecture*, New York: Dover Publications, 1986, p. 282.
3   >*Ibid*., p. 140.
4   >*Ibid*., pp. 144–5.
5   >*Ibid*., p. 134.
6   >David Leatherbarrow and Moshen Mostafavi, *On Weathering*, Cambridge, Massachusetts, London: The MIT Press, 1993.
7   >Vladimir Mayakovsky, cited in Renato Poggioli, *Theory of the Avant-Garde*, trans. G. Fitzgerald, Cambridge, Massachusetts: Harvard University Press, 1968. p. 152.
8   >Filippo Marinetti, *Let's Murder Moonshine: Selected Writings*, ed. R.W. Flint, Los Angeles: Sun and Moon Classics, 1991, p. 87.
9   >David Anink, Chiel Boonstra and Jon Mak, *Handbook of Sustainable Building*, London: James & James (Science) Publishers, 1996, p. 8.
10   >Sim Van der Ryn and Stuart Cowan, *Ecological Design*, Washington, DC: Island Press, 1996, p. 95.
11   >Emanuel Levinas, 'The Old and The New' in *Time and The Other*, trans. R. A. Cohen, Pittsburgh: Duquesne University Press, 1997, p. 128.
12   >*Ibid*., p. 126.
13   >See Ulrich Beck, *Risk Society*, London, New Delhi: SAGE Publications, 1992.
14   >Jeremy Rifkin, *The Biotech Century*, London: Phoenix, 1998, p. 16.

INDEX

404293